Nostalgic Memories

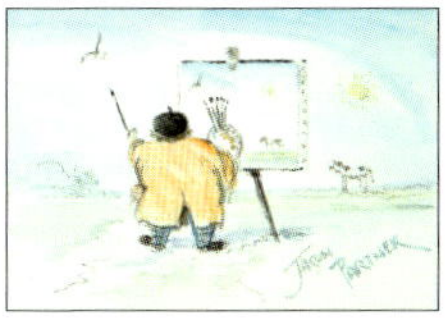

Nostalgic Memories of Jason Partner

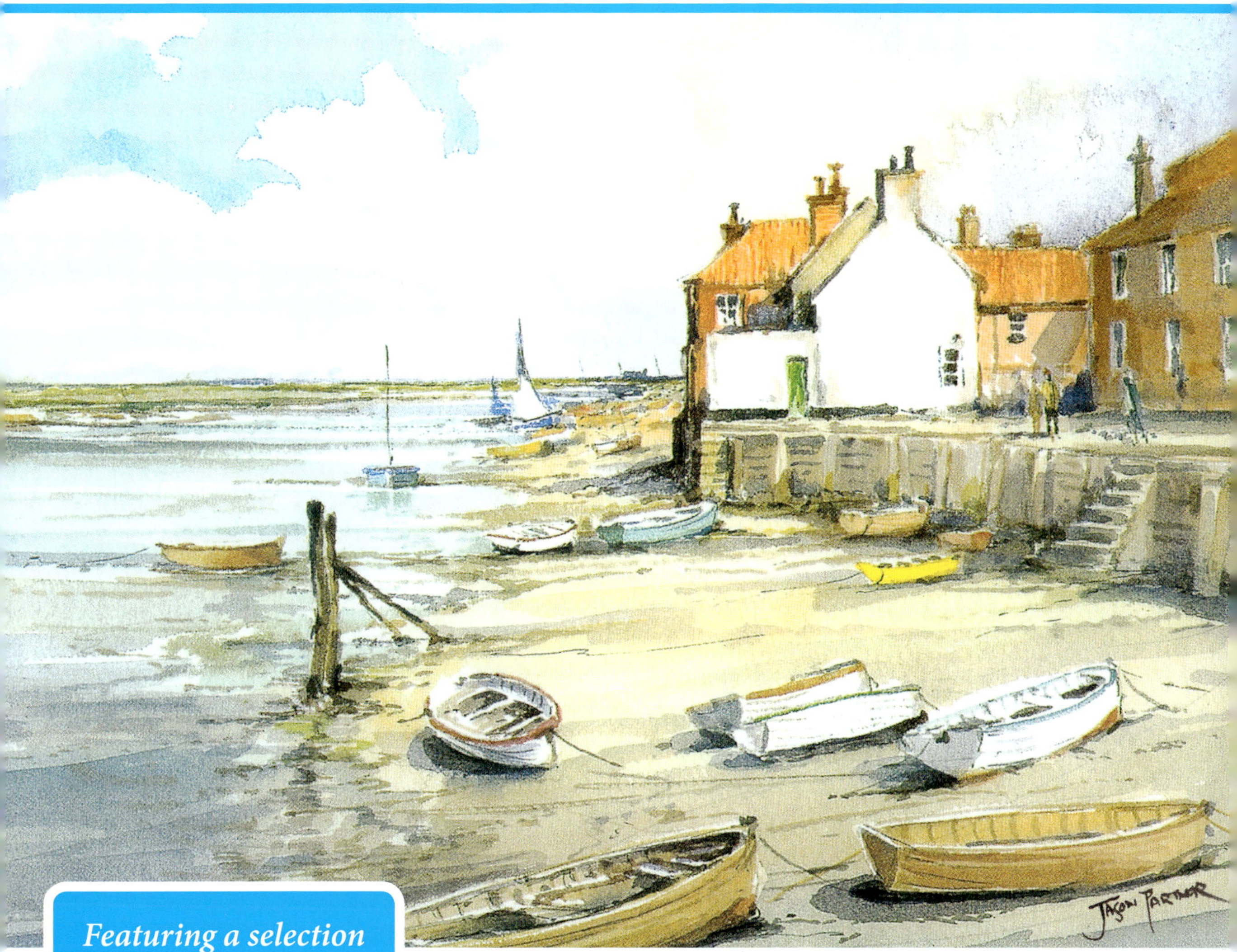

Featuring a selection of his famous Norfolk landscapes, anecdotes and odes

Colin and Mary Nelson

Published by Stanford Press, 11 Siskin Green, Oulton Broad, Lowestoft, Suffolk, NR33 8PP

First published 2015

ISBN: 978-0-9931362-0-7

Odes by Mary Nelson

Design and Origination by The Little Graphic Design Company 01502 584049

Printed and bound in Great Britain by Barnwell Print Ltd 01263 732767

Corrections may be made to future printings

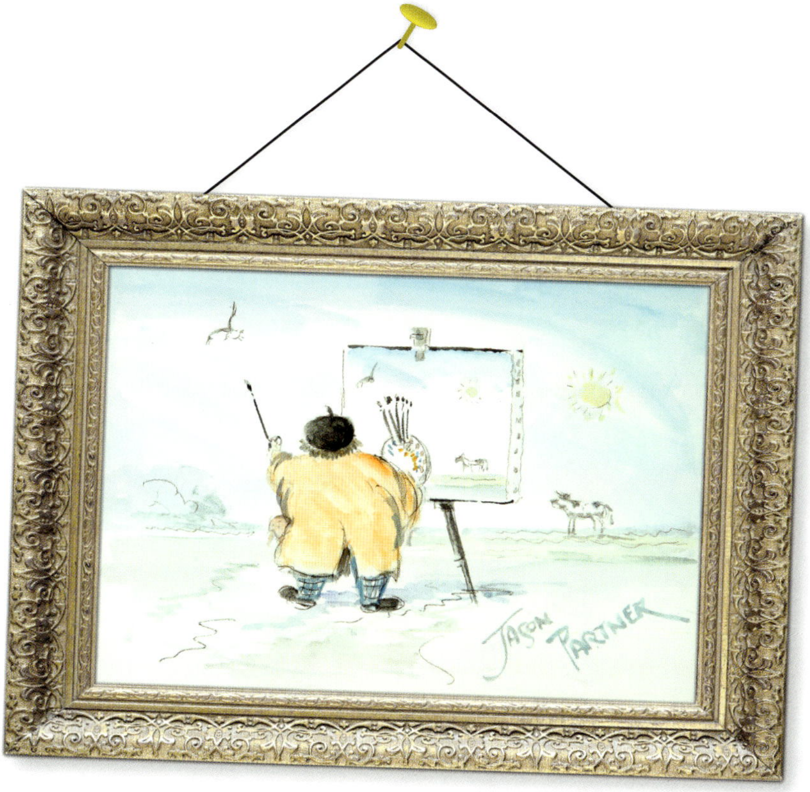

Dedicated to Jason Partner,
without whose exceptional artistic skills
and sense of humour
this book would never have been created.

Jason - if you are looking down on us…
hope you approve 'ole partner'.

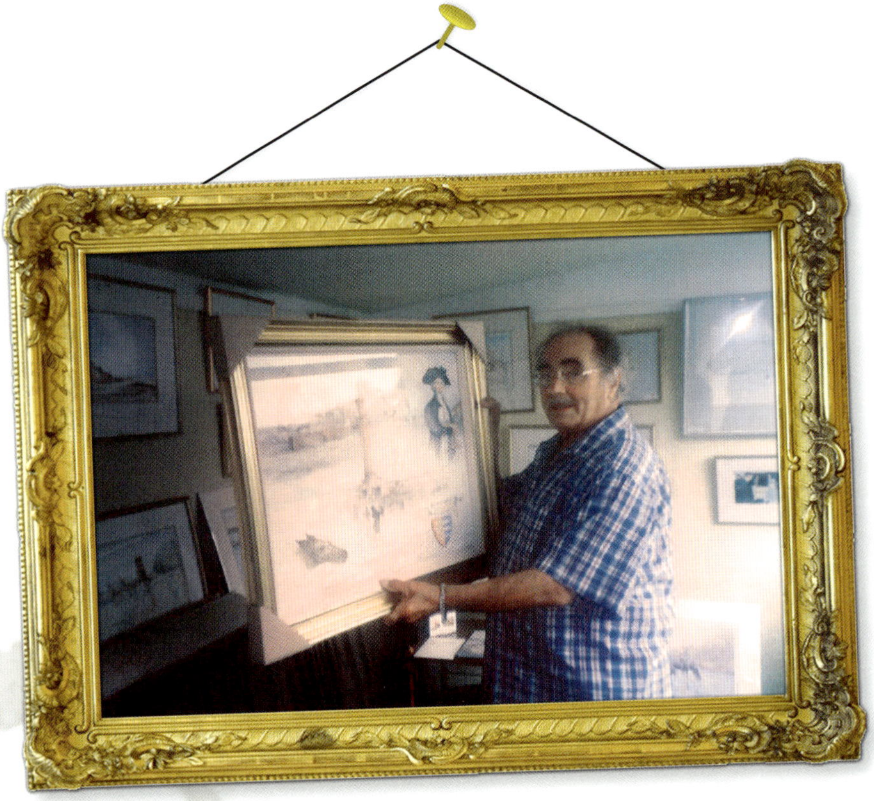

© From an original photograph by Colin Nelson
of Jason in his garden studio.

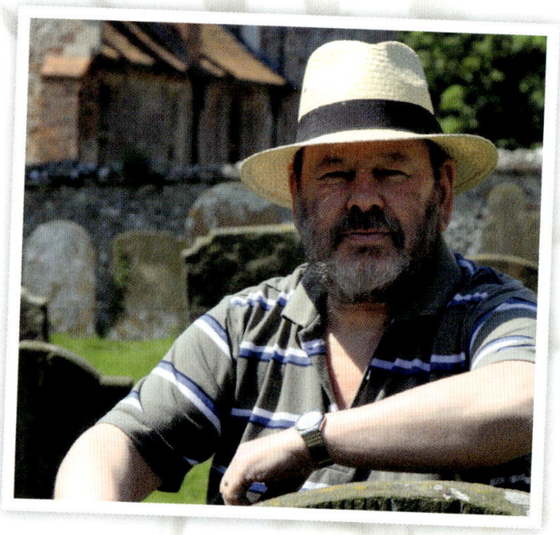

Jason to Keith -

'Reckon we ought to go by bus next time.'

See Foreword on page 8.

Keith Skipper,
Norfolk writer, broadcaster and entertainer.

© Keith Skipper.

Contents

Foreword

Keith Skipper, *Norfolk writer, broadcaster and entertainer.*

I used to call Jason Partner 'one of Norfolk's most eagerly-adopted sons'. He would part company with yet another throaty chortle and suggest that was the nicest thing anyone had ever said about him.

Modesty and mirth came easy to the lad from Leicestershire while he assumed legendary status as a true star in the Norfolk artistic firmament. Yes, he was serious about his work – but an impish laugh and generous spirit remain just as much at the heart of fondest memories.

We first met at one of his exhibitions where he made it all look and sound so easy. He could paint vivid pictures on the wireless as well and we savoured several hearty exchanges over the air at BBC Radio Norfolk.

'My studio is a bit tidier than this,' he would chide as I waded through various piles of paper to get to my chair. 'Yes,' I would respond, 'but you don't have to entertain strange characters for over an hour at a time.'

He hadn't been in Norfolk very long before he tuned in readily to native speech and humour as he walked his dog one balmy evening. A local on similar business waved cheerfully and inquired, 'How yer gittin' on, ole partner?'

Jason shared that incident with anyone who'd listen during the following weeks, expressing both amazement and delight at the way his name was known already in the local community.

My other favourite yarn featuring his irrepressible sense of fun was born out of an offer to act as my chauffeur for the night. He collected me at Cromer for an event at the Museum of the Broads when it was housed at Potter Heigham – it's based now at Stalham Staithe - and we duly fulfilled our respective roles.

Lively banter on the way home degenerated gloriously into a torrent of slightly saucy tales and gales of laughter. We were so busy amusing each other than Jason missed the junction leading to Smallburgh and, eventually, Cromer.

I didn't notice either – and we chuckled on to the outskirts of Wroxham. My driver eventually called for order, turned the car round, asked where I lived and did a splendid impression of a serious artist for nearly 30 seconds.

'Reckon we ought to go by bus next time,' he called as our travelling show concluded with a short hymn of praise for a potent mixture of Leicestershire larks and laughs with normal natter for Norfolk.

Keith Skipper

Meeting Jason

To be honest, neither myself nor my wife, Mary, had heard of Jason Partner. I was looking for a new career and noticed a greeting card business advert in the local paper which interested me. Within a few weeks of reading the advert, I had bought Stanford Press from Jason's brother-in-law, Peter Stanford. So, in March 2002, Mary and I, along with Peter, visited the home of Jason Partner in Aylsham so that we could be introduced as the new owners. Immediately we clicked and although neither of us had any previous experience in selling greeting cards, Jason must have known that we were the right people to take on the business.

It was then that Jason told me to drop in any time to see him and that is how I got to know Jason Partner. If I was in North Norfolk, I would make a point of calling in to see Jason and his wife, Jo. Jason would take me through to his studio and more often than not there would be a new painting he'd been commissioned to do. So he might relate the story behind it. Gazing around the wooden structure I could see various books relating to different artists, photographs, especially one featuring the late Queen Mother being presented with one of Jason's pictures. Also dotted around would be sketch books dating back many years from which Jason got his inspiration; he was 79 years old so was not going out to sketch and paint as often as he used to. The large window faced the garden and Jason made sure the studio was filled with light from early morning, which he thought was the best part of the day. We chatted about art, his life, gardening, family background, and he often gave me ideas of places to contact to see if they would like to sell his greeting cards. I always received a friendly welcome from him.

I learnt about the Old English style of watercolour, using only six colours, and the art was in the mixing of those. Jason mentioned his mentor, Dan Watson of the Leicester School of Art, and how Jason respected him. One thing which Jason learnt from him was not to overcharge for his work and Jason understood this too. From his initial cost of a couple of guineas, depending on size, to hundreds of pounds, Jason's clientele were delighted to have an original at such a good price, so more often than not, they would purchase another one the following year and tell all their friends. For someone who had no art background, I felt it was a privilege to talk to someone with so much knowledge and who just delighted in imparting his love of the medium. He would tell me about the exhibitions in Norwich and Holt, art demonstrations, commissions, people he had met and places he had visited. It was almost like chatting to a favourite uncle and that is how I sum up my relationship with him.

I am proud to say that it was a great pleasure knowing Jason. His work lives on even now and I will not forget the many happy times spent in his company.

Colin & Mary. Nelson

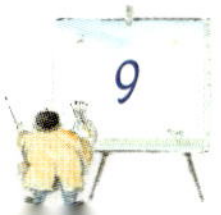

Jason Partner – A brief history

Born in Leicestershire in 1922, the son of a smallholder and a mother herself a keen amateur artist. She was a strong influence in the observance and discovery of nature etc. Educated at Market Bosworth Grammar School, Jason obtained a position at the Leicester School of Art at an early age where he came under the guidance and tuition of Dan Watson, an R.W.S. member and fine artist. Here, with his love of true watercolour and the traditional masters to study, it was a period of development of sound composition and mastering of the difficult medium, long hours in front of nature observing her moods, changing lights etc.

Alongside his work on paintings, Jason began publishing greeting cards in the 1960s, selling to friends and local farmers. However, when he held exhibitions and commissions followed, Jason asked friends and close relatives to take on the card business for him.

In the 1970s Jason was invited to visit the USA and Canada by Lord Beaverbrook. Whilst there, Jason did demonstrations in the Old English Style. He exhibited his work in Boston and Canada and both proved popular.

He was commissioned to paint for the late Queen Mother, the Duke of Edinburgh and former Prime Minister John Major. During his career he was a prolific artist and was invited to local art groups. Jason would make his demonstrations enjoyable using some witty stories and had a great sense of humour. His originals were never overpriced and his clients often bought more than one painting at a time.

In April 2005 Jason died at the age of 82 after a career spanning nearly half a century. Many art lovers and ordinary people mourned his loss. Jason's legacy was that he was a family man and an artist whose love of Norfolk came across in his work. His memory will live on in each of his paintings and every one has a story to tell.

'How yer gittin' on, ole partner?'

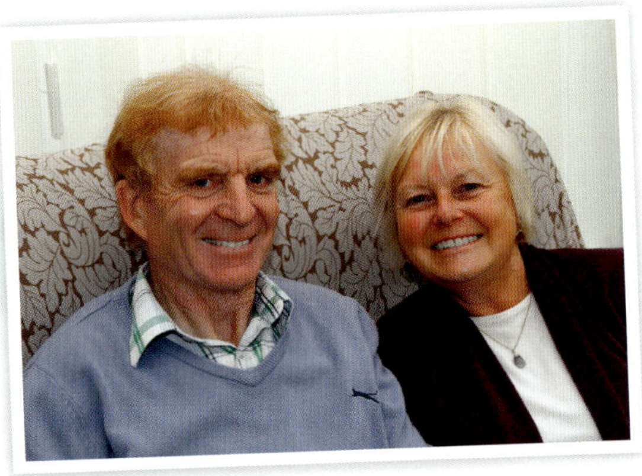

Colin and Mary Nelson,
Stanford Press.

Twelve favourite Locations

Although Jason painted scenes from all over East Anglia he did have his favourite locations. These were mostly in North Norfolk and approximate locations are shown in the map below.

1 - Cley Mill, Cley-next-the-Sea, Norfolk - *see page 12*
2 - Mill on the Ant, near Ludham, Norfolk - *see page 13*
3 - Wells-next-the-Sea, Norfolk - *see page 14*
4 - Market Place, Aylsham, Norfolk - *see page 15*
5 - Blakeney High Street, Norfolk - *see page 16*
6 - The Moorings, Norfolk - *see page 17*
7 - Burnham Overy Staithe, Norfolk - *see page 18*
8 - West end of Quay, Wells-next-the-Sea, Norfolk - *see page 19*
9 - Blakeney Quay, Norfolk - *see page 20*
10 - Hunstanton Beach, North Norfolk - *see page 21*
11 - Blickling Hall, Blickling, Norfolk - *see page 22*
12 - Low tide at Morston, Norfolk - *see page 23*

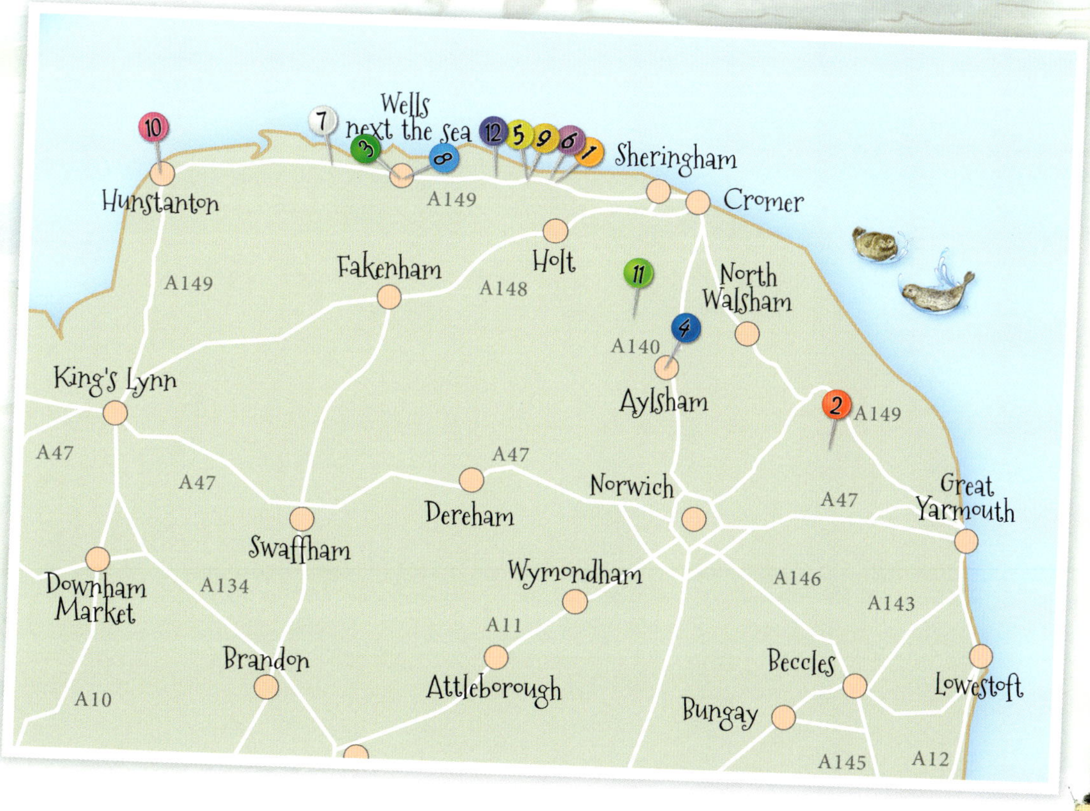

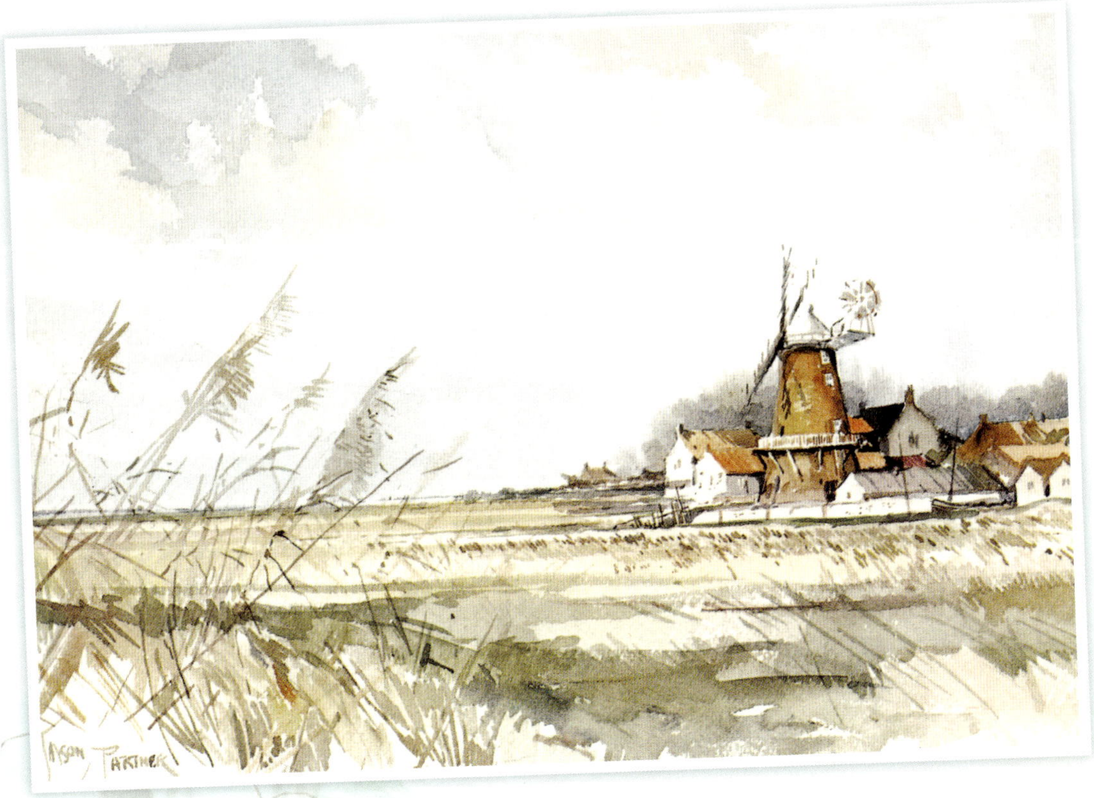

Cley Mill, Cley-next-the-Sea, Norfolk

© From an original watercolour by Jason Partner.

Cley is a place where time stands still.
In the pretty village is a mill.
Throughout the year, visitors you'll find,
And many will be of the feathered kind.

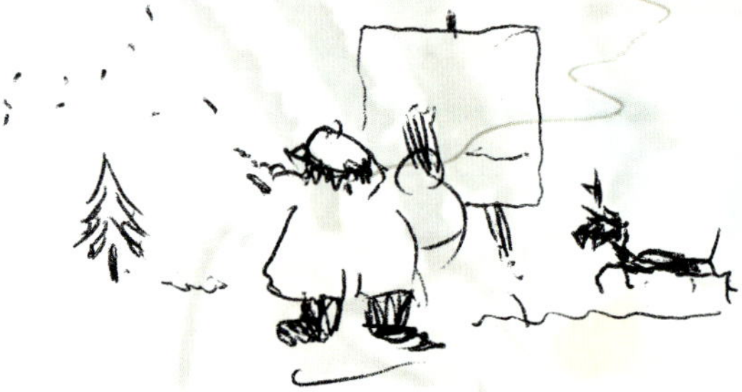

Mill on the Ant, Norfolk

© From an original watercolour by Jason Partner.

The river Ant forms part of the Norfolk Broads,
Where water takes over from winding roads.
Near to the beautiful setting of How Hill,
A place of peace and tranquility.
The area is noted for its flora and fauna,
Mother nature's magic is everywhere adorned.

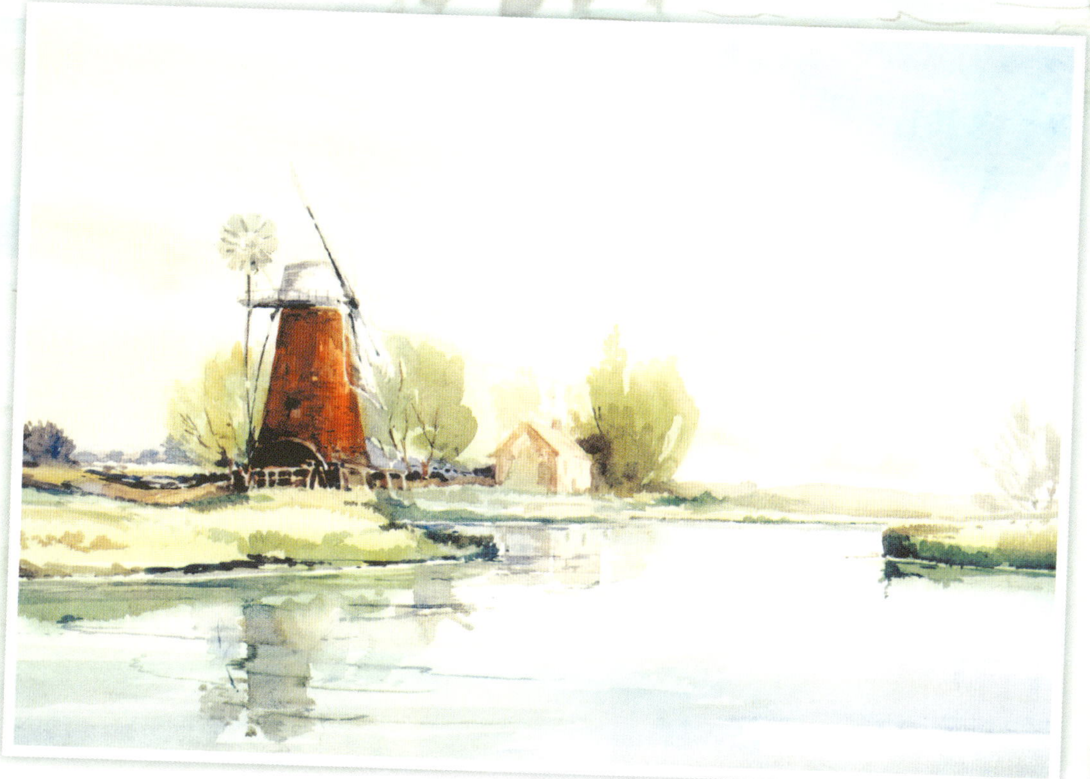

Wells-next-the-Sea, Norfolk

When Jason was out painting, he would often chat to people and be told stories of the places he was painting.

Wells-next-the-Sea has a story of the pub which was very close to the Custom and Excise office. Word has it that vast amounts of illicit liquor were consumed in this pub, under the very noses of the officers.

Wells-next-the-Sea is on
the Norfolk coast,

in years past, of cockles
it did boast.

Small boats ferried people
away from dry land,

where the tasty shellfish
were hiding beneath the sand.

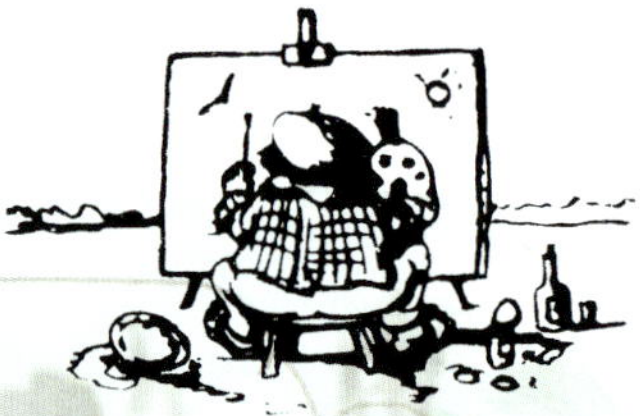

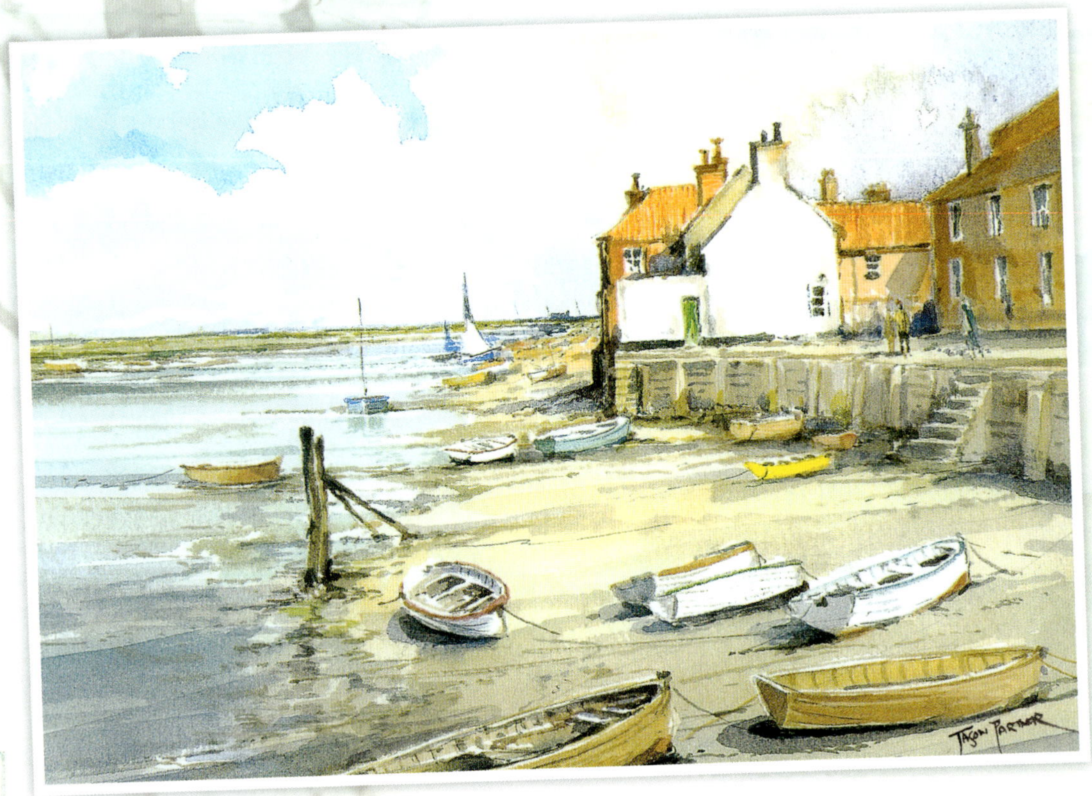

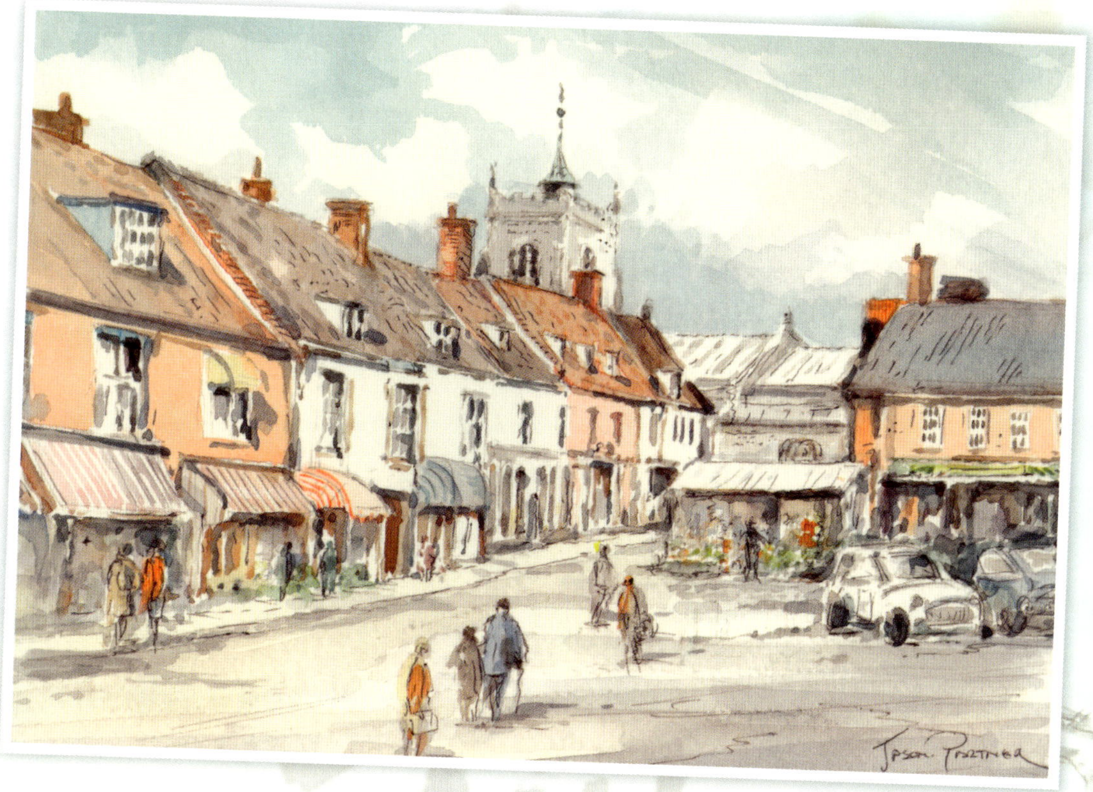

Market Place, Aylsham, Norfolk

© From an original watercolour by Jason Partner.

Aylsham has a bustling market place,

packed with stalls and friendly faces.

There is so much to do and see,

it's an important part of the community.

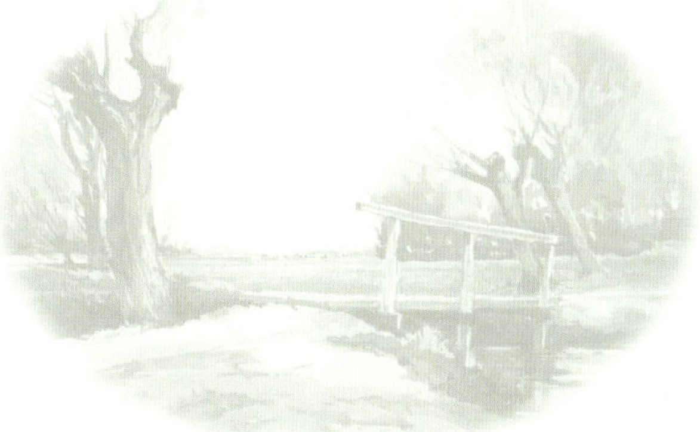

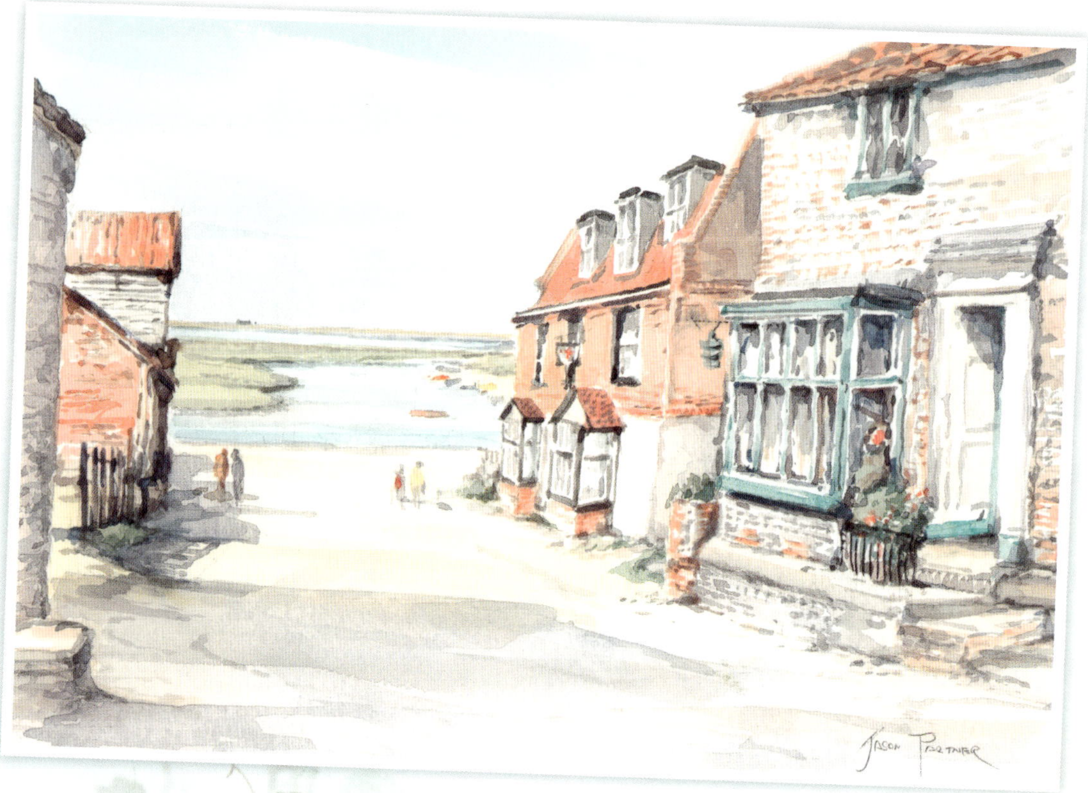

Blakeney High Street, Norfolk

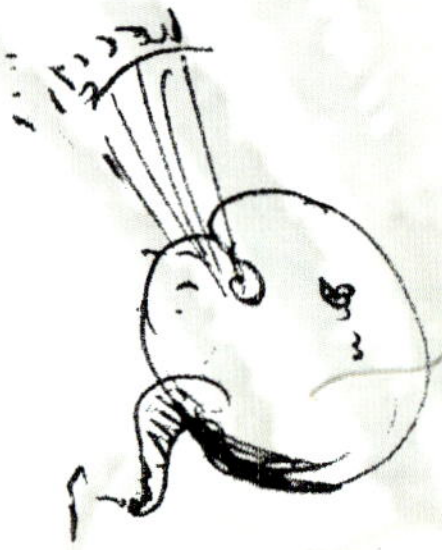

The High Street is lined with quaint houses,
together with shops where you can browse.
Seal trip boats wait at the quay,
many journeys they make in a day.
There is nowhere so delightful
as Blakeney.

The Moorings, Norfolk

© From an original oil on board by Jason Partner.

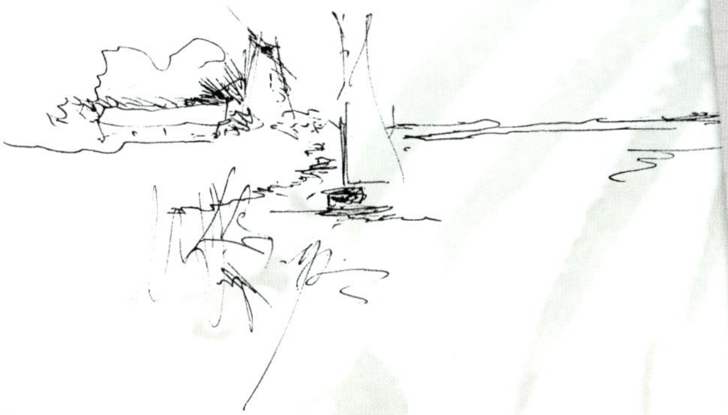

Along the Norfolk coast
this image you will see,

It conjures up a restful time
and fills you with ease,

The many inlets and staithes
which cover this coastline

Have a special peaceful quality
that really is sublime.

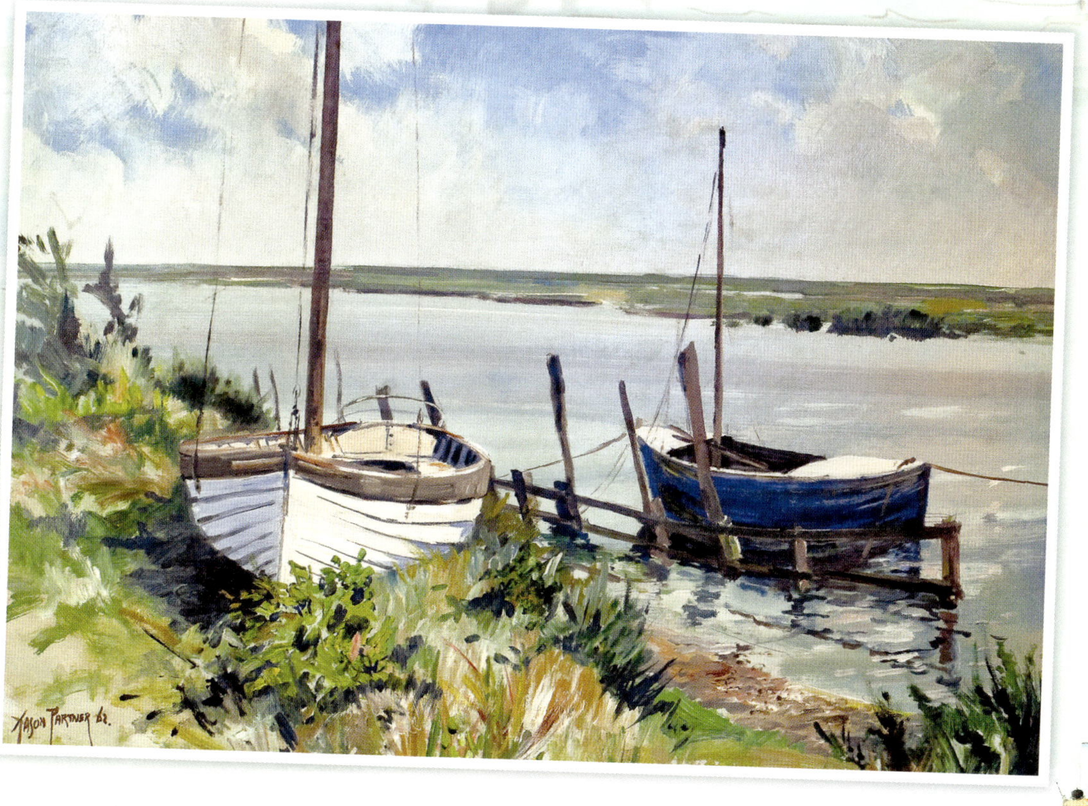

Burnham Overy Staithe, Norfolk

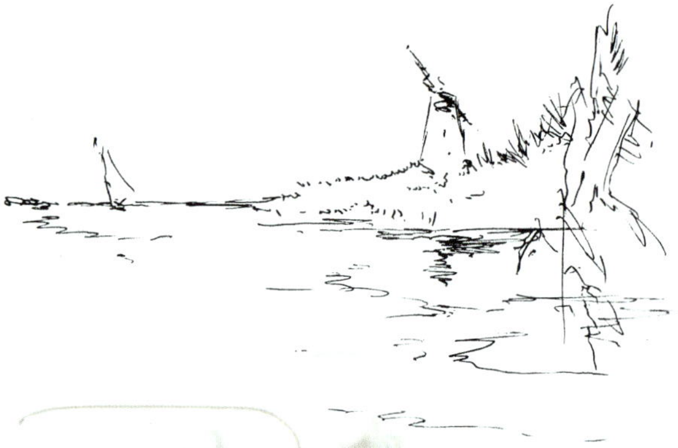

Where the Norfolk Coastal walk
meets Peddars Way,

you'll come across Burnham Overy Staithe.

Once a middle-ages port,
now known for water sports.

Possibly, where Nelson first learnt to sail.

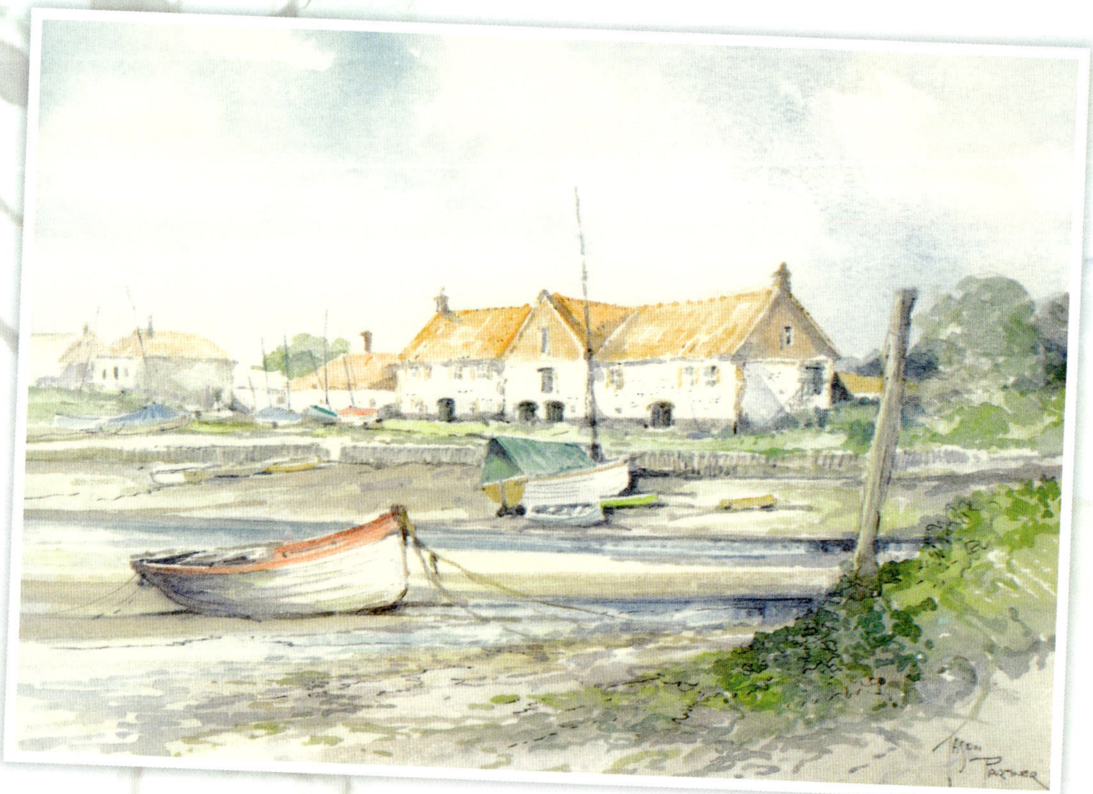

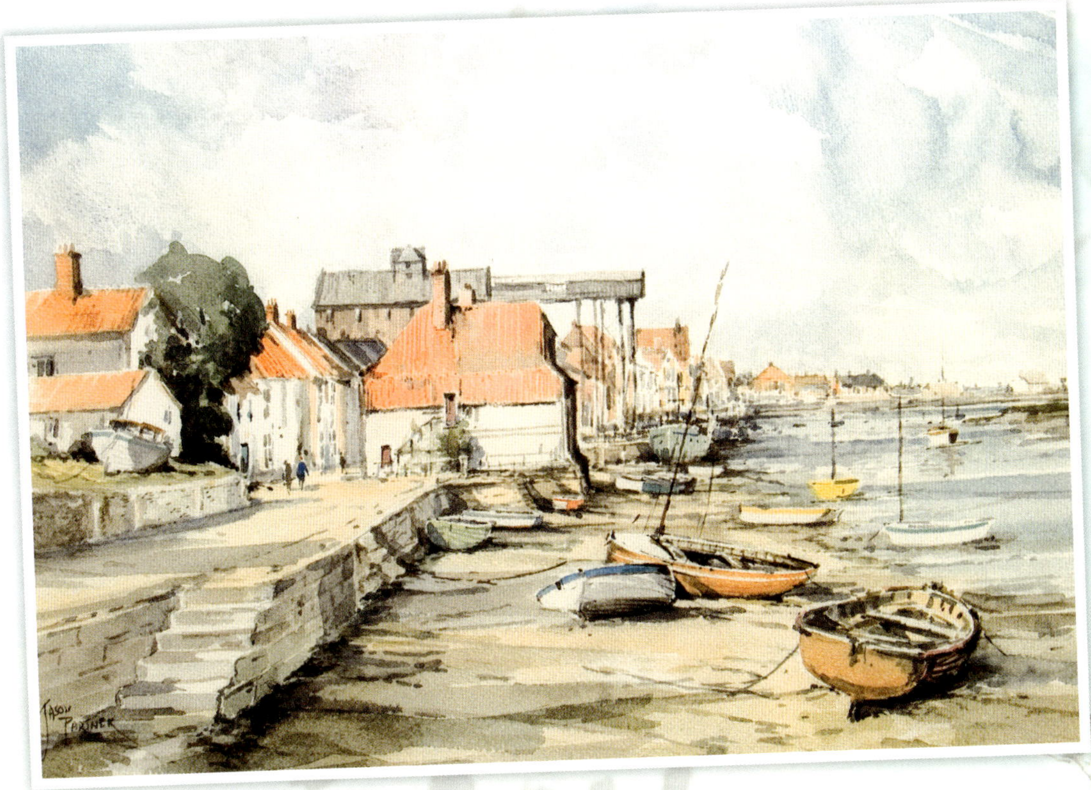

West end of Quay, Wells-next-the-Sea, Norfolk

© From an original watercolour by Jason Partner.

Well known for its quay
is Wells-next-the-Sea.
A pleasant walk is all it takes to reach
the lovely sandy stretch of beach.

Watercolour pigments ...

...The Old English style of watercolour became prominent in the 18th century.

Although there are variations regarding how many colours to use when painting in the Old English style, Jason usually used only six.

Prussian Blue, Yellow Ochre, Burnt Umber, Burnt Sienna, Ultramarine, and Scarlet Red.

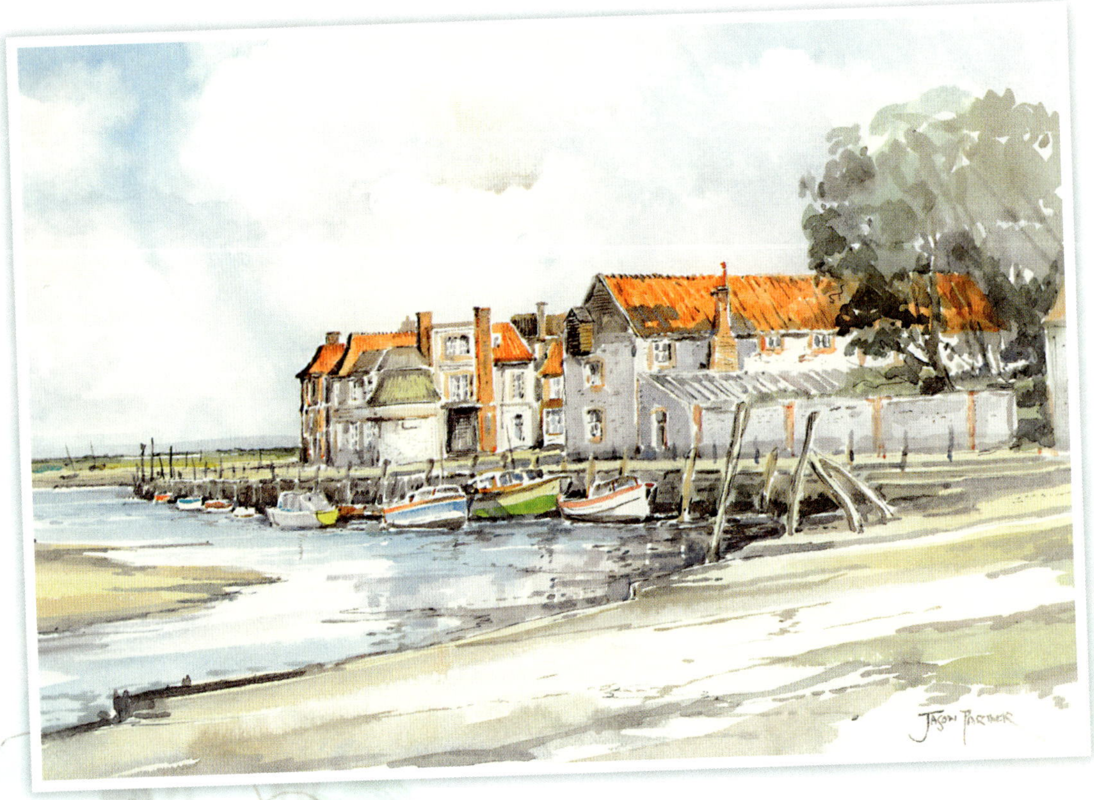

Blakeney Quay, Norfolk

© From an original watercolour by Jason Partner.

Blakeney is familiar to those
who, when it comes to birds, are in the know.
Whether the weather be rain, wind or snow,
for bird watchers, Blakeney is the place to go.

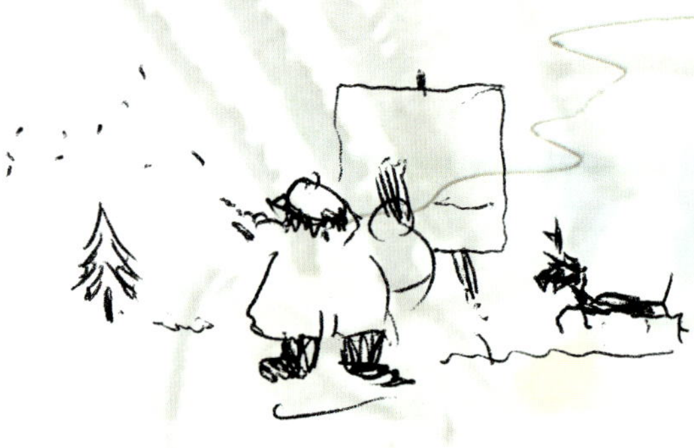

Beach scene, Hunstanton, North Norfolk

© From an original watercolour by Jason Partner.

With miles of sand and sparkling sea,
children playing happily.
This makes Hunstanton a
great place for all the family.

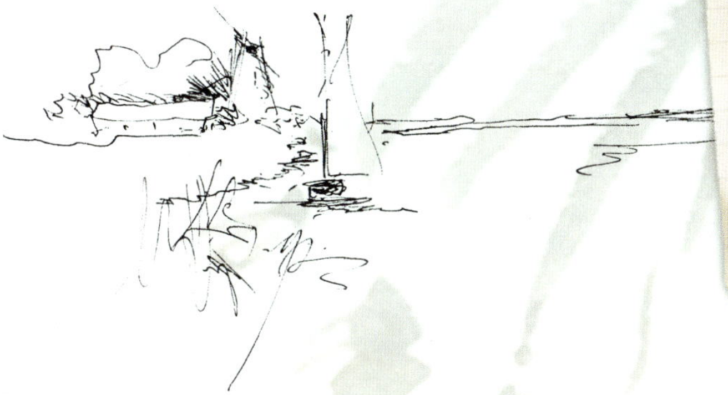

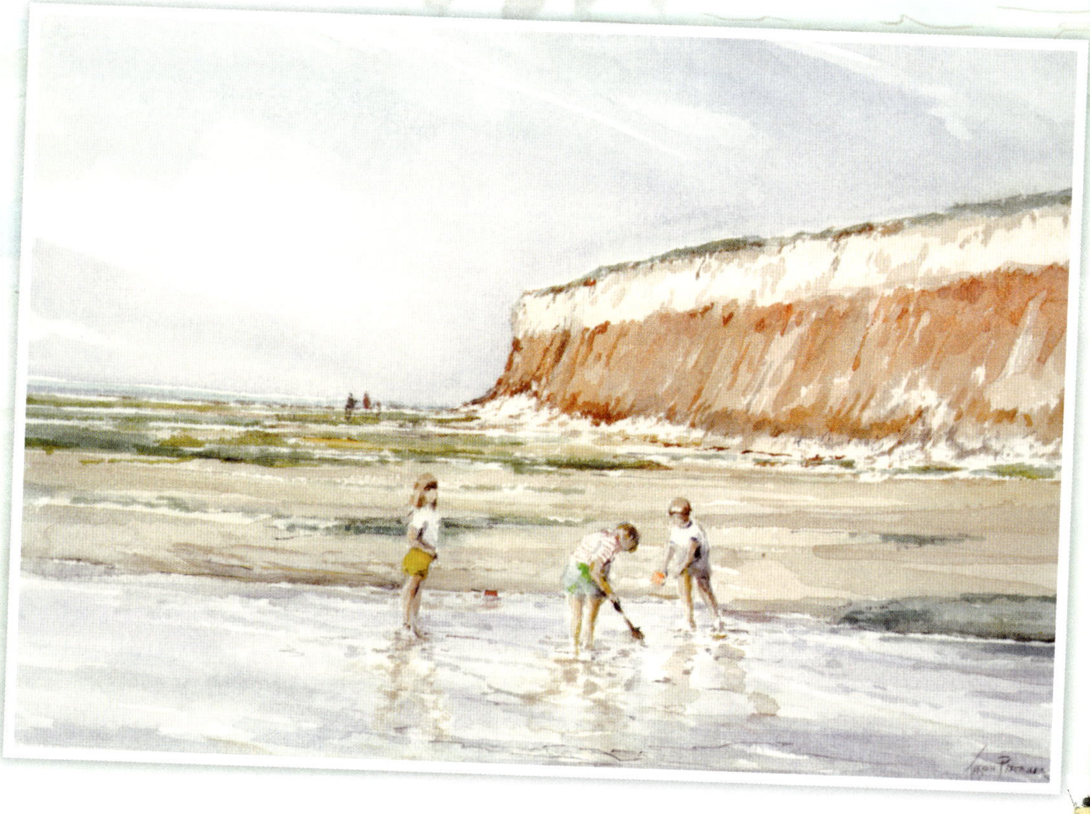

Blickling Hall, Norfolk

© From an original watercolour by Jason Partner.

Like many stately homes,
Blickling has its place in history.

At one time,
home of the Boleyn family.

Anne became the second wife
of Henry the Eighth,

being beheaded was her fate.

Now the beautiful hall
and gardens are a must,

and you'll be welcomed
by the National Trust.

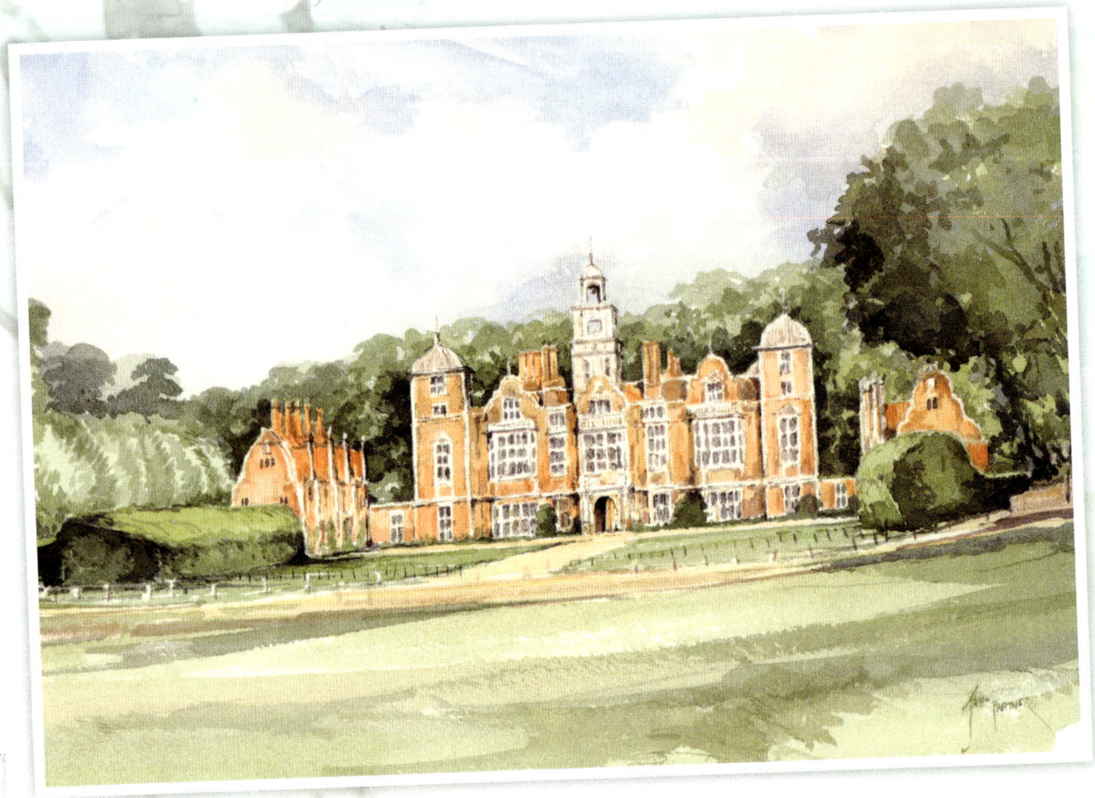

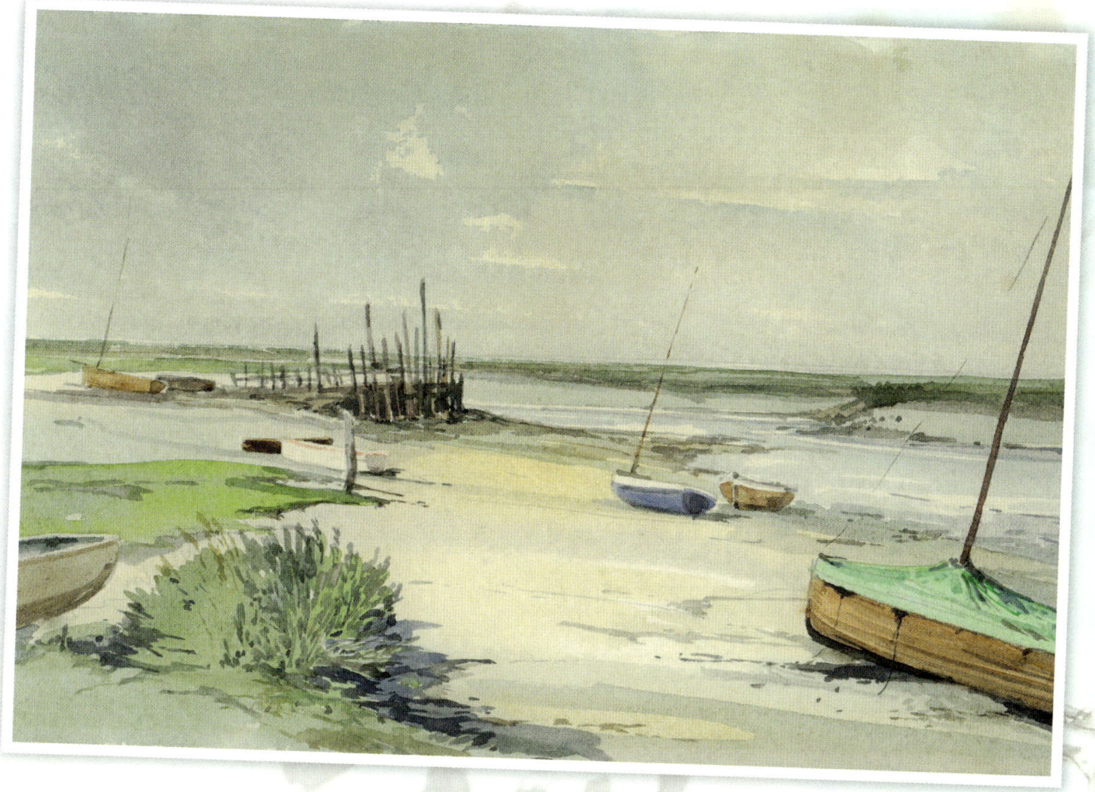

Low tide, Morston, Norfolk

© From an original watercolour by Jason Partner.

Jason Partner loved the county of Norfolk and became a well loved artist who captured the stunning landscapes and big skies.

A favourite spot for Jason to paint was in the Morston and Blakeney area and often people would stop and talk to him.

When they found out what he was doing they would give him ideas about the local area, for instance, interesting places to paint etc.

Although the parish of Morston covers around
three square miles, there is so much to see.

In the past, like Blakeney, it was a major port,
so a busy place to be.

Now-a-days smaller craft are seen
going back and forth; for sailing it's ideal.

That is why this part of Norfolk's coast
has so much appeal.

It sticks in our minds...

Jason's wife, Jo, said that Jason sometimes felt nervous before an art demonstration as he thought he might talk too much.
He always asked Jo to signal him if she thought the audience was getting restless.
On one occasion, Jo made a sign to Jason, who then asked the group - 'My wife has just signalled to me - am I talking too much?' - 'No,' came the reply, and all the audience turned and stared at Jo in disapproval!

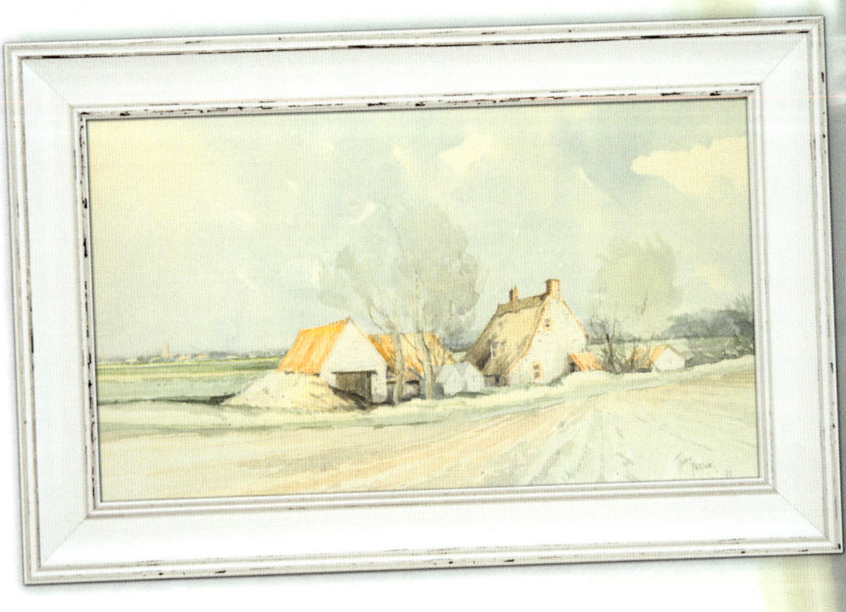

HAPPISBURGH

One of the quieter coastal resorts in Norfolk, well known for the red and white striped lighthouse.

This, being painted in 1979, is a typical scene of farm buildings and church in the distance which may not have changed much since Jason painted the image.

Original watercolour © Jason Partner.
By kind permission of
Colin and Mary Nelson.

Broadland scenes

A selection of Broadland scenes painted by Jason.
These were mostly in and around the Norfolk Broads area and
approximate locations are shown in the map below.

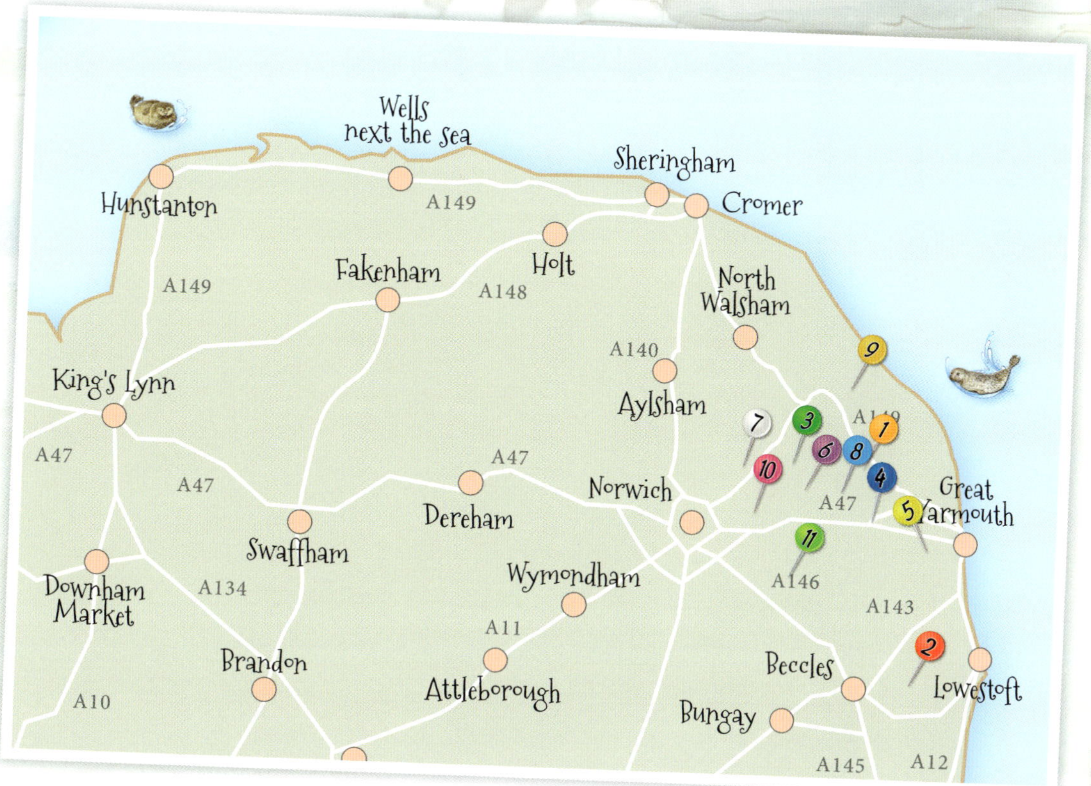

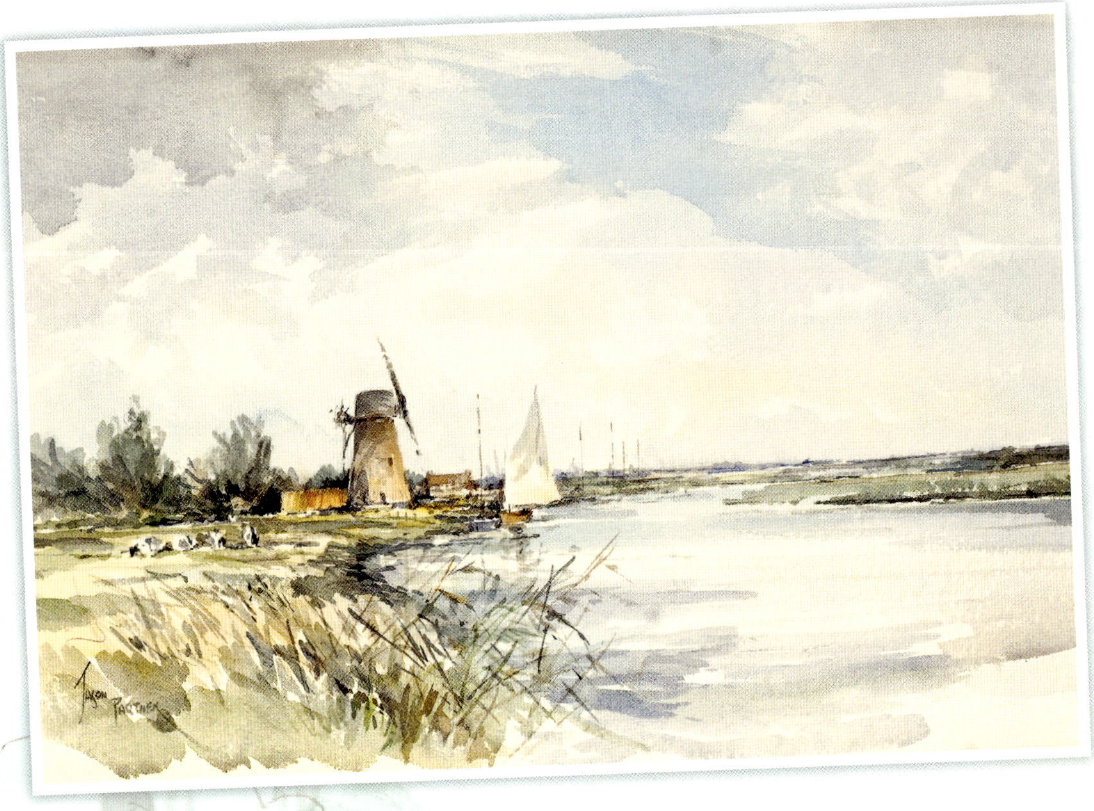

Norfolk Treasures

Norfolk is well known for its varied
coastal areas and waterways,

where locals and the many visitors
love to spend their days.

Whether you travel by car, on the water
or even on wheels of two,

Norfolk is a place that promises
rest and relaxation for me and you.

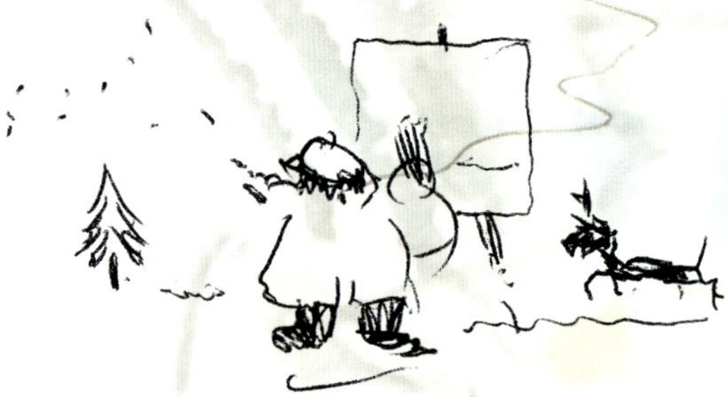

Wherry on the Waveney

© From an original watercolour by Jason Partner.

The area surrounding the River Waveney
is a very popular place to be.

For sailors, scenic views that cannot be matched,
for anglers, plenty of fish to catch.

Flora and fauna live in harmony,
as the river makes its way down to the sea.

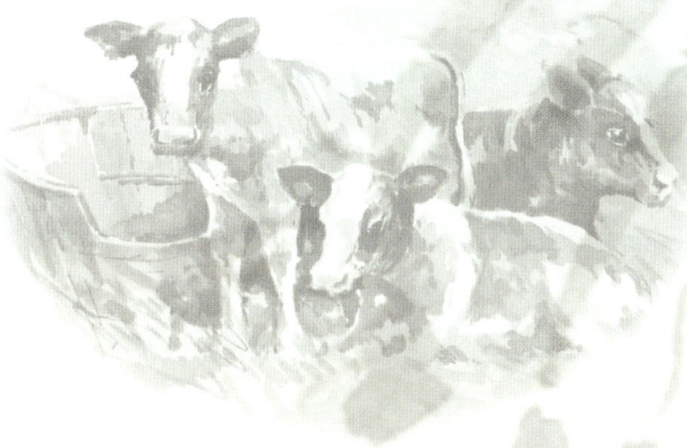

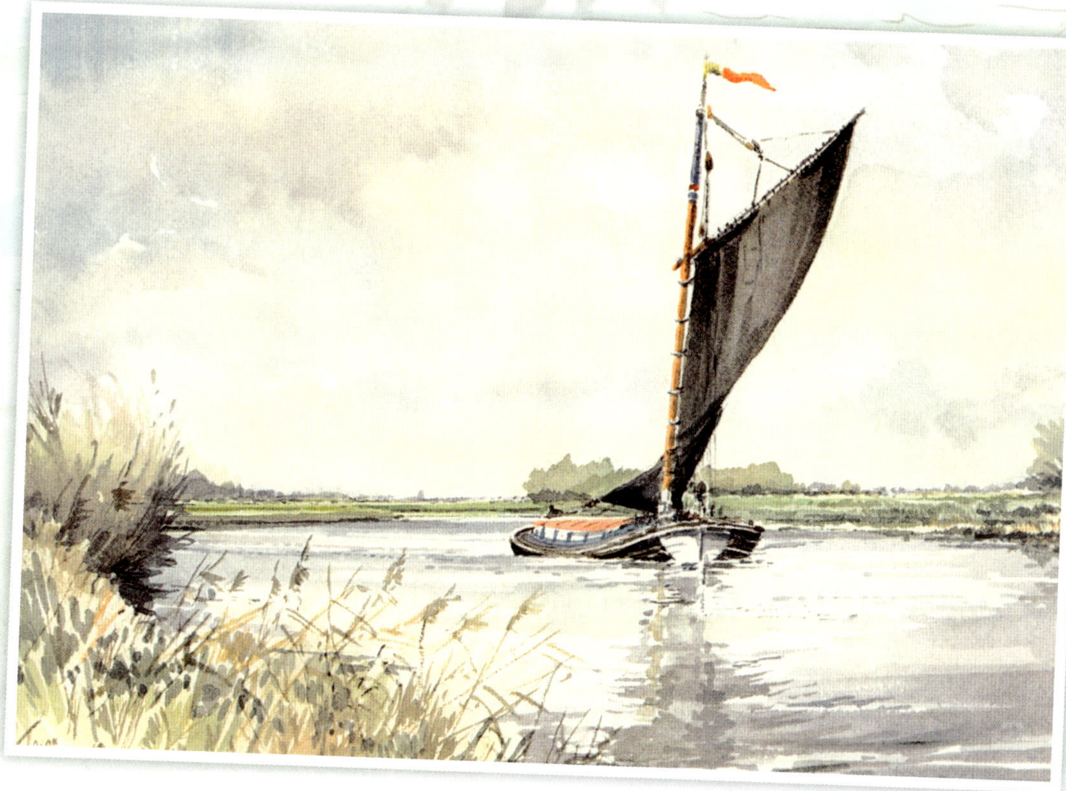

Horning, River Bure, Norfolk

When the wind catches the sails,
it never fails to excite.

There are scenic views you can cruise,
watching anglers waiting for their first bite.

Wildlife abounds and you'll see
pleasure craft chugging past,

keeping their distance as
motor boats give way to mast.

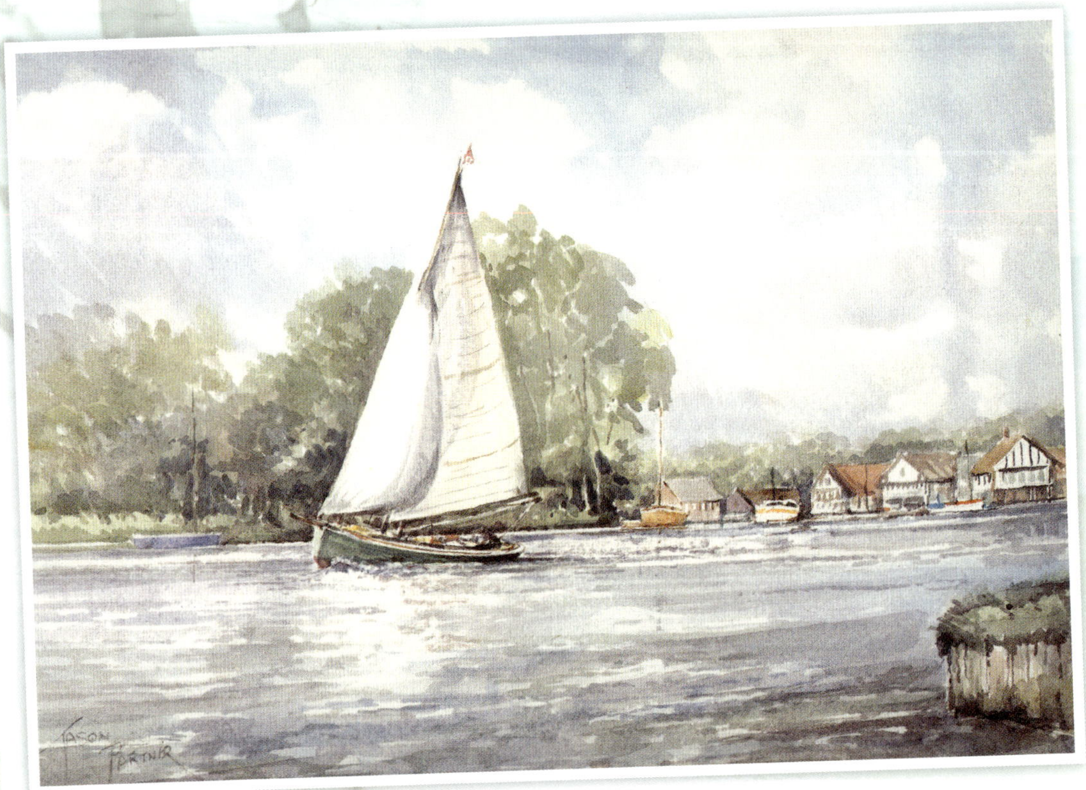

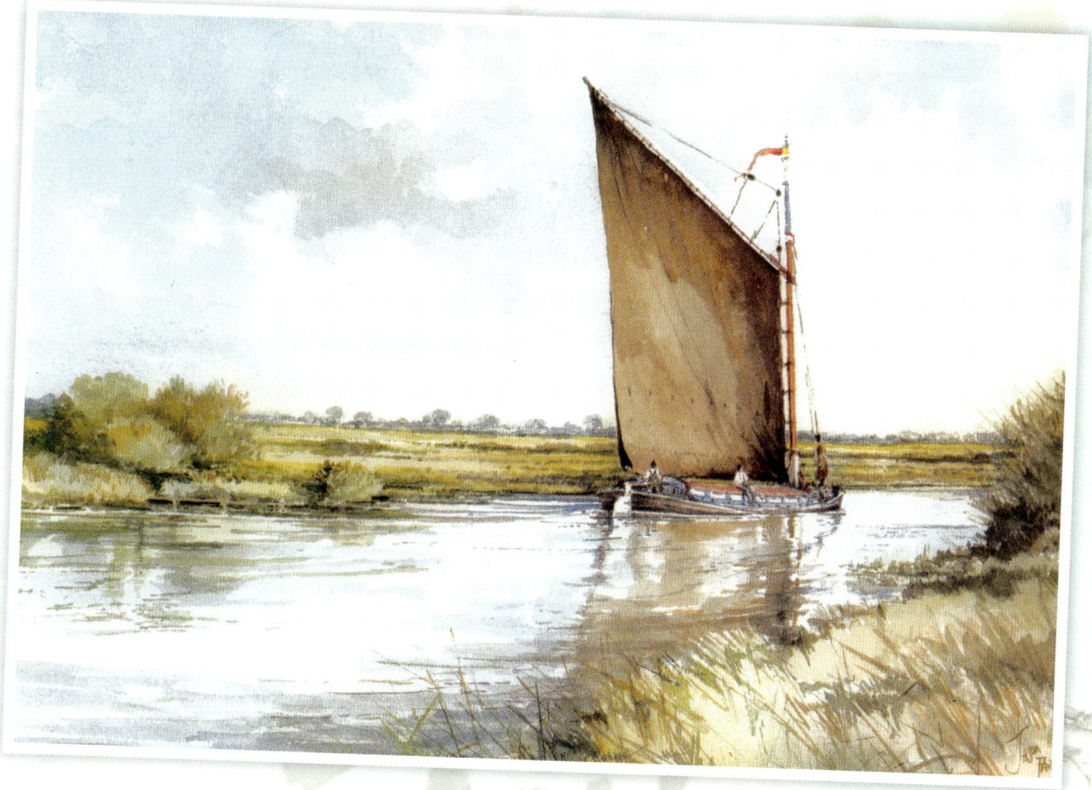

Wherry at Acle

© From an original watercolour by Jason Partner.

Years ago Wherries plied their trade
along the Broads,
many journeys they made.

They travelled at a gentle pace,
now huge lorries
have taken their place.

Prussian Blue ...

...synthetically produced
and also called Berlin Blue.

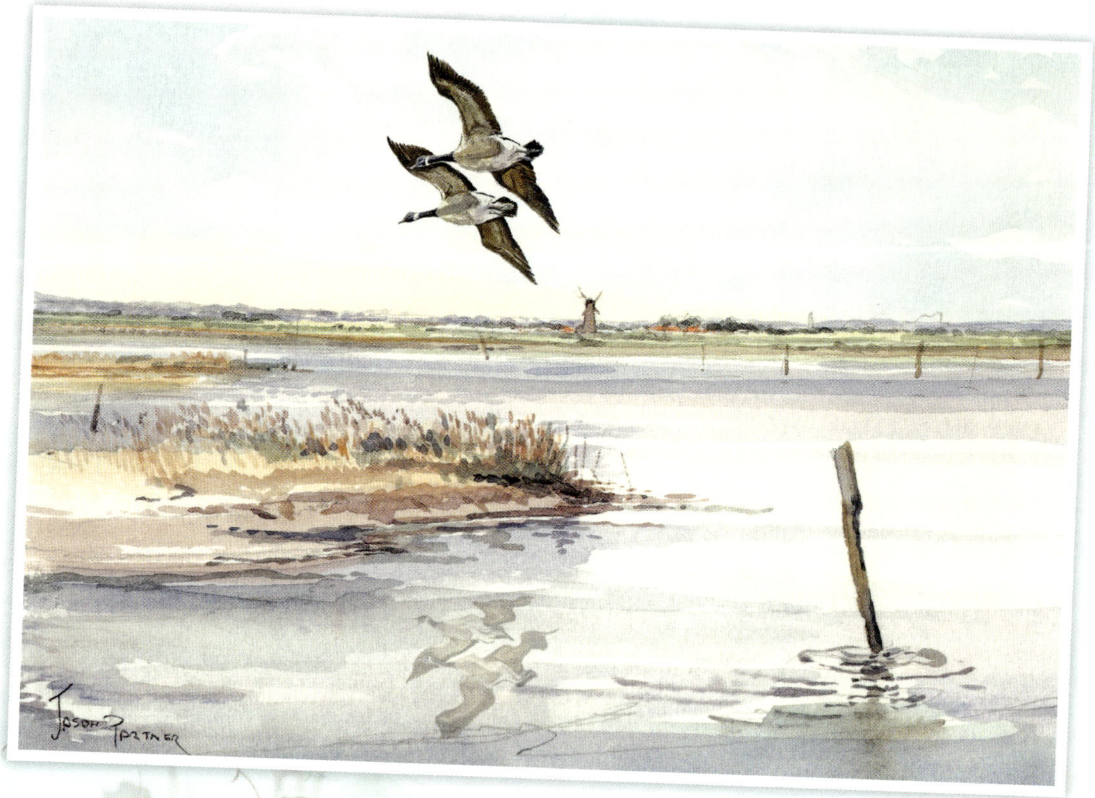

Breydon Water, Norfolk

© From an original watercolour by Jason Partner.

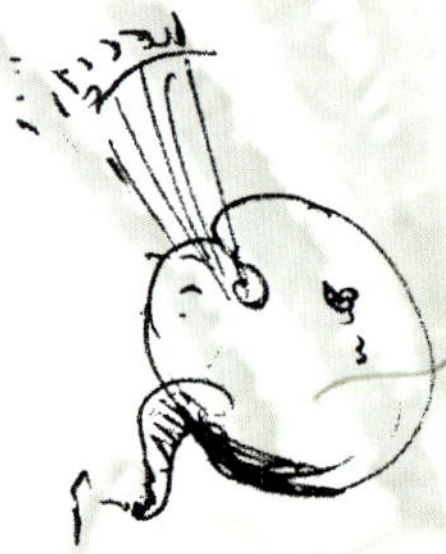

From the hustle and the bustle of
Great Yarmouth's port, cruisers and other boats leave

And head across Breydon Water,
a gateway to many rivers and historic places to see.

Along the way you may spot native or migratory birds
which have flown many hundreds of miles

And, with 'Weaver's Way' on its northern bank,
it is a perfect place to walk or rest awhile.

Ranworth Church, Norfolk

© From an original watercolour by Jason Partner.

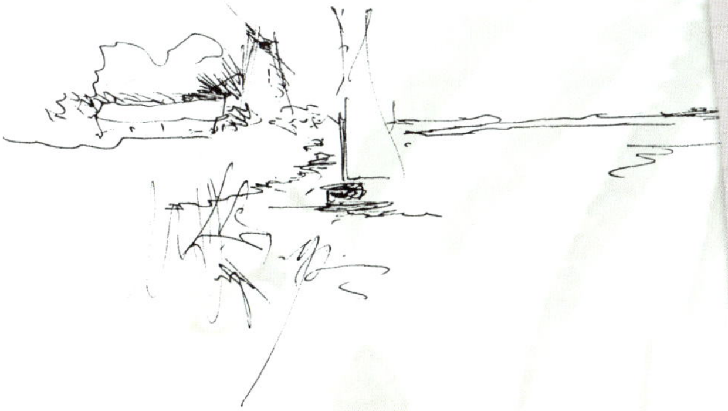

Ranworth is a broadland beauty spot,

it's a popular place for tourists to stop.

Visit the Norfolk Wildlife Reserve for an hour or two,

then climb St Helen's church to admire the view.

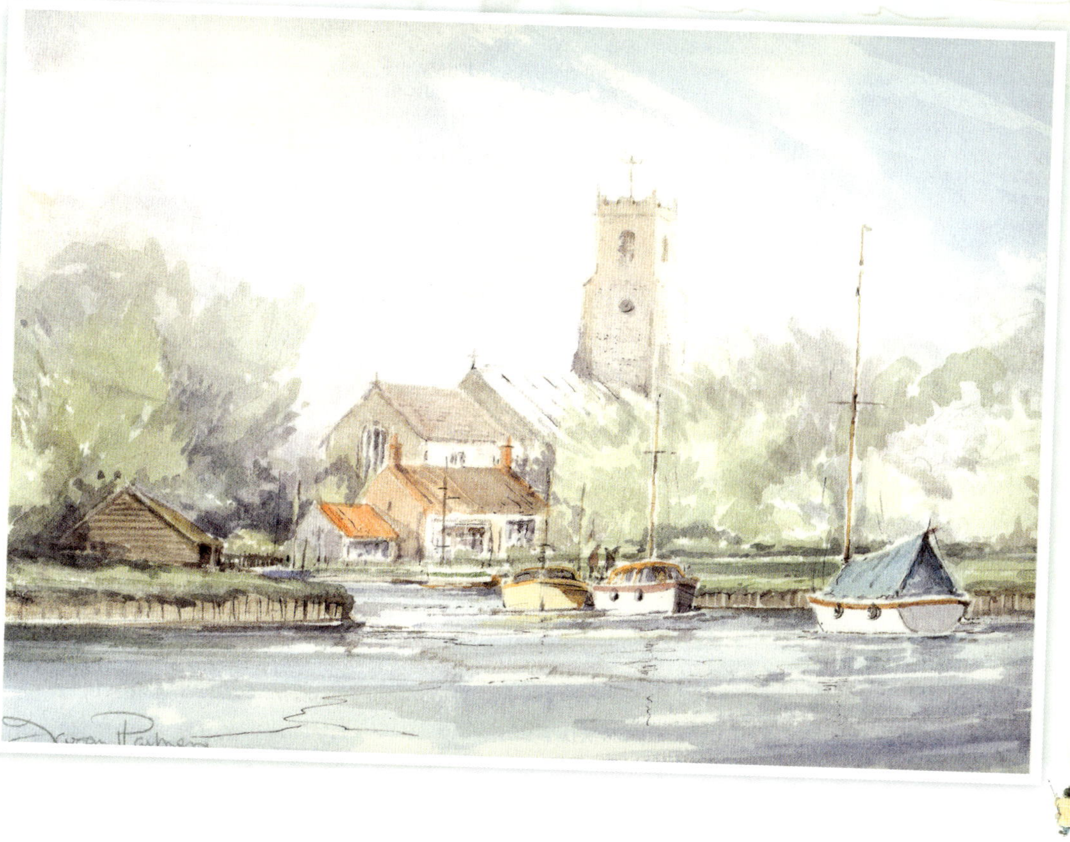

Wroxham, Norfolk

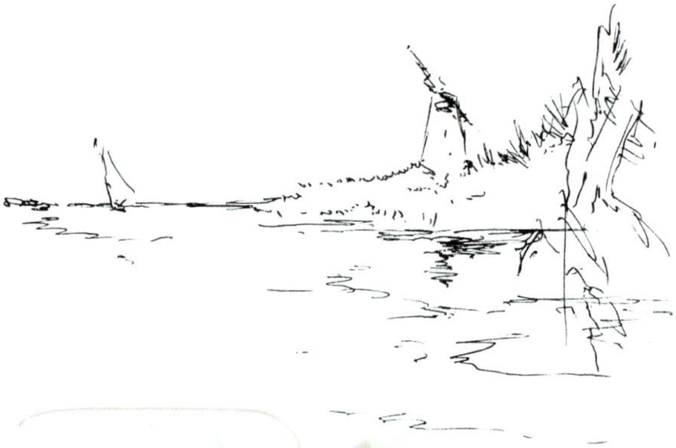

Wroxham is at the heart of the Broads,
you can get there by rail, sail or road.

On view there are many kinds of boats,
from yachts that glide to cruisers that float.

In the village there are plenty of places
to buy your supplies,

in fact, it is a shoppers' paradise.

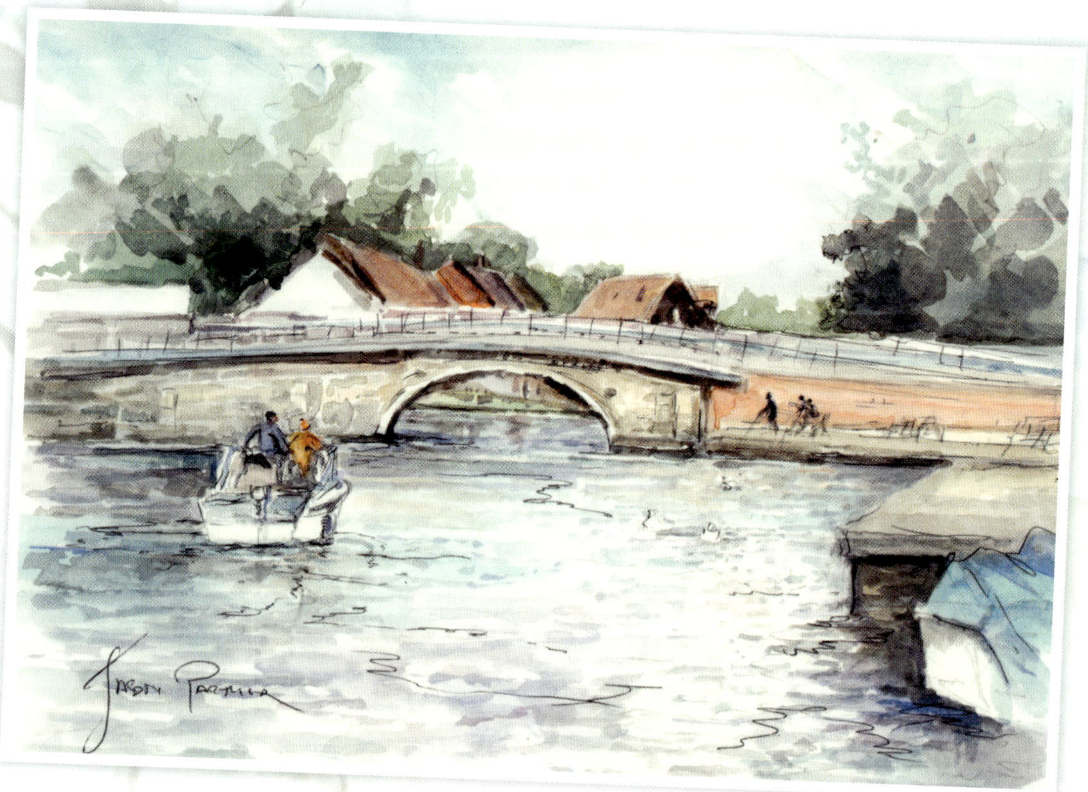

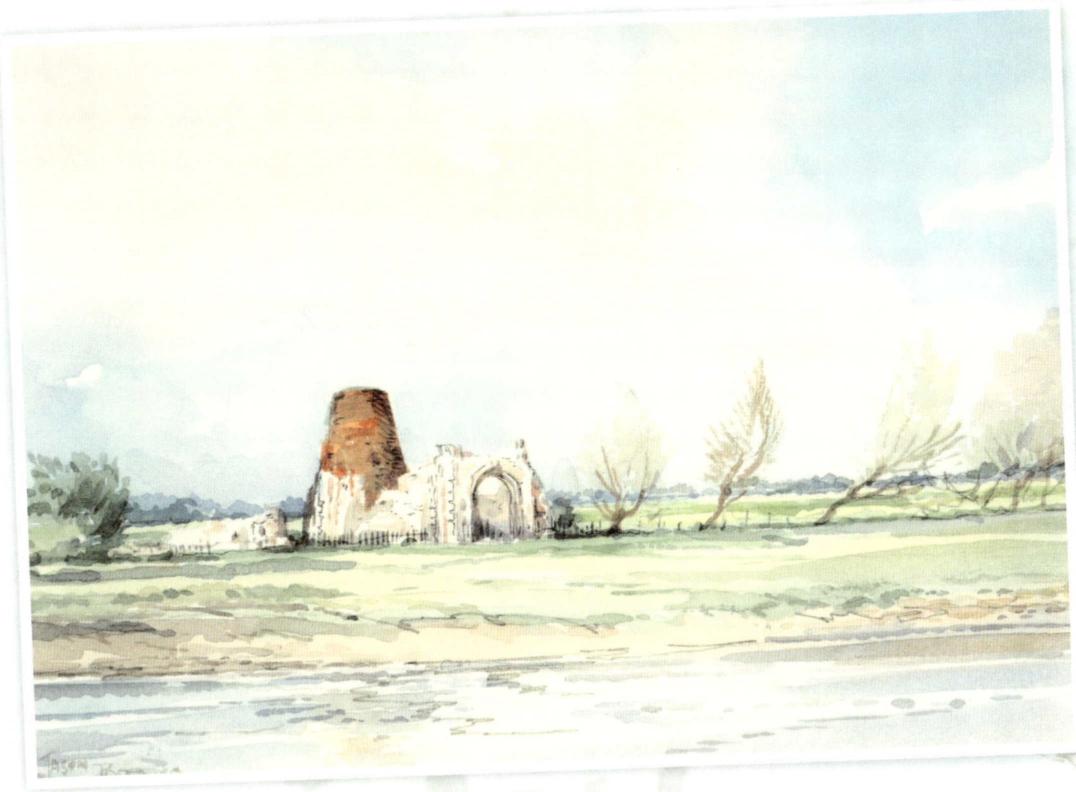

St Benet's Abbey, Norfolk

© From an original watercolour by Jason Partner.

St Benet's Abbey lies beside
the banks of the river Bure.

An Anglo-Saxon monastery,
which has been left undisturbed.

A place of worship
and an area of archaeology,

St Benet's Abbey
is a magical place to be.

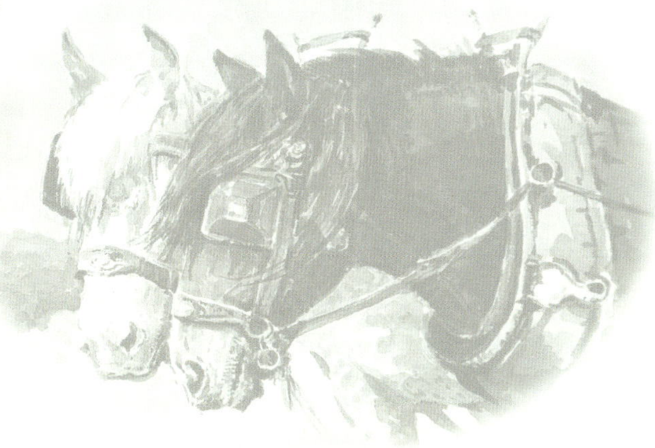

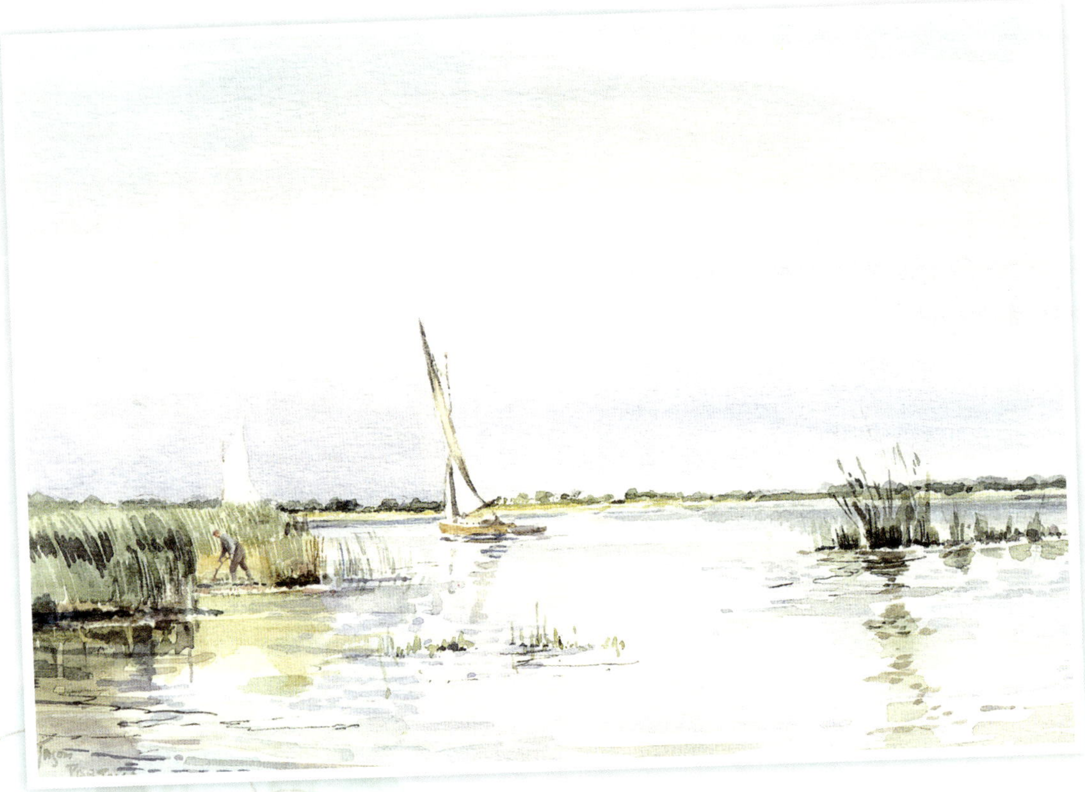

Beautiful Broadland, Norfolk

© From an original watercolour by Jason Partner.

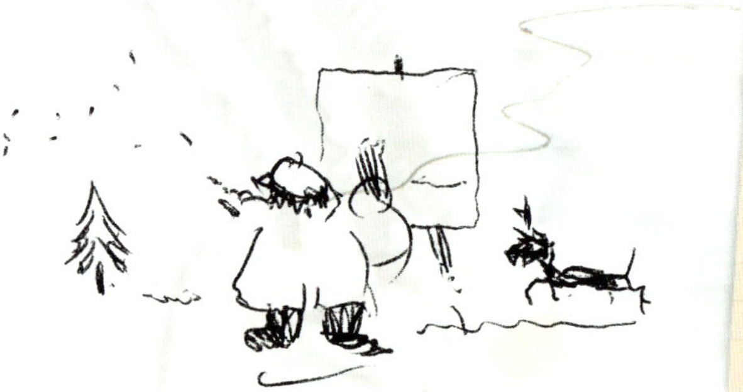

The Broads in Norfolk are a magical place;
of roads and power lines there is no trace.

Centuries ago these waterways were used
to deliver goods

by Norfolk Wherries which carried everything
from coal to animal food.

On the marshes men cut, bundled and dried the reed;
each one scythed the crop with speed.

All this history is still on view today,
making it an area of outstanding beauty.

Wherry on the Broads, Norfolk

There's nothing more pleasurable
than travelling by sail,

even more so when the wind does prevail.

So much of the riverbank
can be seen and admired,

and by the landscape you will be inspired.

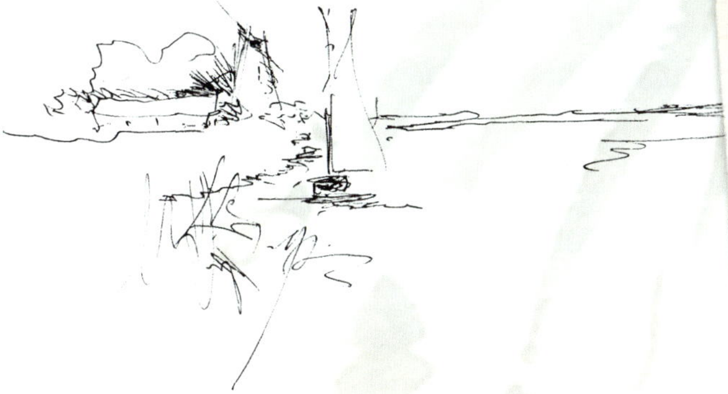

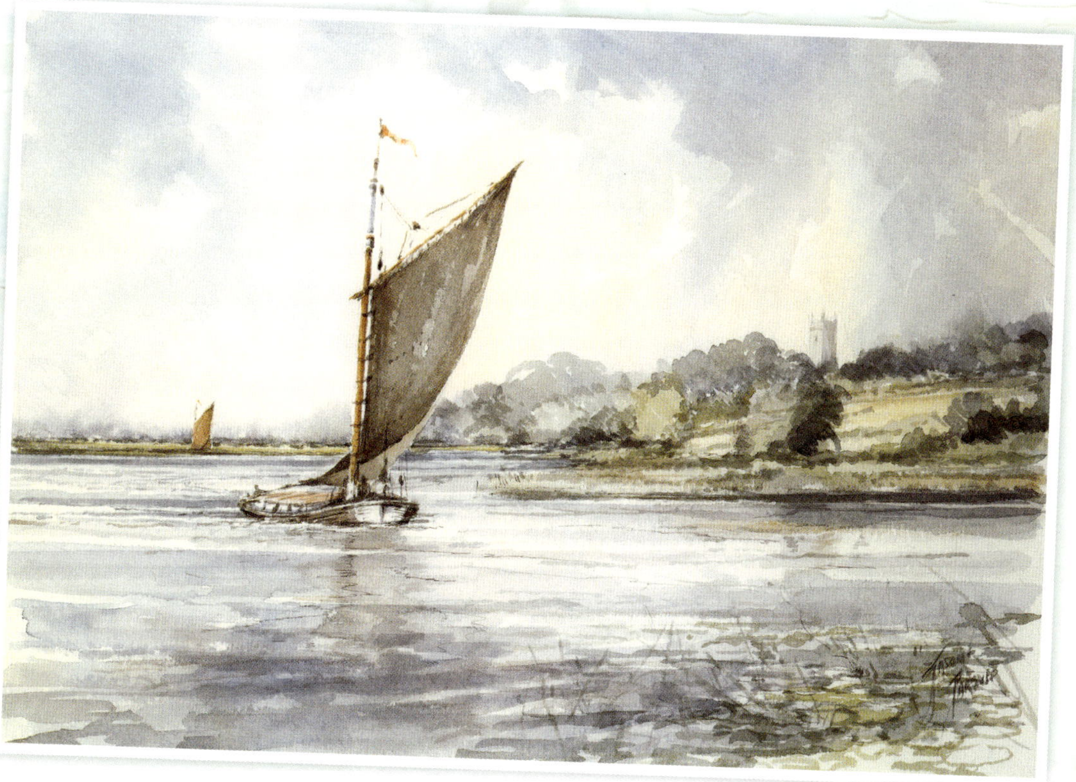

Reedcutter, Norfolk

© From an original watercolour by Jason Partner.

Around the country in villages and towns,
buildings with thatch roofs are adorned.
A testament to a traditional art
in which reed cutters make a vital part.

It is during the Winter months
that the reed cutting begins,
working on marshland
in rain and biting winds.

The reed cutter cuts and stacks the reed
then it is left to dry.
A job that scores of men have done,
over the centuries.

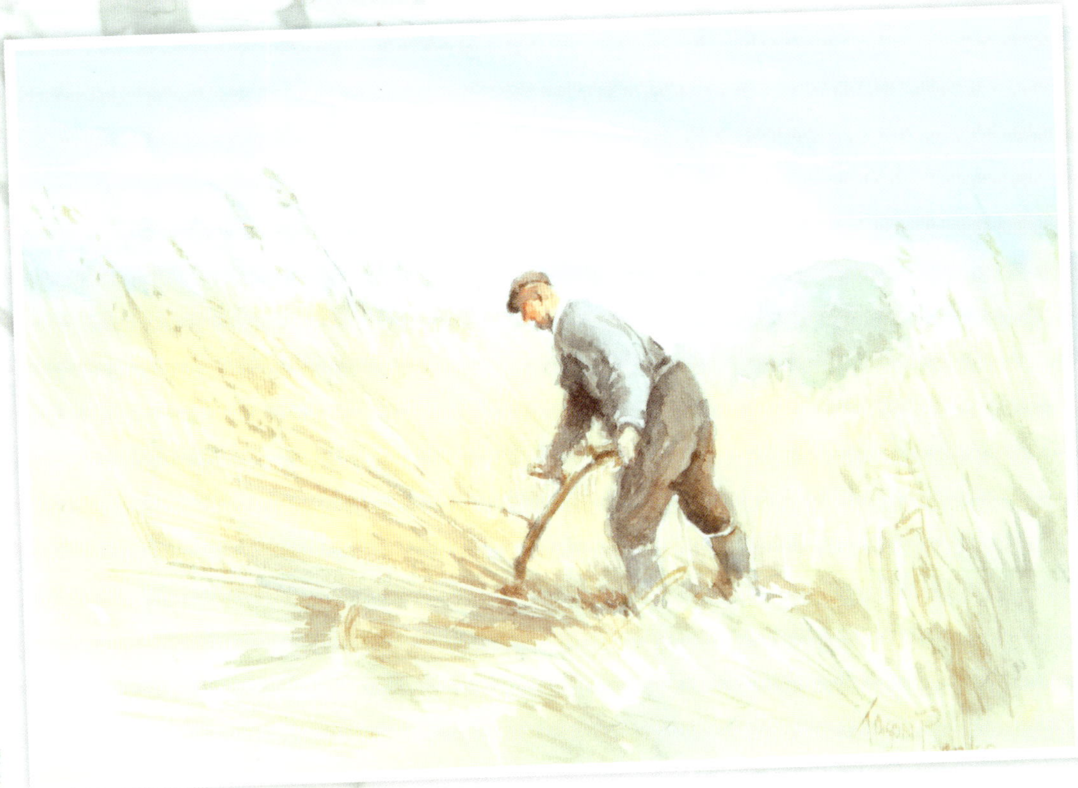

Mills in East Anglia

A selection of mill scenes painted by Jason.
These were mostly in and around the Norfolk Broads area and
approximate locations are shown in the map below.

1 - Burnham Overy Windmill, Norfolk - *see page 38*
2 - Dawke's Hide, Cley-next-the-Sea, Norfolk - *see page 39*
3 - White Mill, Thurne, Norfolk - *see page 40*
4 - Horsey Mill, Norfolk - *see page 41*
5 - Six Mile House, Norfolk - *see page 42*
6 - Billingford Mill, Norfolk - *see page 43*
7 - Cley Mill, Cley-next-the-Sea, Norfolk - *see page 44*
8 - Drainage Mill, Nordelph, Norfolk - *see page 45*
9 - Onion Top Mill, Barnack, Cambridgeshire - *see page 46*

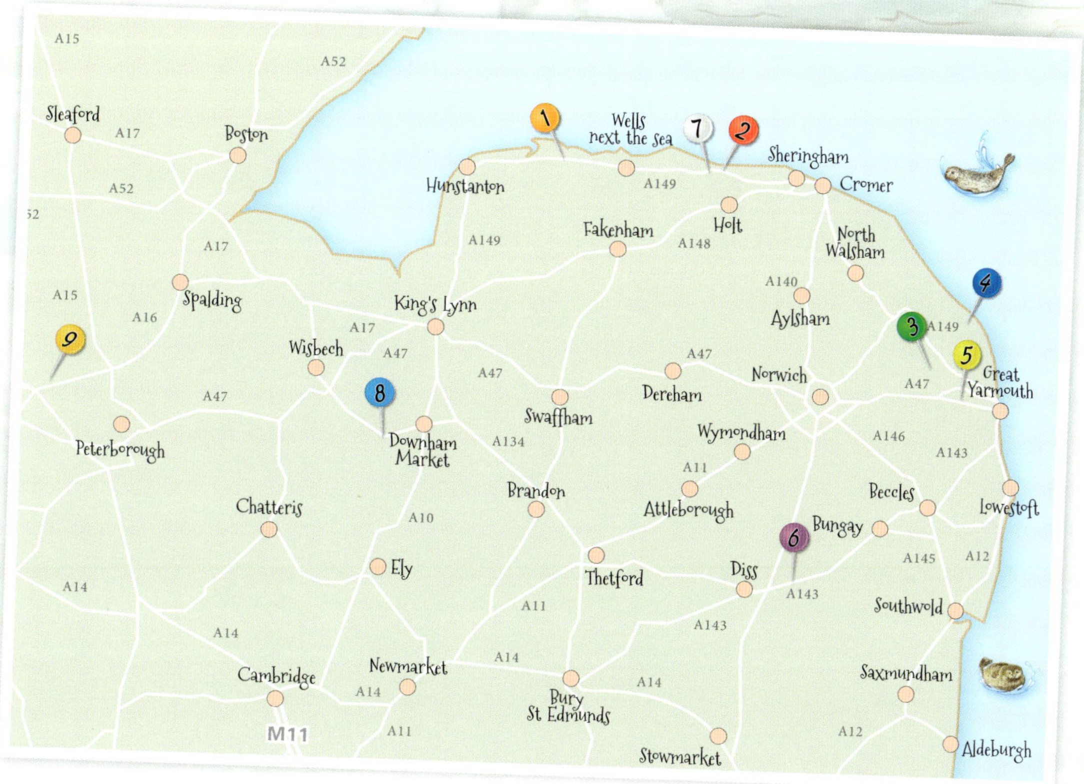

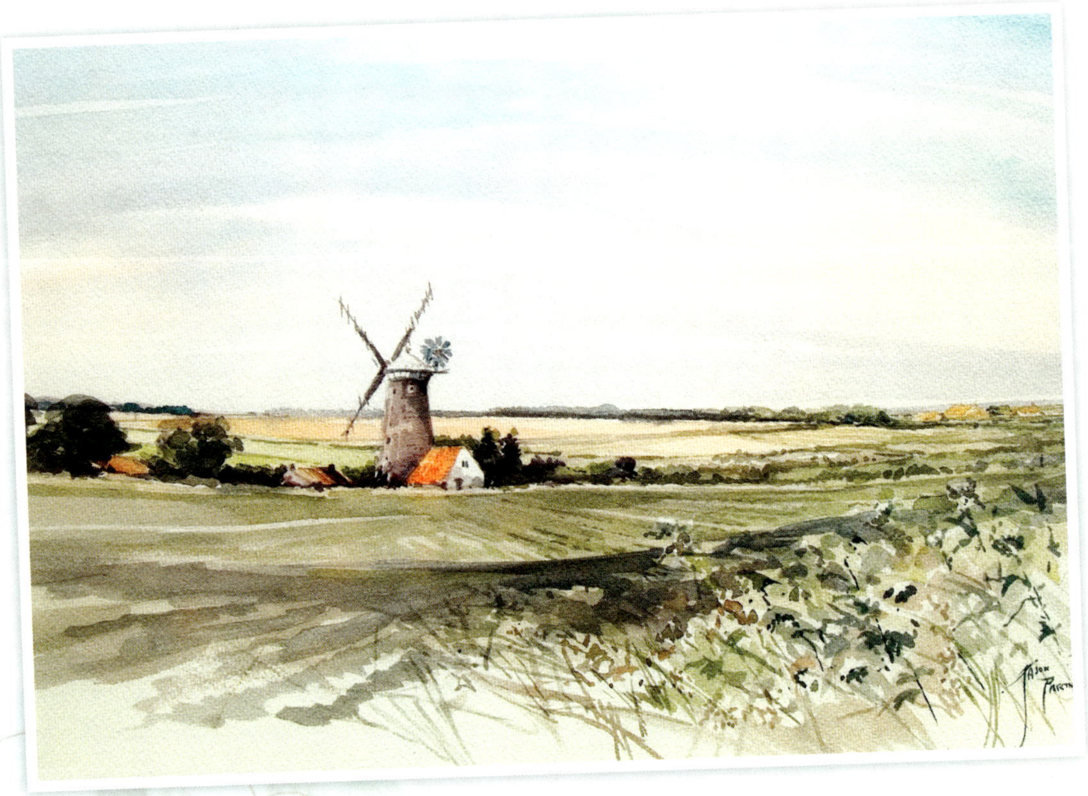

Burnham Overy Windmill, Norfolk

© From an original watercolour by Jason Partner.

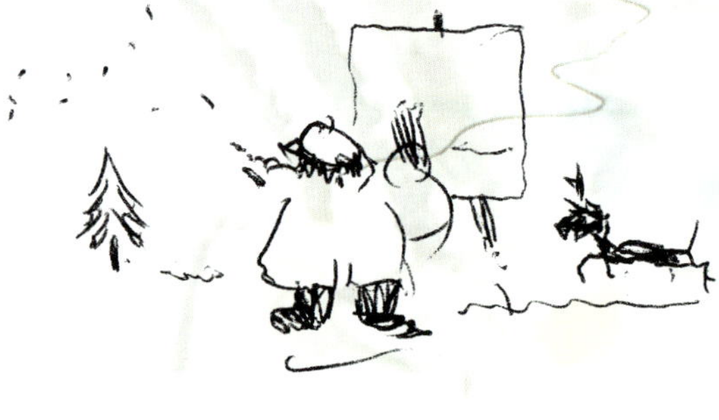

In North Norfolk there is a cluster of Burnhams,
they are very popular for people to come.

Burnham Overy being one;
a village where time is easily forgot.

And at the Staithe you'll see sailors
in their dinghies and yachts.

Dawke's Hide, Cley-next-the-Sea, Norfolk

© From an original watercolour by Jason Partner.

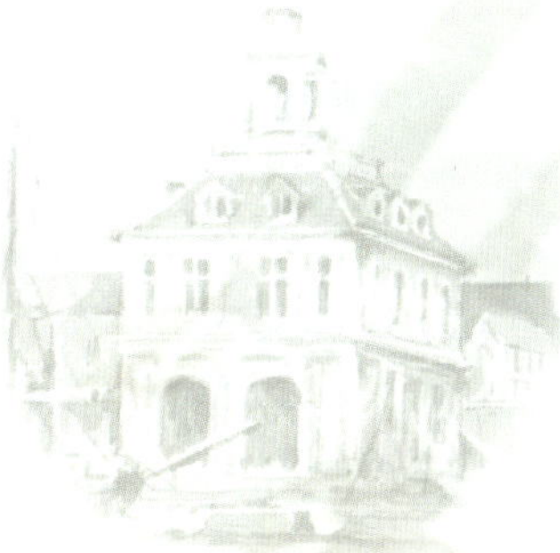

Hush!!

Please keep very still and quiet!

The hide is not the place to cause a riot.

Patience and concentration
help to focus the mind.

Then you'll get the chance
to spot birds of all different kinds.

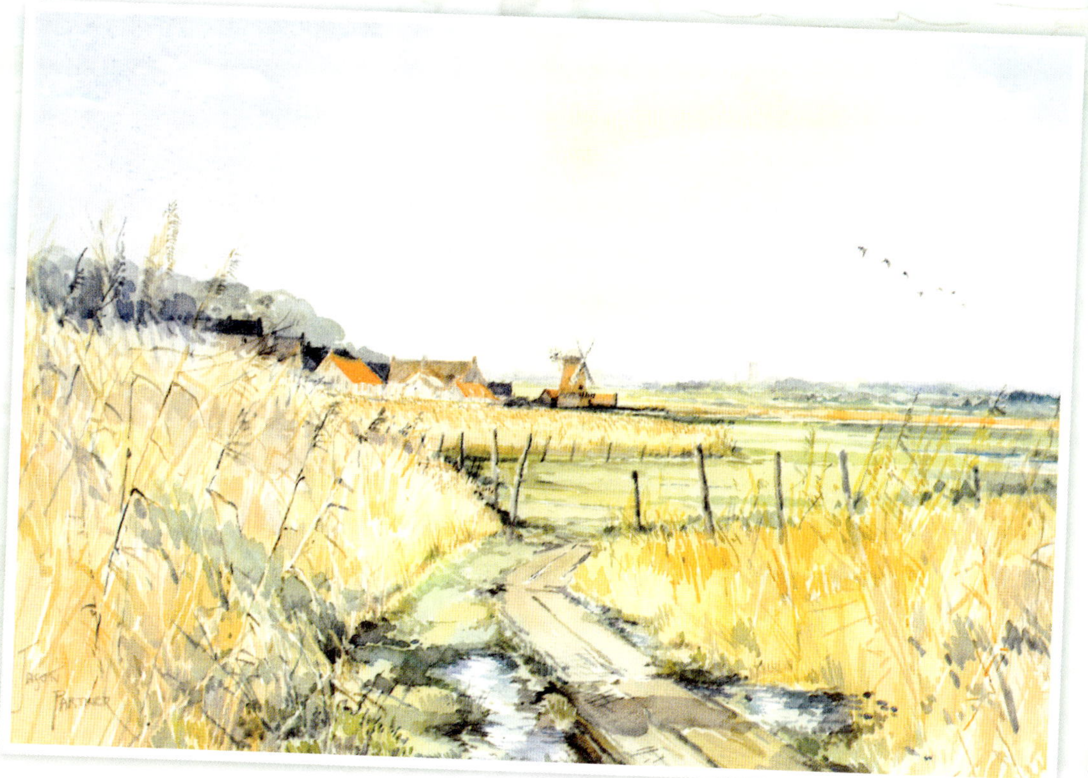

White Mill, Thurne, Norfolk

The white mill at Thurne, as many would say,
is a hidden treasure of the Broad's waterways.
There are places for your boat to moor,
in fact it is a lovely place to explore.

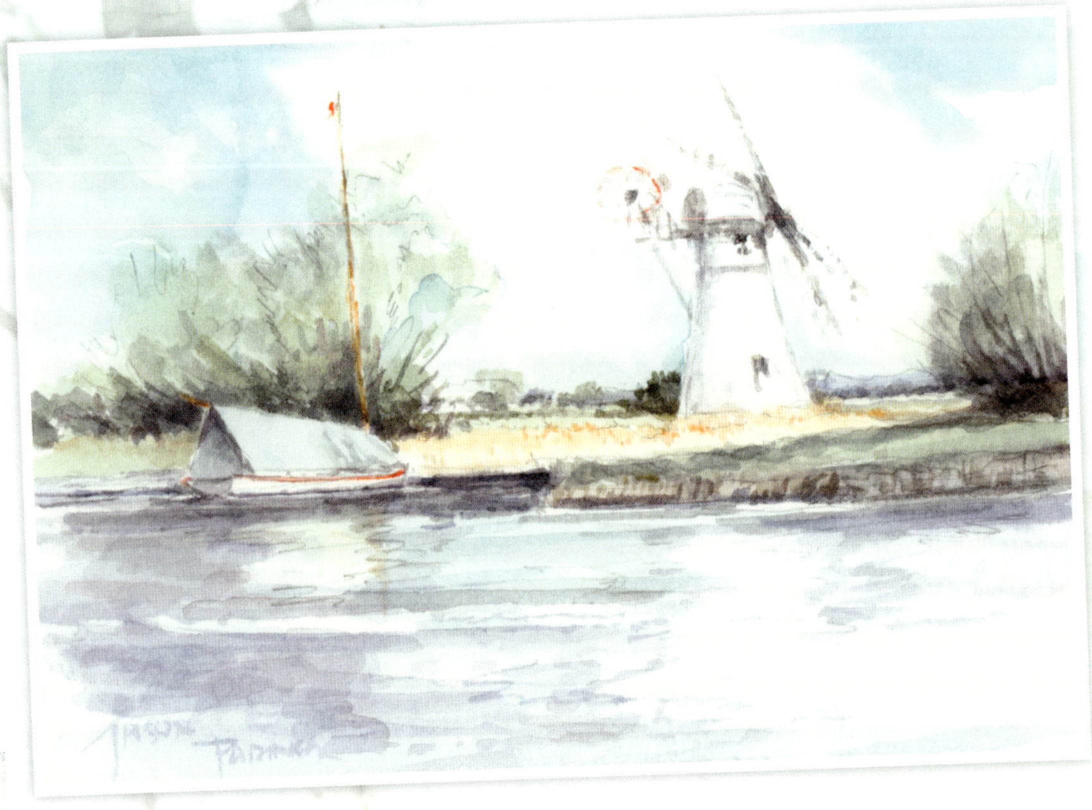

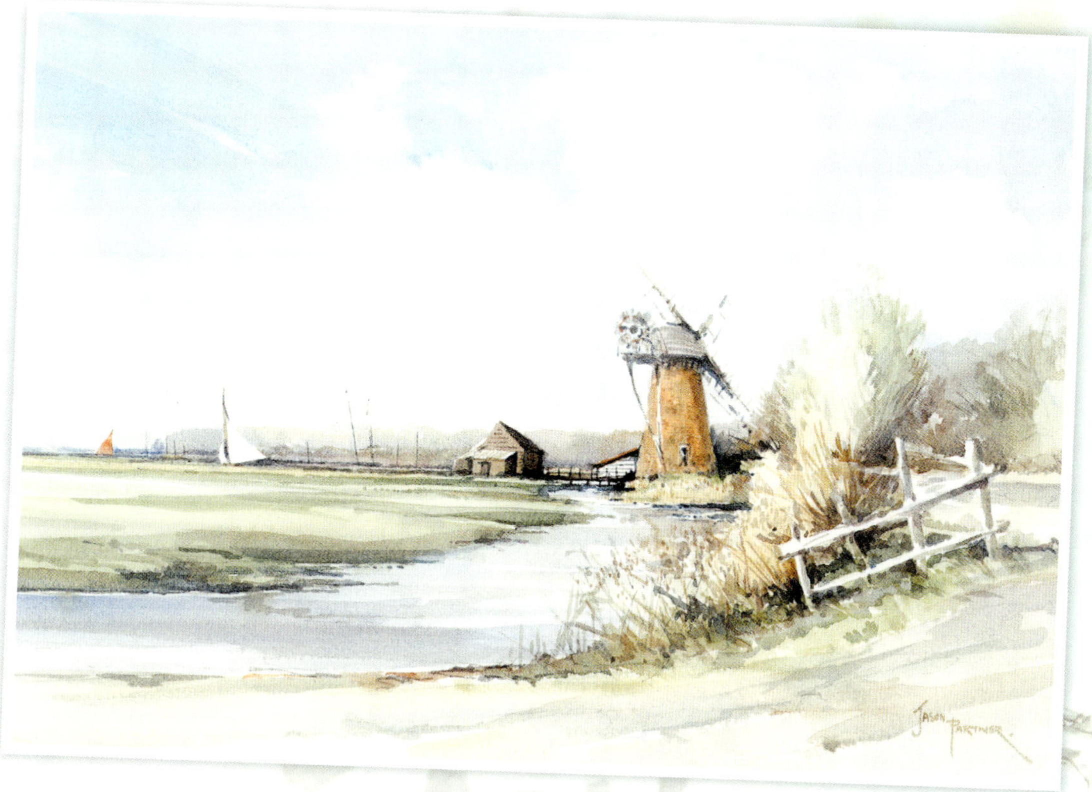

Horsey Mill, Norfolk

Close to where the 21st century turbines stand,
not built to give power, rather to drain the land,

With pleasant surroundings, where reeds gently sway,
is the picturesque mill at Horsey Staithe.

A very popular place, for boats to moor,
for visitors an ideal area to explore.

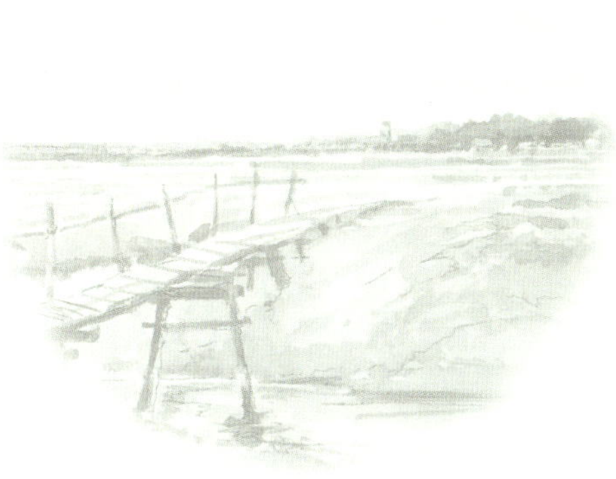

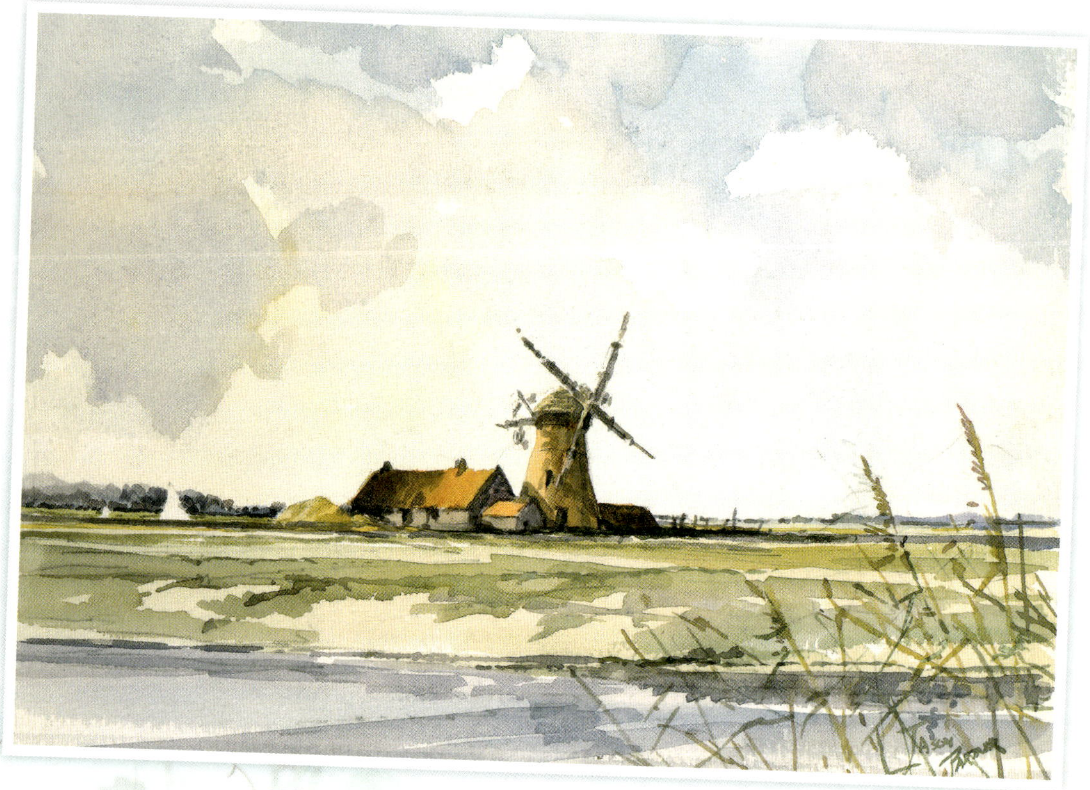

Six Mile House, Norfolk

© From an original watercolour by Jason Partner.

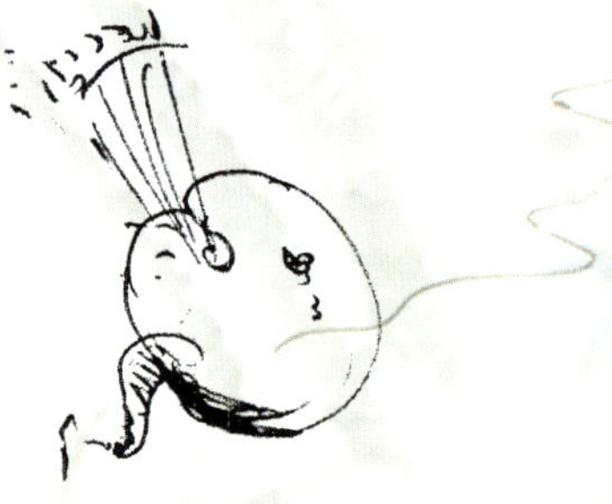

Throughout Norfolk, especially around
the Broads, you'll see

Drainage mills which form part
of an historic legacy.

These mills worked hard
to keep the marshland dry

So cattle and sheep safely graze
and watch the world go by.

Billingford Mill, Norfolk

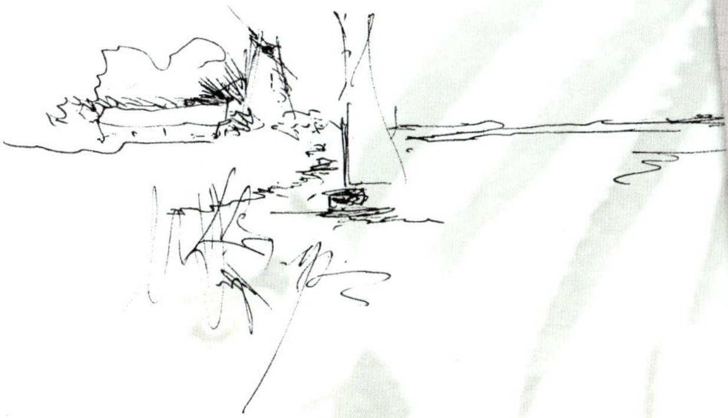

On the borders of Norfolk and Suffolk,
Billingford lies.

Where an impressive mill
dominates the skies.

Over the years grain
was ground into flour.

The sails being turned
by the force of wind power.

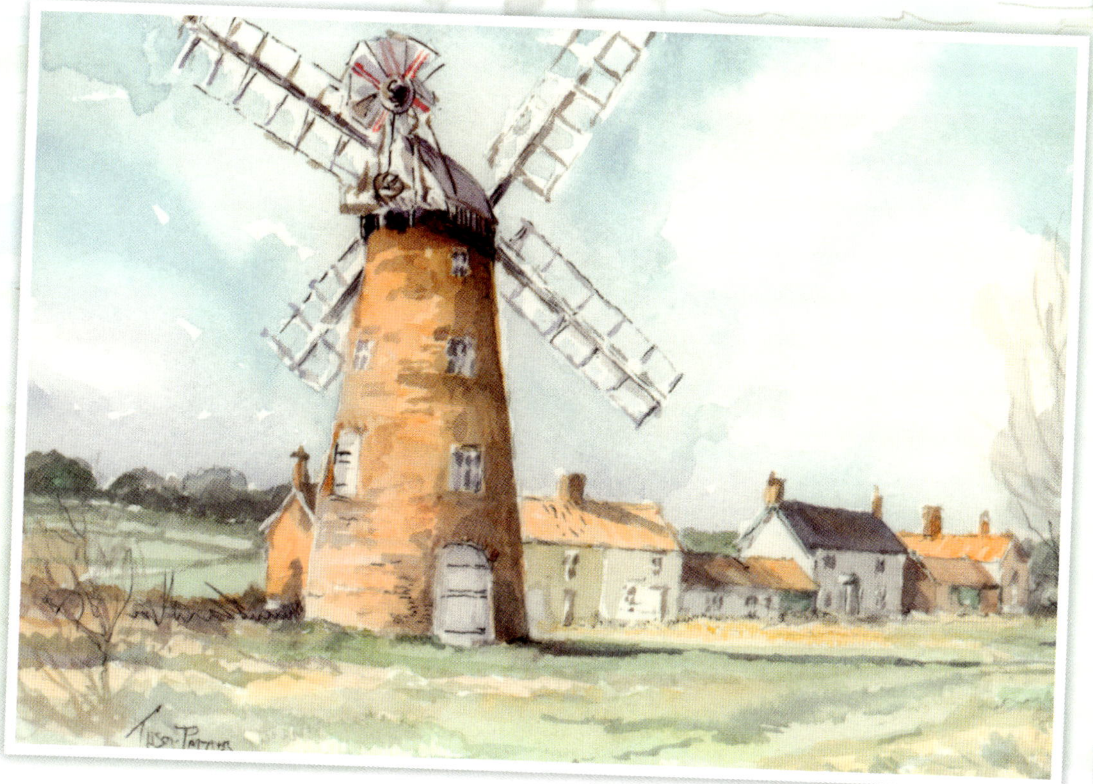

Cley Mill, Cley-next-the-Sea, Norfolk

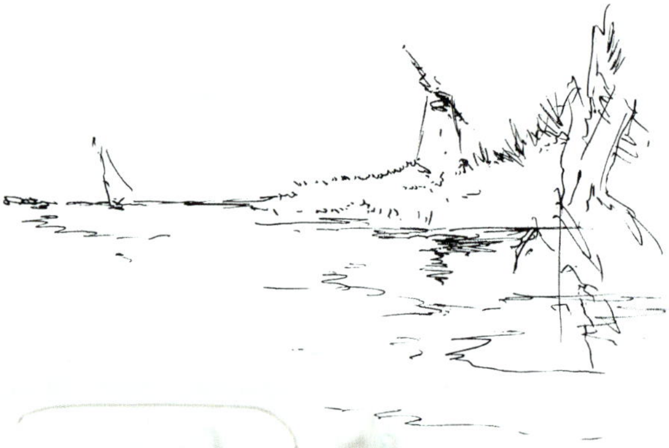

The scenery around Cley attracts people
from far and near.

Especially when a rare feathered
visitor appears.

Apart from the wildlife, there is much
to be explored,

And, for artists,
Cley is very much adored.

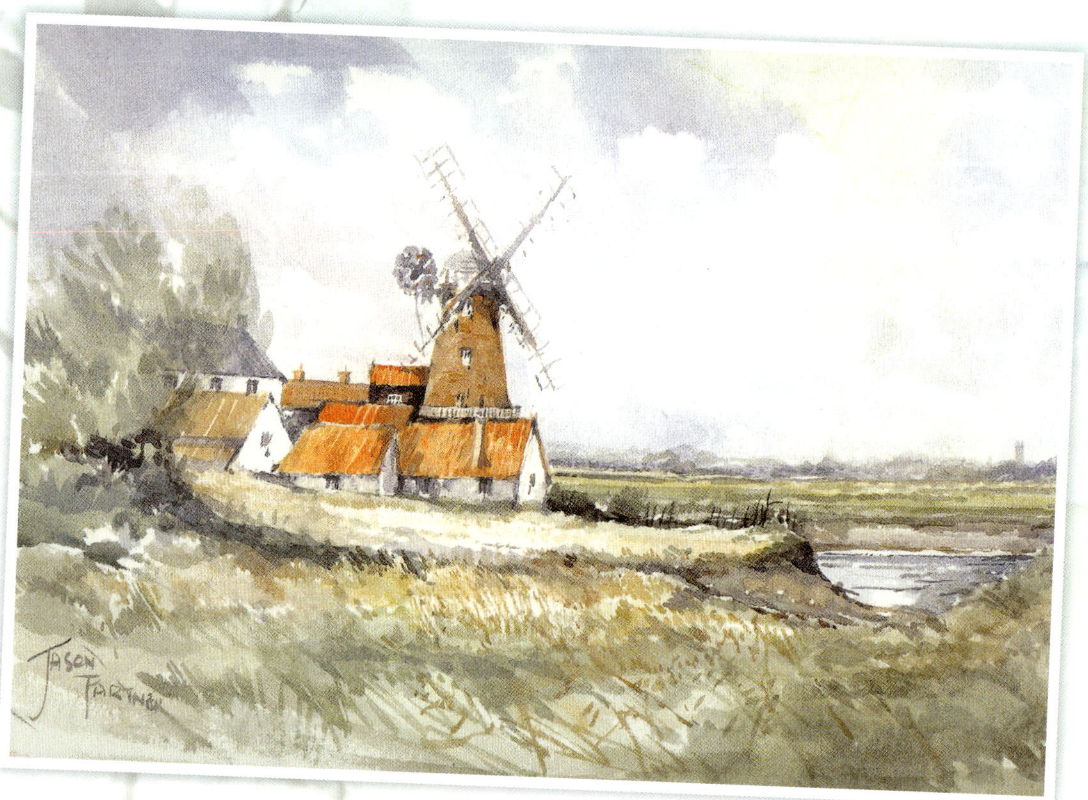

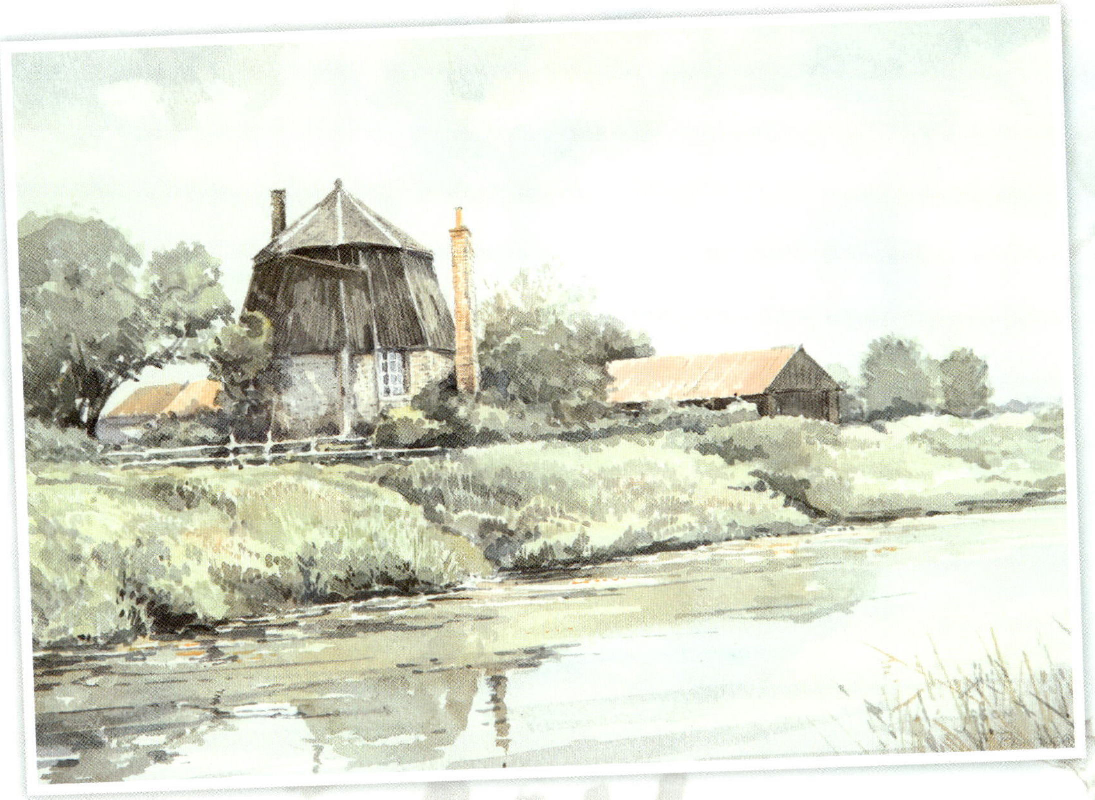

Drainage Mill, Nordelph, Norfolk

© From an original watercolour by Jason Partner.

In this quiet location close to Downham Market
is where you'll see this mill.

Although for many years the machinery etc
has stood still.

This smock mill, in days long gone,
helped to drain the land.

Now, as a testament to centuries past,
it proudly stands.

Yellow Ochre ...

...a natural earth colour which can range from yellow to deep orange.

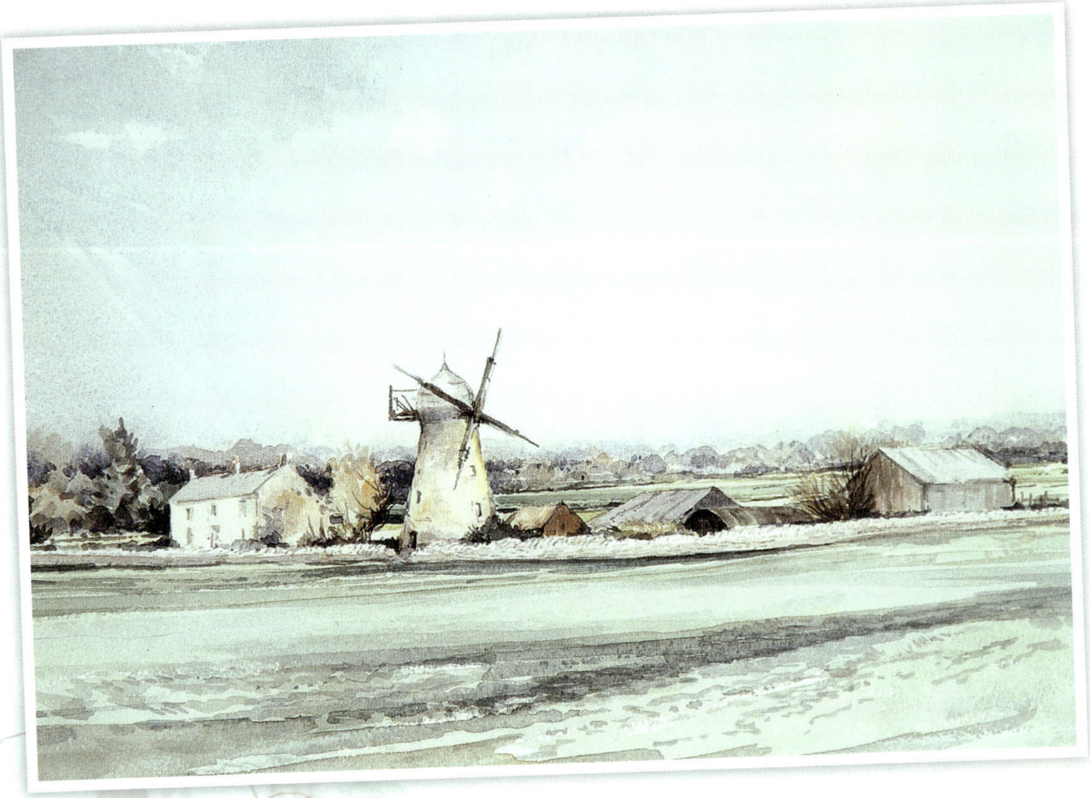

Onion Top Mill, Barnack, Cambridgeshire

© From an original watercolour by Jason Partner.

You may not have heard of Barnack
or know where it is,

But its limestone was used for buildings
by the Romans.

The 18th century mill has been restored
for posterity,

As it showcases three hundred years
of history.

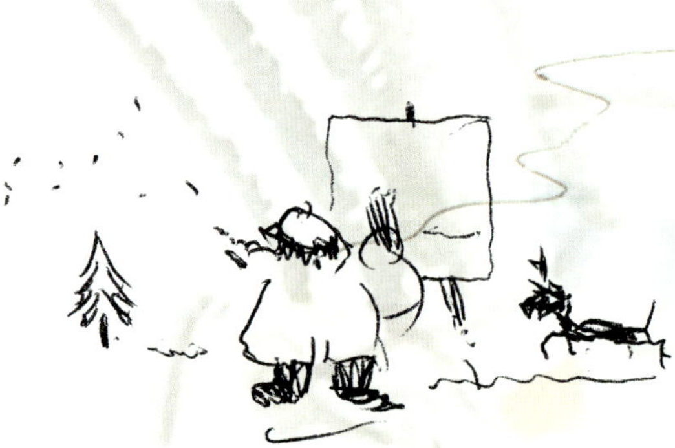

Farming Scenes

A selection of farming scenes painted by Jason.
These were mostly in and around the East Anglia region.

Jason's grandfather had a smallholding of land, so many a time was spent observing what the farm labourers did during the year and painting images as a record.

During this time Jason became friendly with the foreman, Alf, whom Jason admired. He also got to know the other farm hands, including Reuben, who had some sort of learning disability. Alf made sure that Jason respected Reuben as much as the other people working on the farm. In later life, when Jason returned to his grandfather's farm he would visit Alf's grave, too, as a mark of respect and gratitude for all he had been taught in his youth.

In the 1930s, well before mechanisation of farming, men and horses did all the work. So the labourers would first make sure the horses were fit, fed and ready for the day ahead.

From harrowing (making sure any lumps of soil had been broken down and made into a tilth), to ploughing, planting, and harvesting, the work was arduous for both man and horse.

The busiest of times was the harvest, when every farm worker, plus women and children, gave a helping hand to make sure the crop of cereal etc was cut, baled and stored whilst the weather and daylight were still good.

From dawn to dusk the people worked, but during the hottest part of the day, a well deserved break was taken. Oats and water were on hand for the horses, whilst the men ate bread and cheese. Once the day's work came to an end, the horses might be lucky enough to be taken to a nearby stream to cool down and have a refreshing drink.

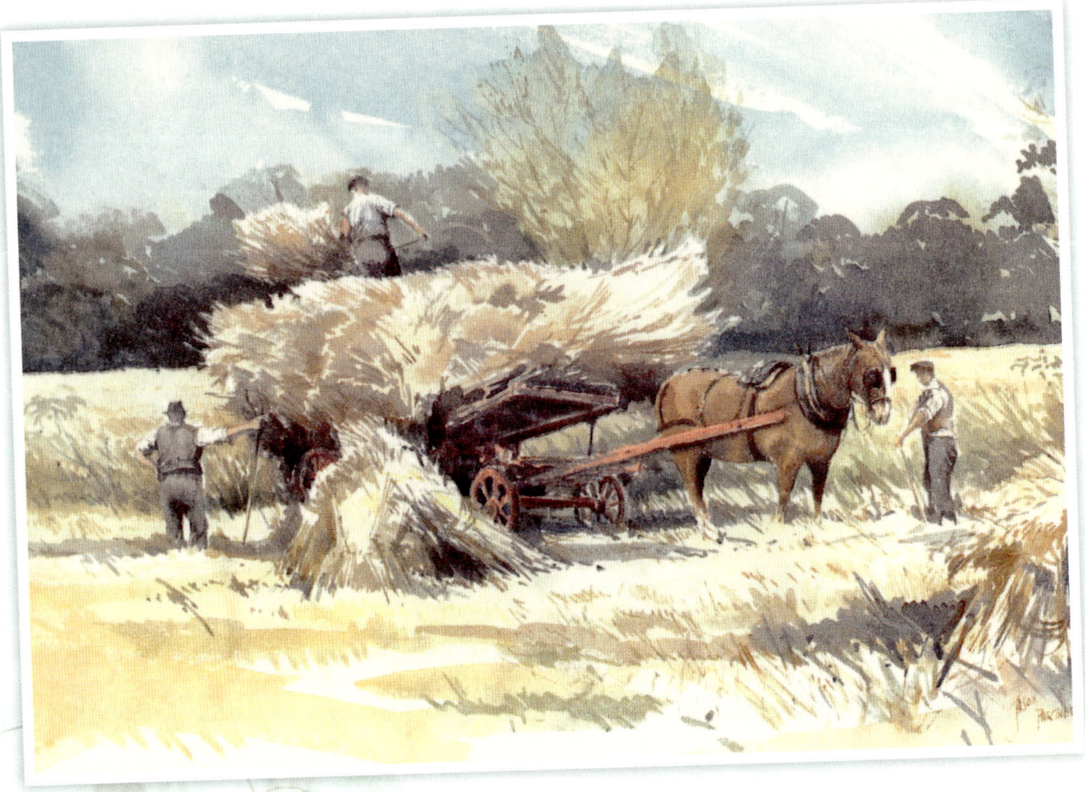

Corn carting

© From an original watercolour by Jason Partner.

Neighbours and family
used to help harvest the corn,

starting the hard work
in the early dawn.

Hand tools and horse-drawn carts
have long since made way

as combine harvesters have come
to the farm workers' aid.

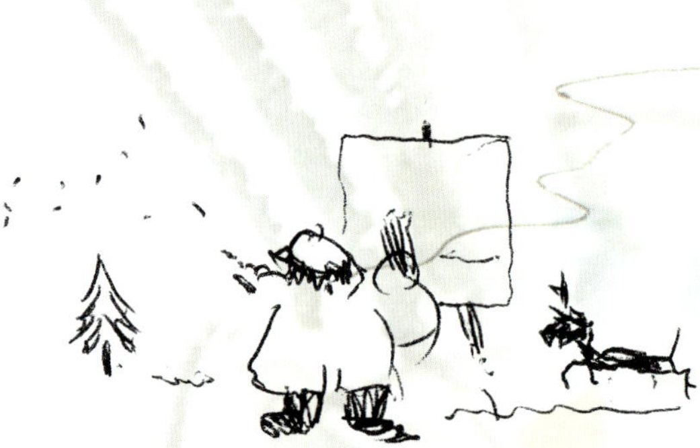

At the end of the day

© From an original watercolour by Jason Partner.

Many hours we have toiled,
working acres of soil.

Now in the stream,
our hooves we dip,

and from the refreshing water,
we sip.

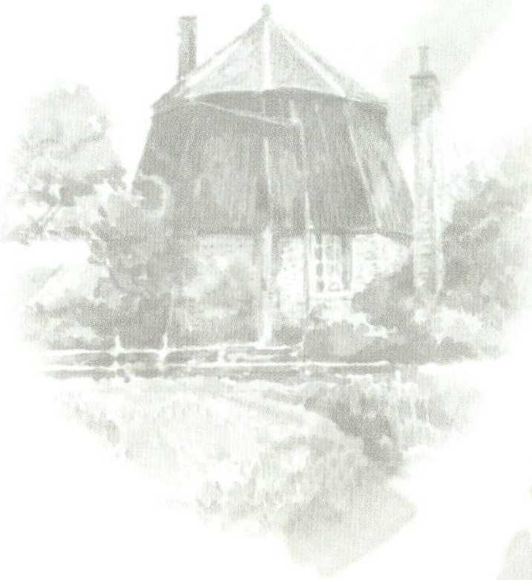

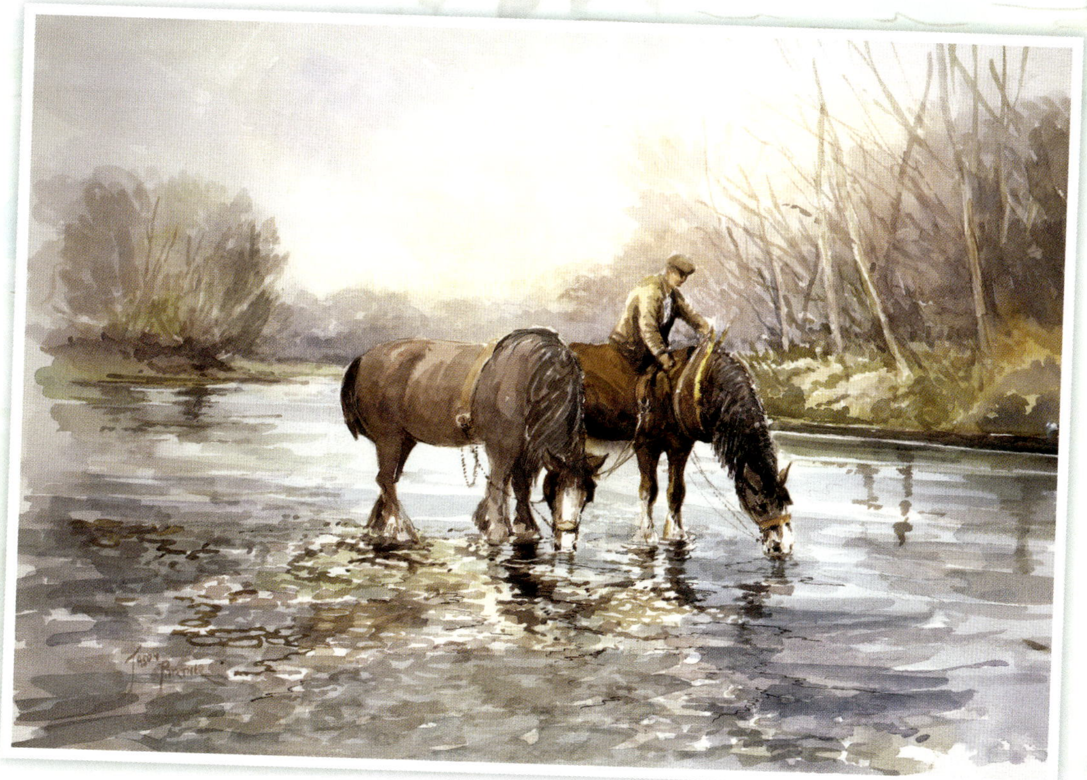

Diamond and Boxer

© From an original watercolour by Jason Partner

As Jason's family in Leicestershire had a smallholding much of his young life was watching the workers on the land and he became friendly with Alf and Reuben. The image of 'Diamond and Boxer' really depicts the time before the Second World War when farm work was undertaken by a large group of men, and horses were an integral part. This period of the 1930s is also seen in 'At the end of the day' and 'Corn carting'.

Walking backwards and forwards, always in line,
whilst Joe, with the reins, trudges behind.
Harrowing the field, making the ground level, the soil stirred,
whilst overhead the chorus of singing birds is heard.
Diamond and Boxer working hard through the day,
once the job is completed, they'll need plenty of hay.

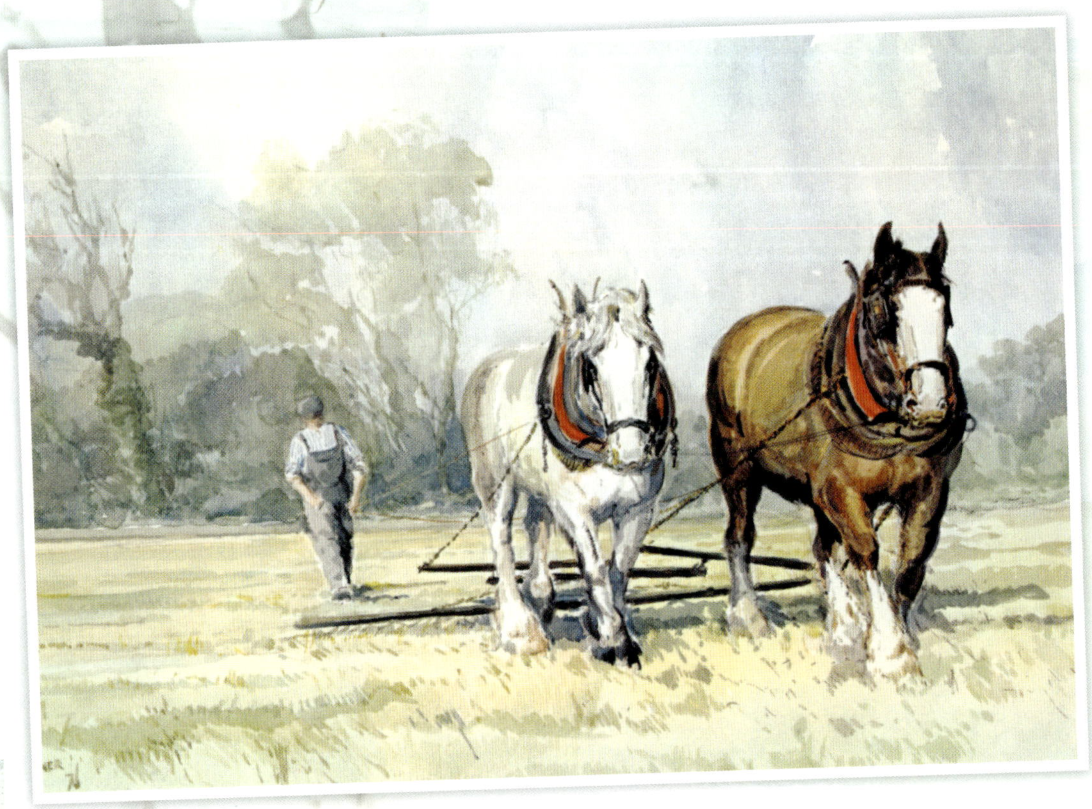

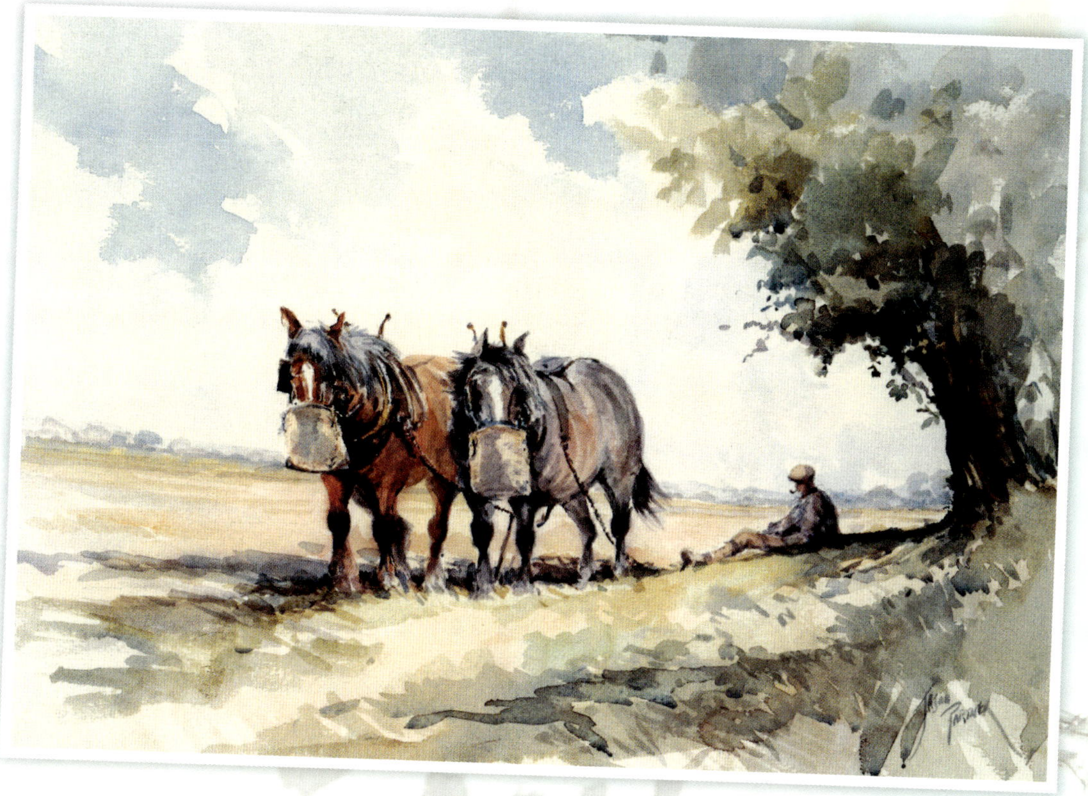

Noon day break

© From an original watercolour by Jason Partner.

It's time for a break for the horses and me.

They have their bags of hay
and I have bread and cheese.

Whilst we have a rest and shelter from the sun,

I am very pleased how much work has been done.

And, although I'd love to sit here all day,

if the work's not finished,
I will not get my pay.

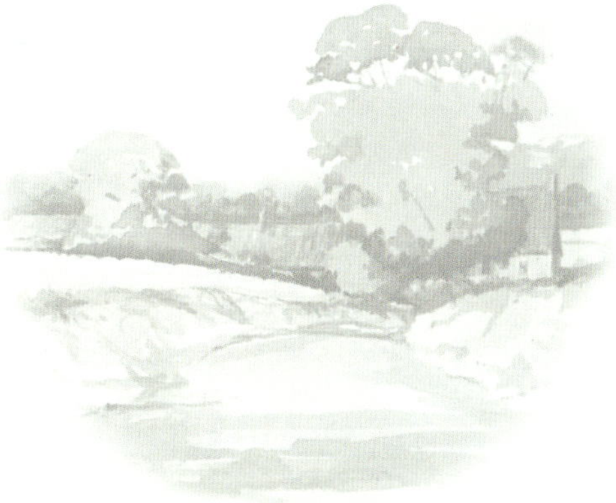

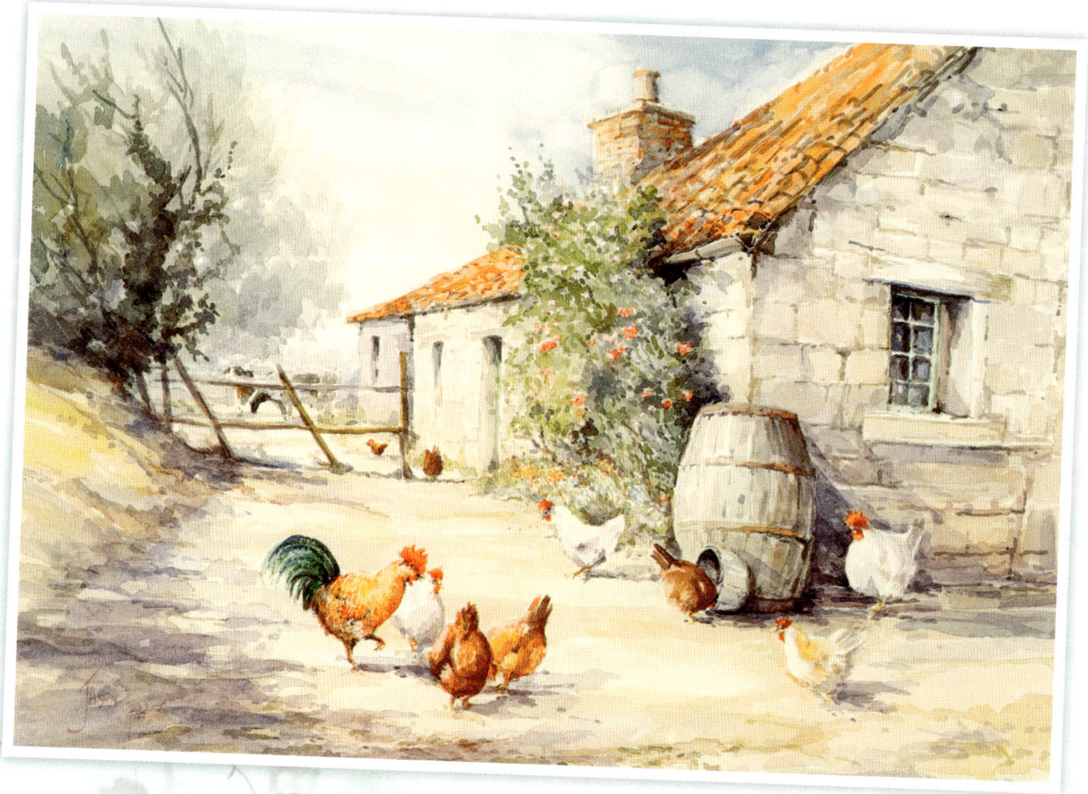

Suffolk Farmyard

© From an original watercolour by Jason Partner.

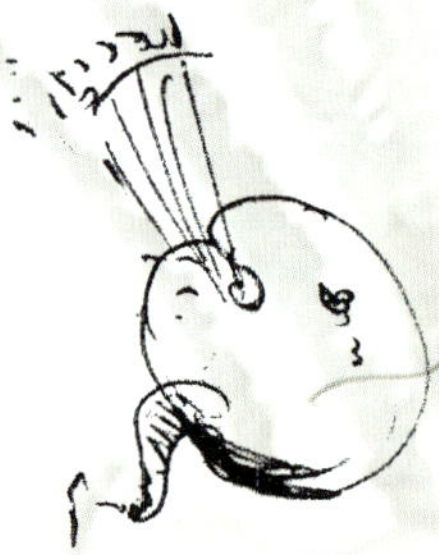

Chickens in the driveway, cattle just beyond.
On this farm you'll be working all day long.
With a cockerel crowing as the sun begins to rise,
you'll not need an alarm clock to open up your eyes!

Village smithy

© From an original watercolour by Jason Partner.

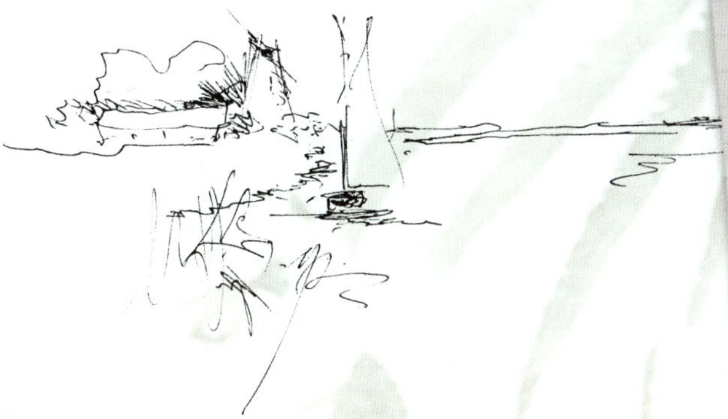

If an owner needed new shoes
for their horses,

They'd head straight for the local smithy,
of course.

Nowadays appointments are made
by email or phone,

And the smithy will make a visit
to the horse owner's home.

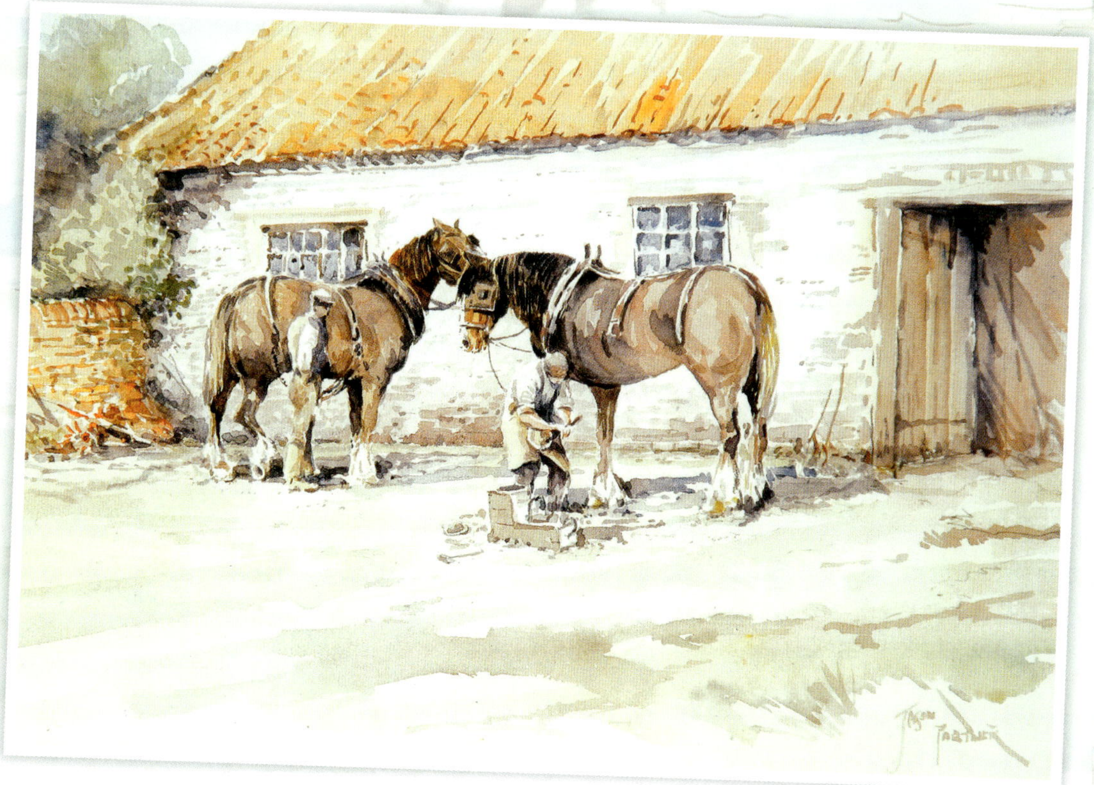

Back from the fields

© From an original watercolour by Jason Partner.

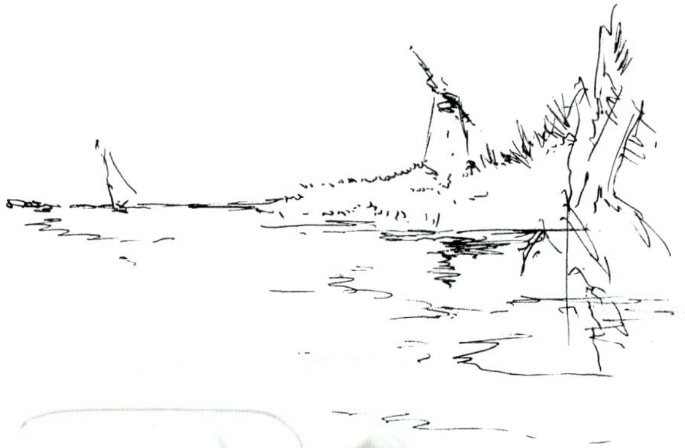

Up before the sunrise,
back home by dusk.

Feeling worn out
and clothes full of dust.

This farmer is glad to be
heading home once more,

Met by Bob, his dog,
who had been waiting by the door.

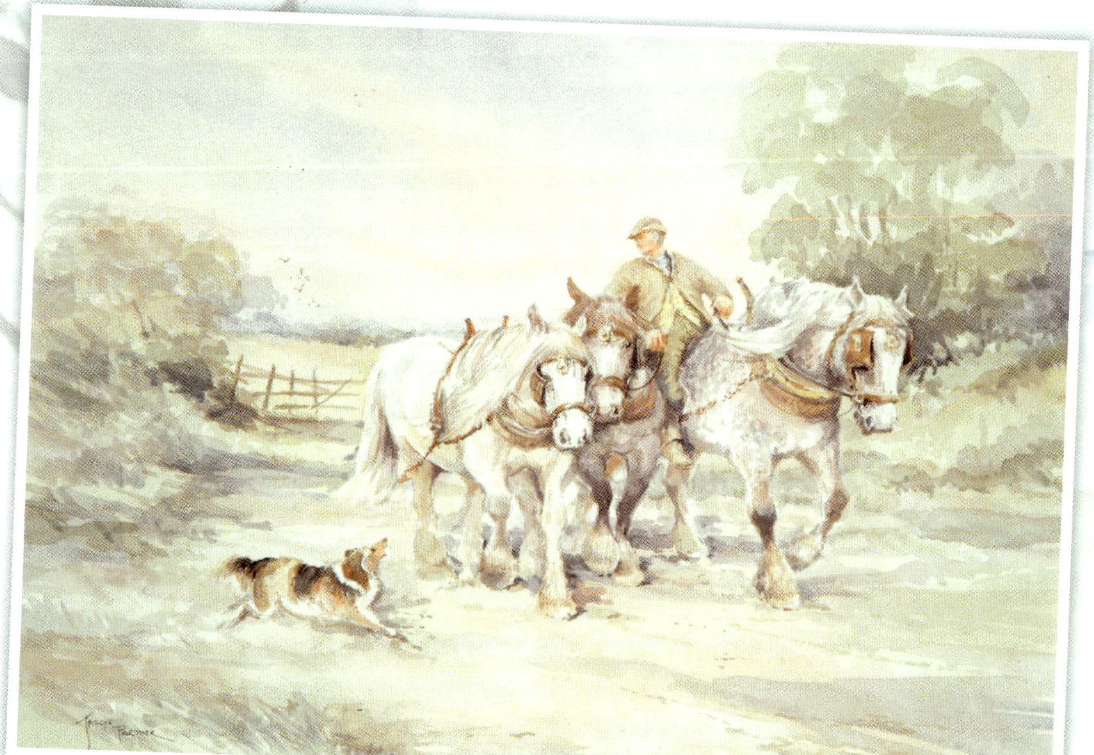

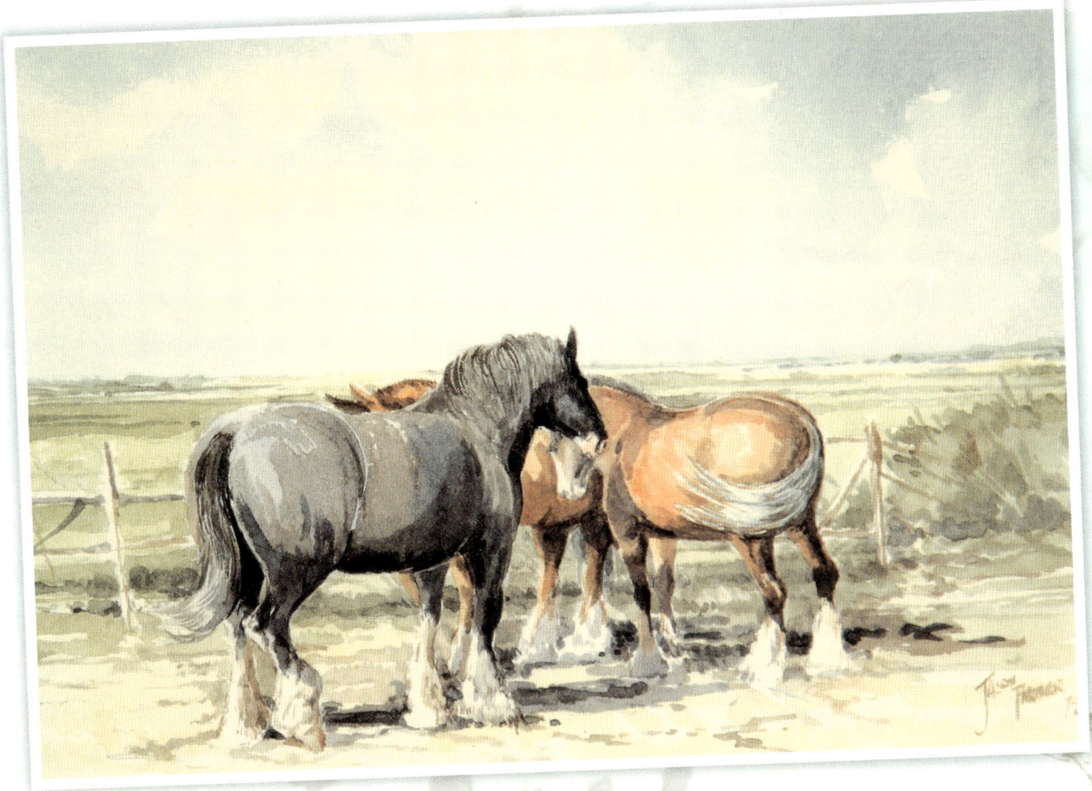

Horses in the Fens

© From an original watercolour by Jason Partner.

The Fens, a vast area
where the soil is most fertile,

From root crops to cereals
cover mile after mile.

This land was drained
many centuries ago,

So that all kinds of vegetables
and flowers could be grown.

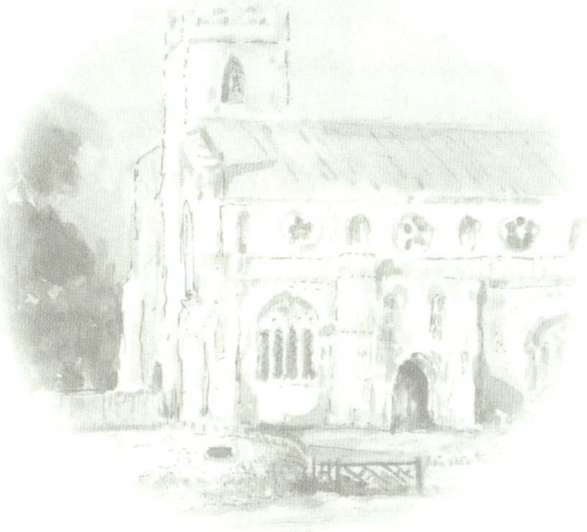

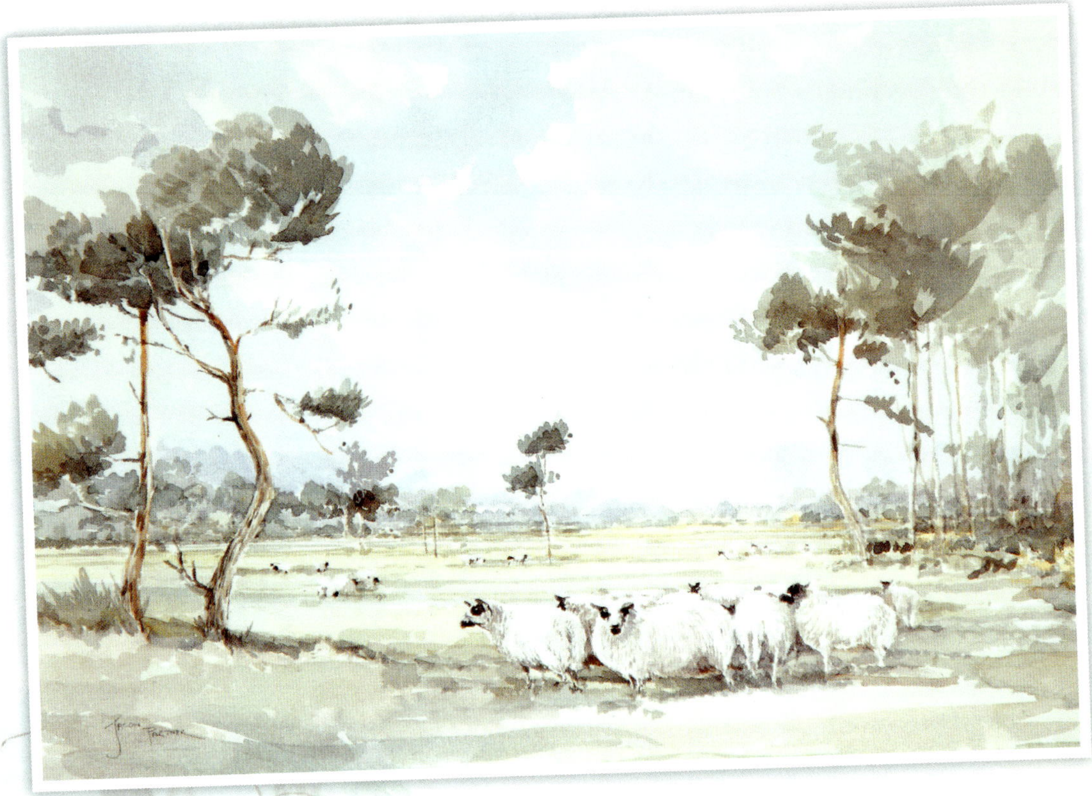

Sheep in Breckland

© From an original watercolour by Jason Partner.

The Brecks, in west Norfolk,
is a place full of surprises,

Where flint knapping skills were used
to make tools of all sizes.

Grazing and forestry
go side by side,

And a place where an abundance
of wildlife abides.

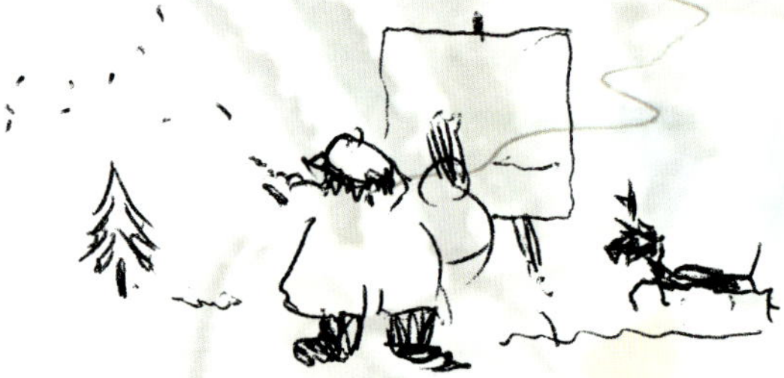

Ploughing horses' heads

For many years these powerful animals
were worth their weight in gold.

Strong, with a good temperament,
they did as they were told.

Throughout the farming year
they worked upon the land.

Following the farm labourers'
every command.

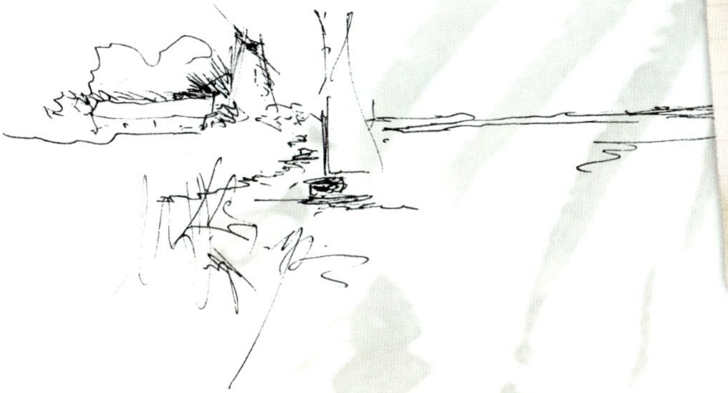

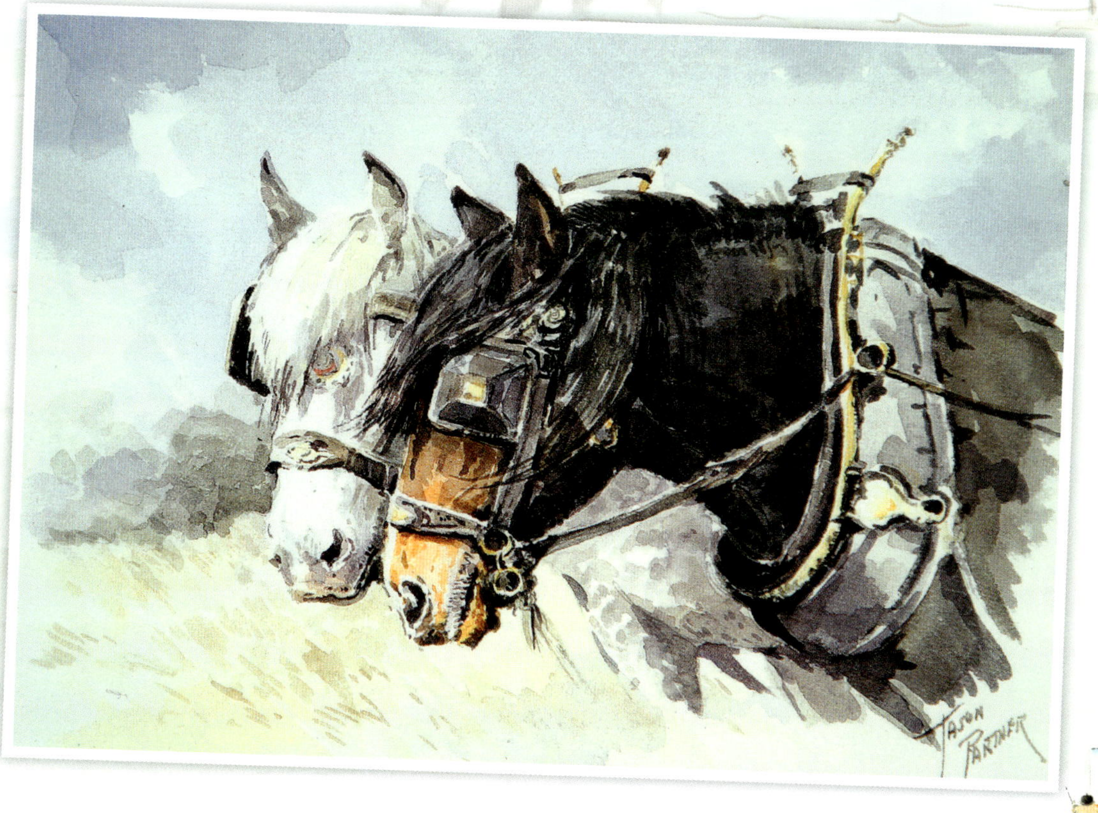

The village blacksmith

This trade is no longer seen as much as it used to be.

In many country villages the forge was a hive of activity.

The blacksmith would beat softened iron using hammer blows.

To make pots, pans, and a variety of farming tools.

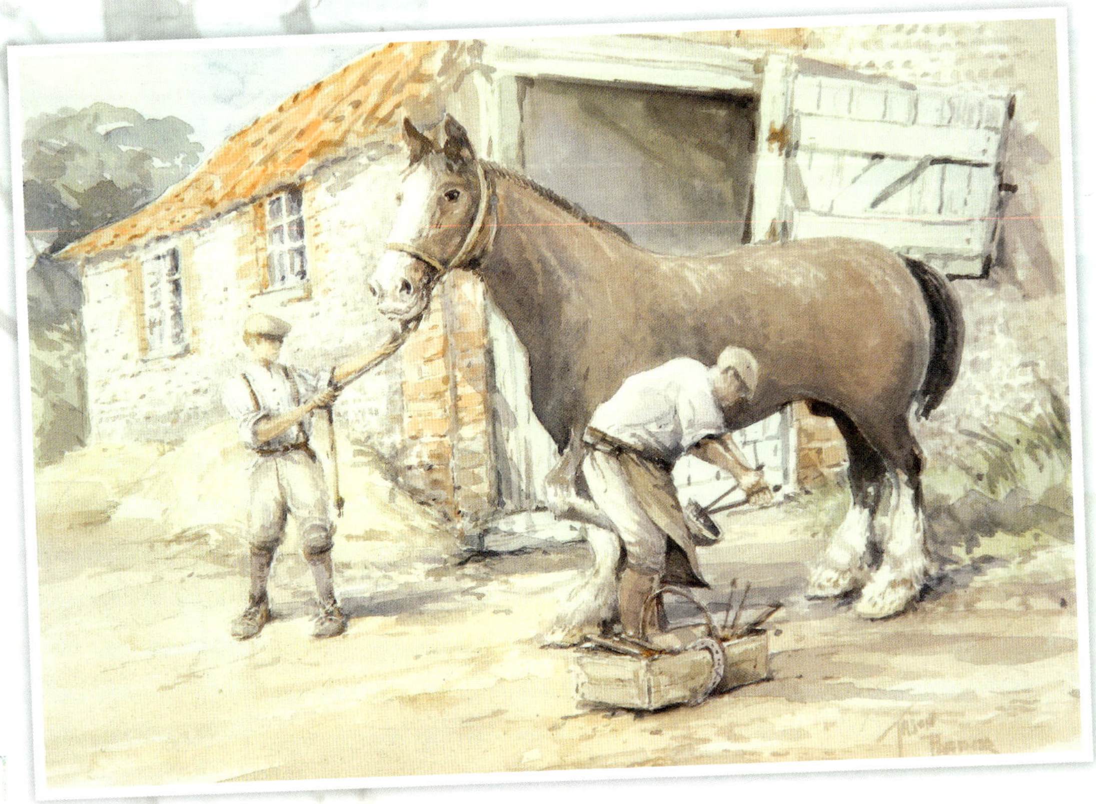

Seascapes

A selection of seascapes painted by Jason.
These were mostly in and around the East Anglia region and
approximate locations are shown in the map below.

1 - Brancaster Staithe, Norfolk - *see page 60*
2 - Pin Mill, Suffolk - *see page 61*
3 - Southwold Quay, Suffolk - *see page 62*
4 - Thornham, Norfolk - *see page 63*
5 - Pakefield, Suffolk - *see page 64*
6 - Morston, Norfolk - *see page 65*
7 - Lowestoft, Suffolk - *see page 66*
8 - Low tide, Brancaster, Norfolk - *see page 67*
9 - Southwold Harbour, Suffolk - *see page 68*
10 - Sea lavender, Morston, Norfolk - *see page 69*

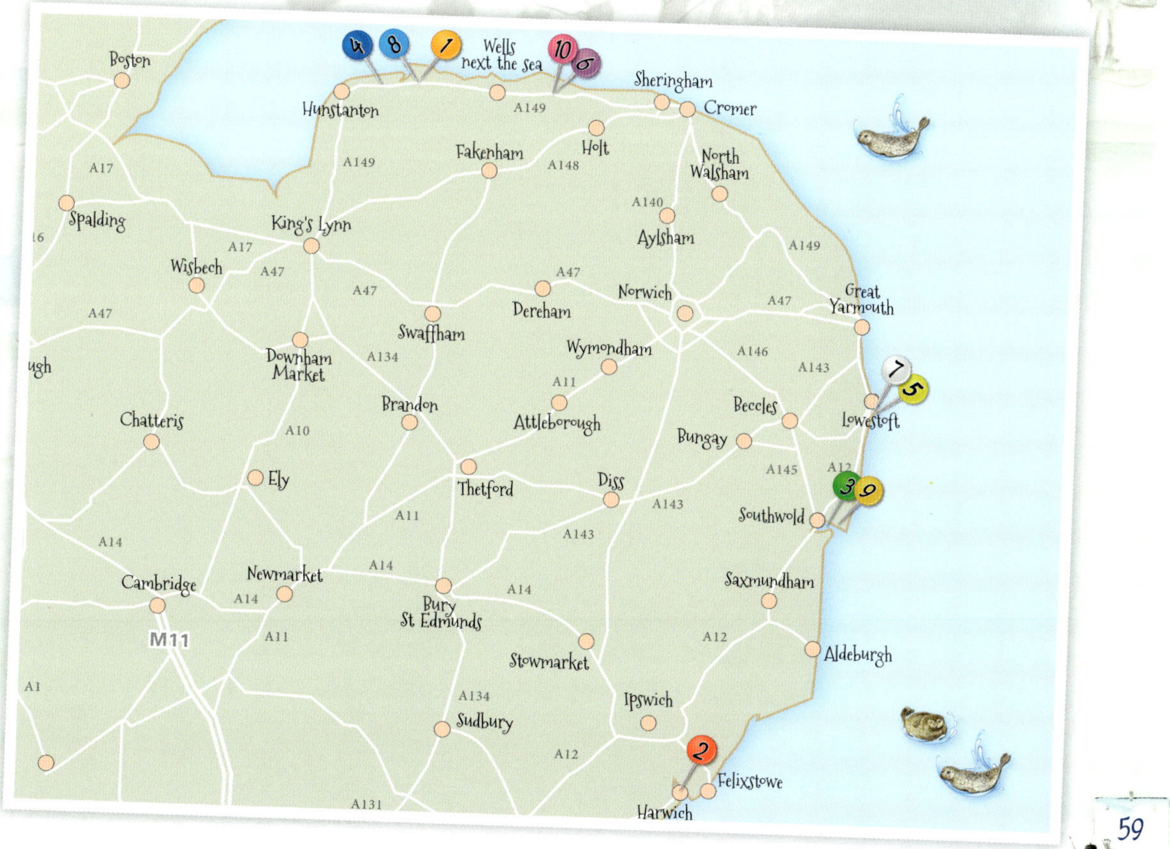

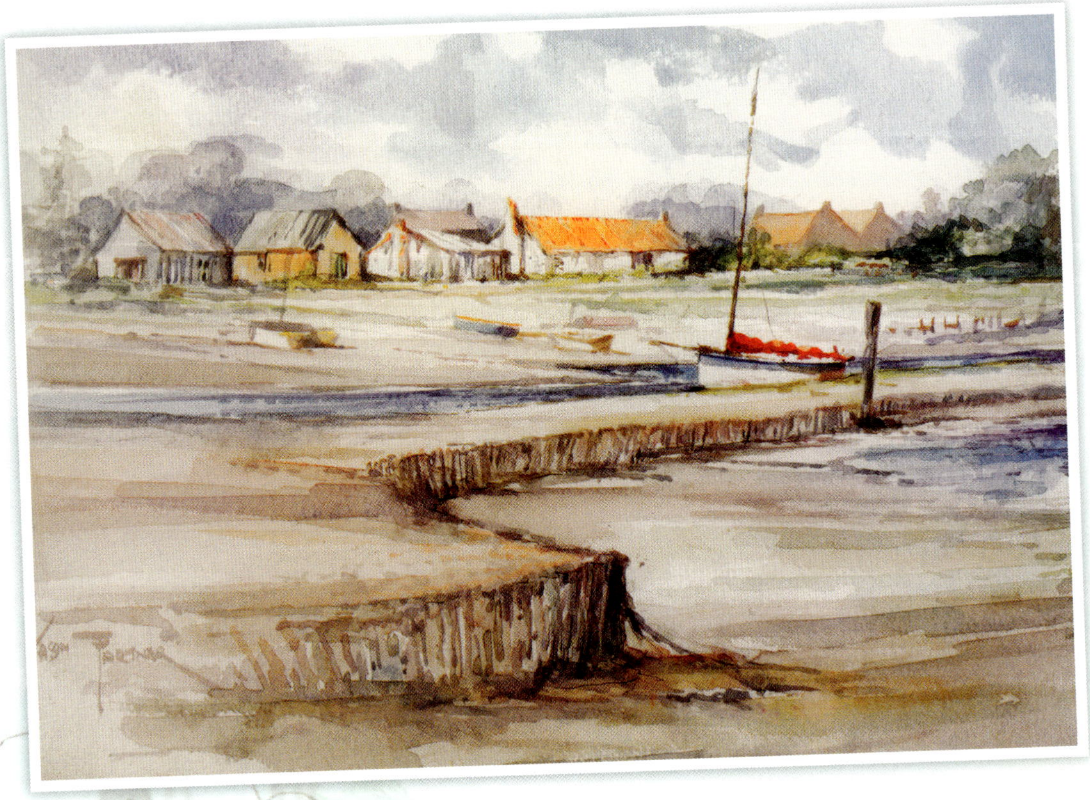

Brancaster Staithe, Norfolk

Along the North Norfolk coast,
where the sun gently bathes,
countless numbers of boats
you will see at Brancaster Staithe.

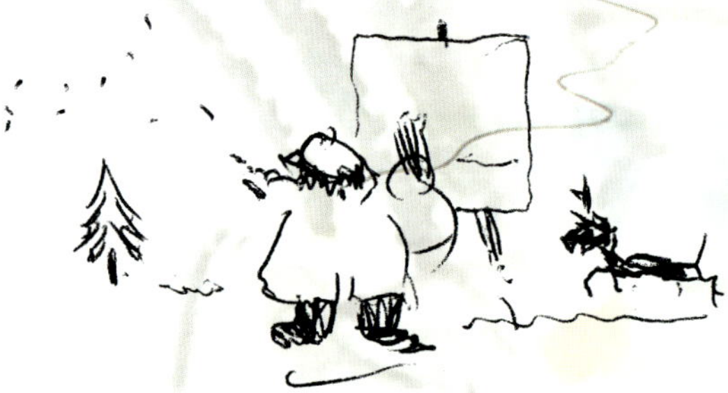

Pin Mill, Suffolk

© From an original watercolour by Jason Partner.

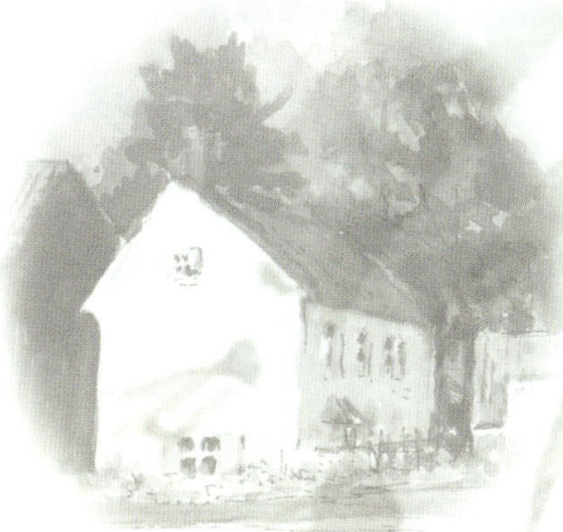

The London Barge looks majestical,
with its sails billowing from the mast.
In races, they are a spectacle,
as they elegantly glide past.

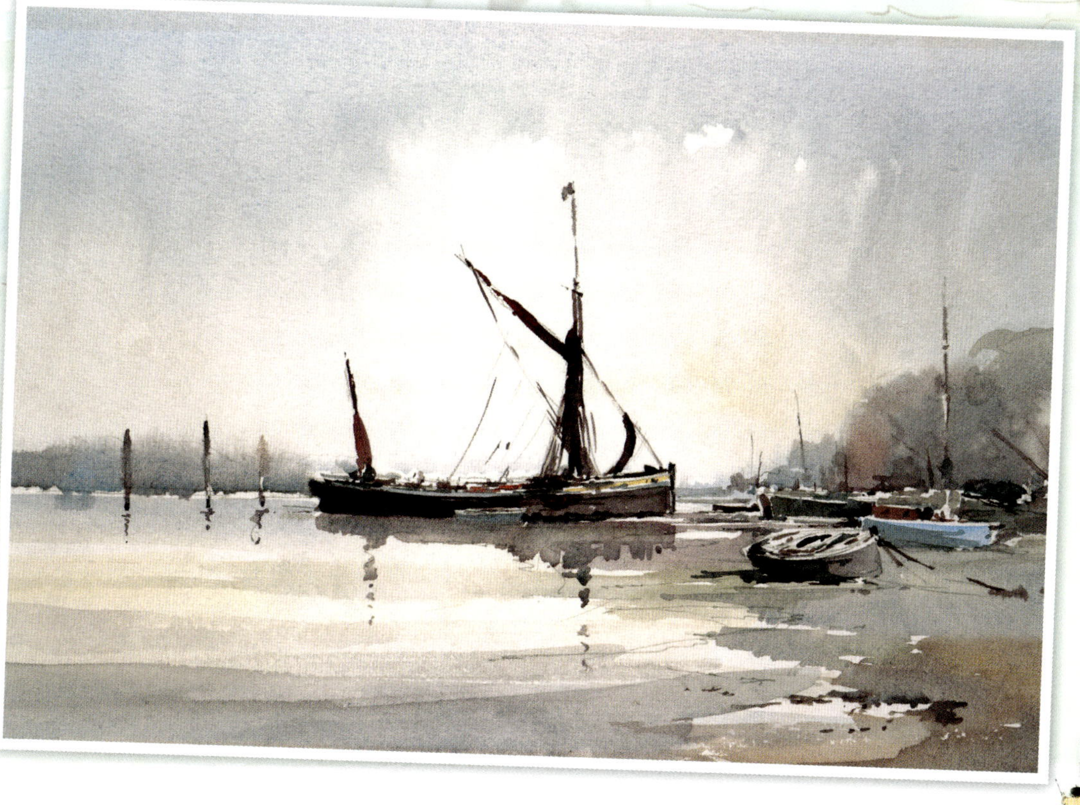

Southwold Quay, Suffolk

If you love getting outdoors
and feeling the fresh air on your face,

or prefer window shopping,
then Southwold is just the place.

Play golf on the Common,
take a brisk walk along the dunes,

hunt out craft and boutique shops,
there are plenty to choose.

Once you've spent time in this North Suffolk gem,

you'll understand why people want to return again.

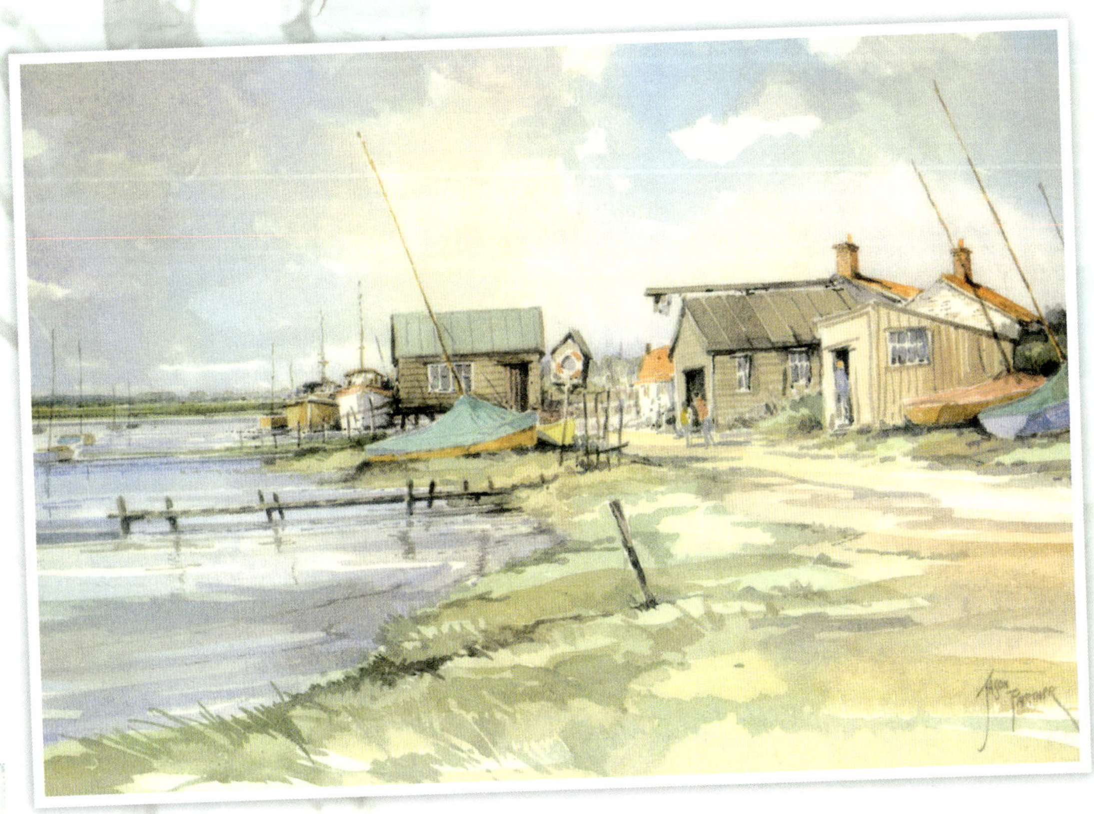

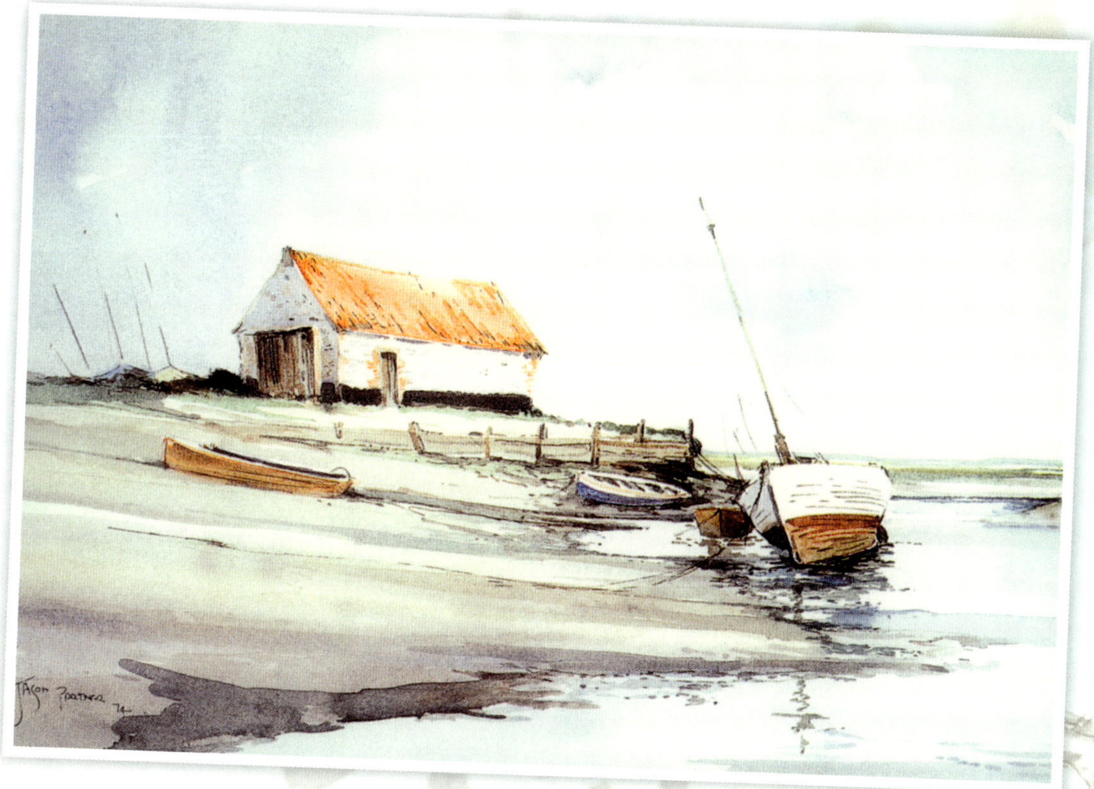

Thornham Creek, Norfolk

© From an original watercolour by Jason Partner.

Betwixt Hunstanton and Wells
lies Thornham Creek.
On visitors it casts a spell
And of Thornham people highly speak.

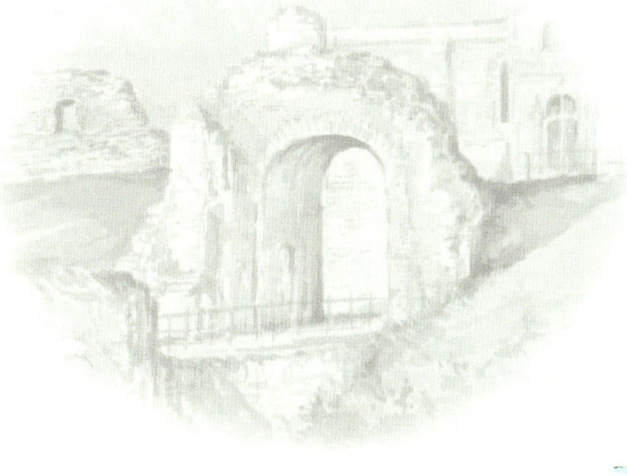

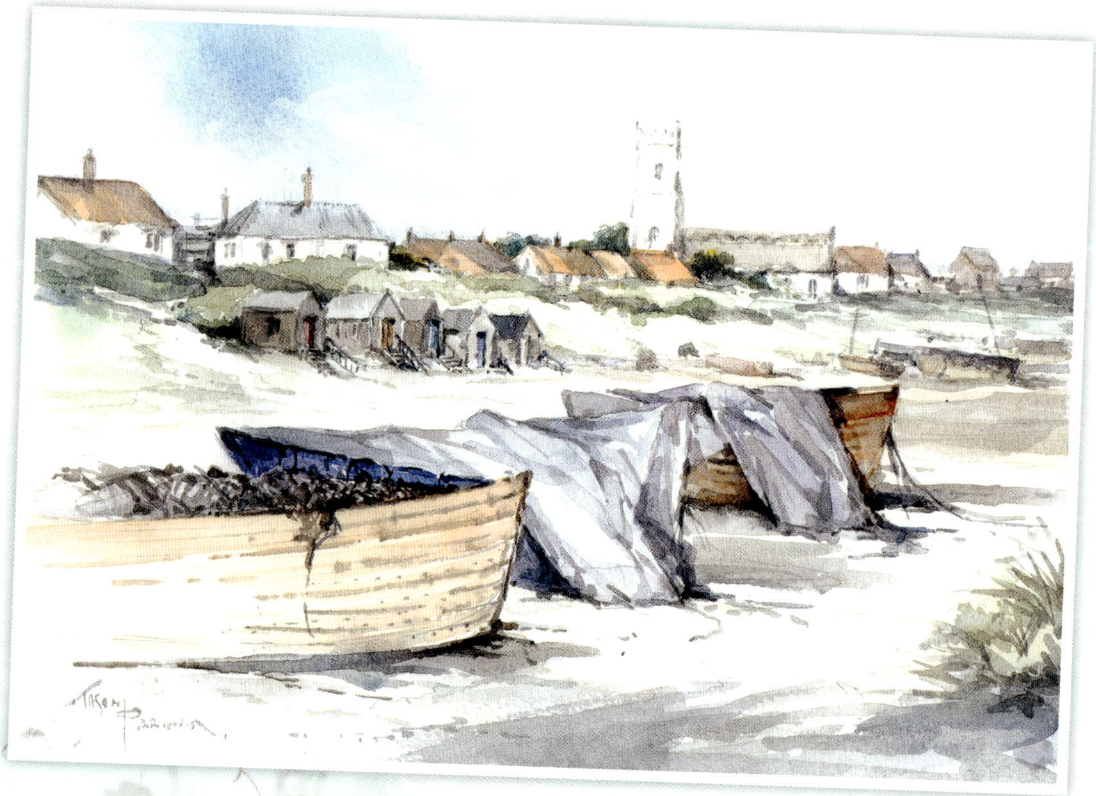

Pakefield Beach, Suffolk

© From an original watercolour by Jason Partner.

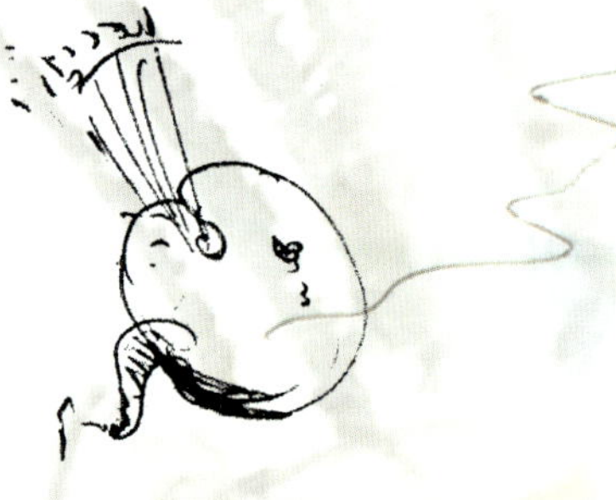

Pakefield is now a place of tranquility,
but years ago a large area was lost to the sea.
Pebbles and dunes stretch along the coastline,
resembling a village lost in time.

Waiting for the tide, Morston, Norfolk

© From an original watercolour by Jason Partner.

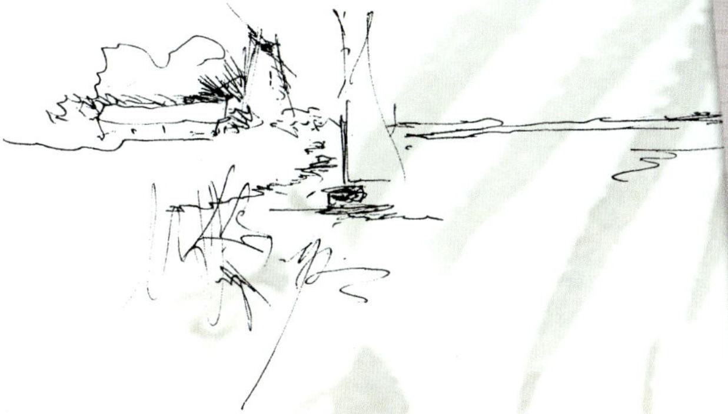

For young and old,
Morston has lots of appeal.

Walking, sailing and a chance
to watch the seals.

North Norfolk has so many treasures,

that give everyone so much pleasure.

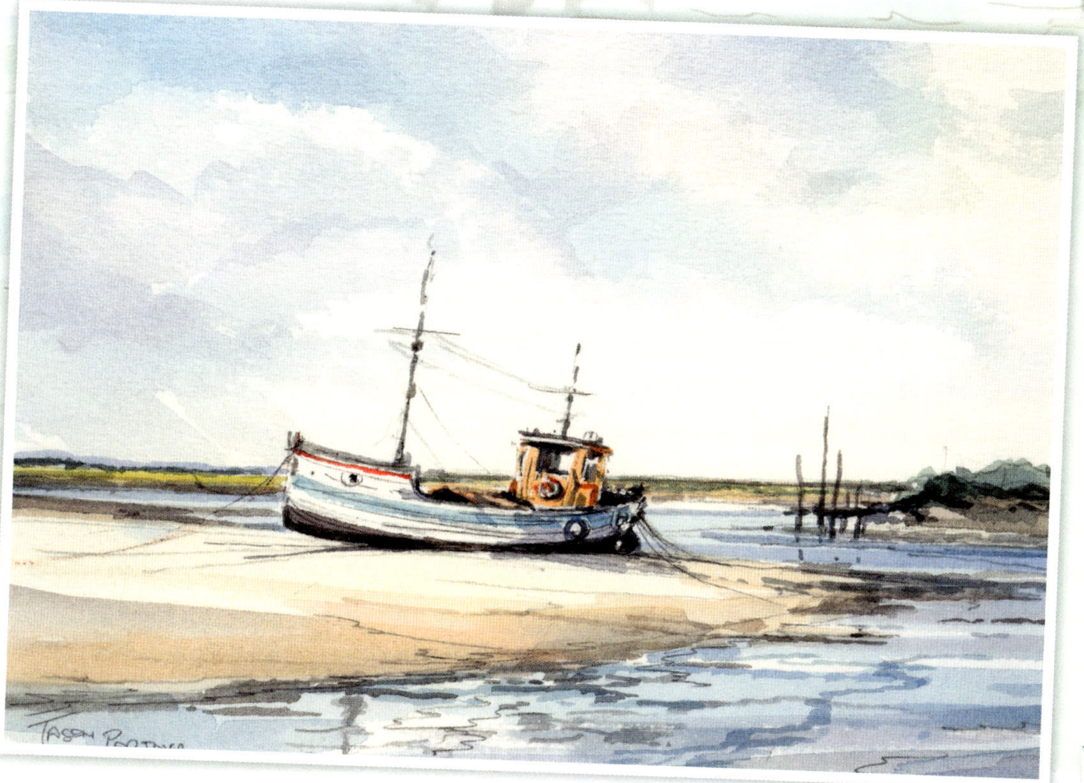

Lowestoft Harbour, Suffolk

© From an original watercolour by Jason Partner.

A fishing smack disappears out to sea,

braving the weather to bring back fish for our tea.

On the docks the women would fillet the fish, knives honed,

speedily cleaning, cutting to the bone.

These were common sights in the 20th century.

Now these images form an important part of our history.

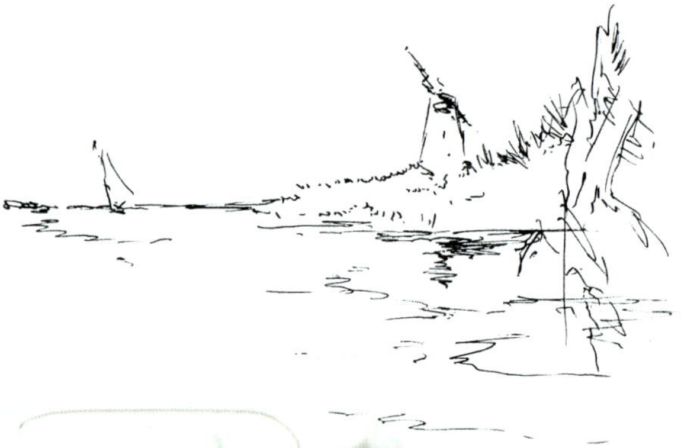

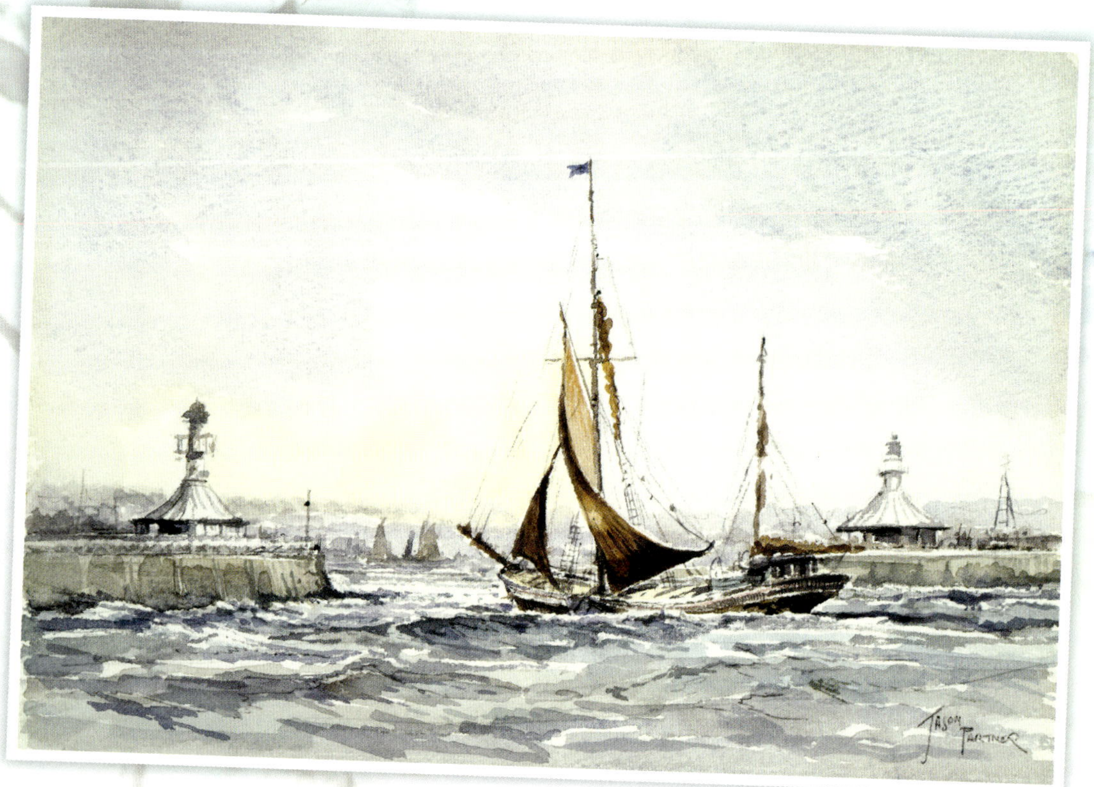

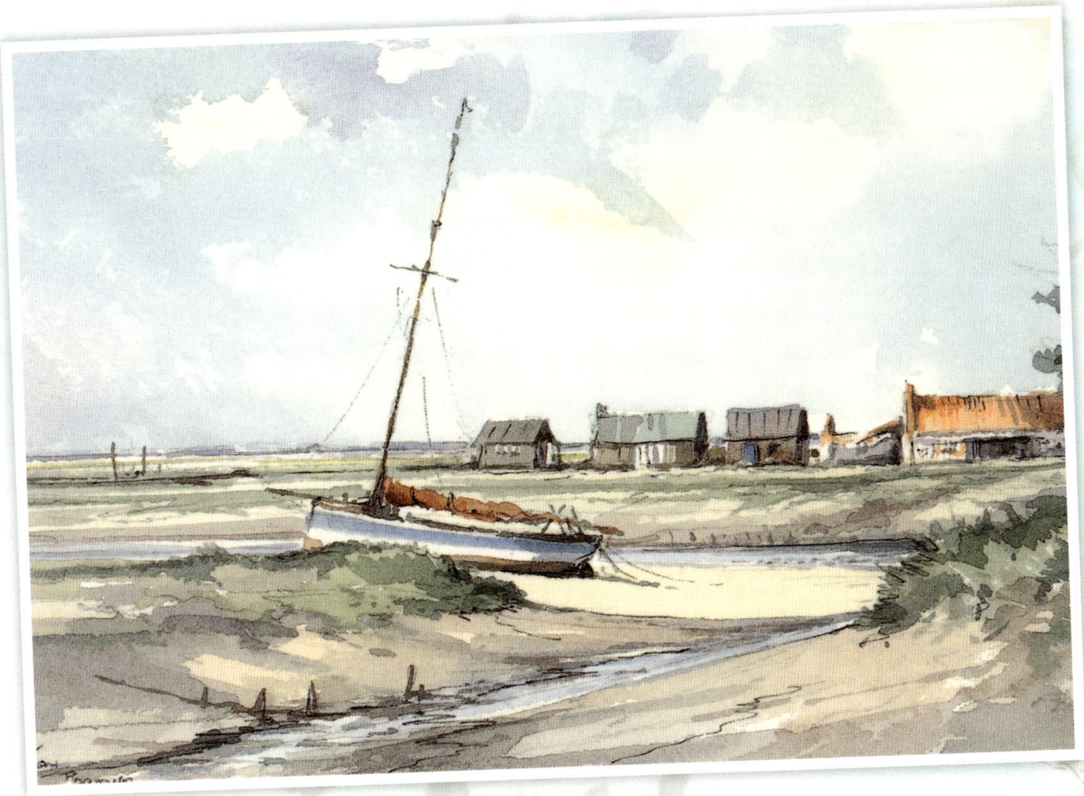

Low tide, Brancaster Staithe, Norfolk

© From an original watercolour by Jason Partner.

This scenic part of Norfolk
is a magnet for visitors.

People can relax here
and their lifestyle be restored.

Away from the hustle and bustle,
to peace and calm,

leaving everyone hypnotised
by its charm.

Burnt Umber ...

...this brown colour is made
by heating raw umber,
'earth of Umbria'.

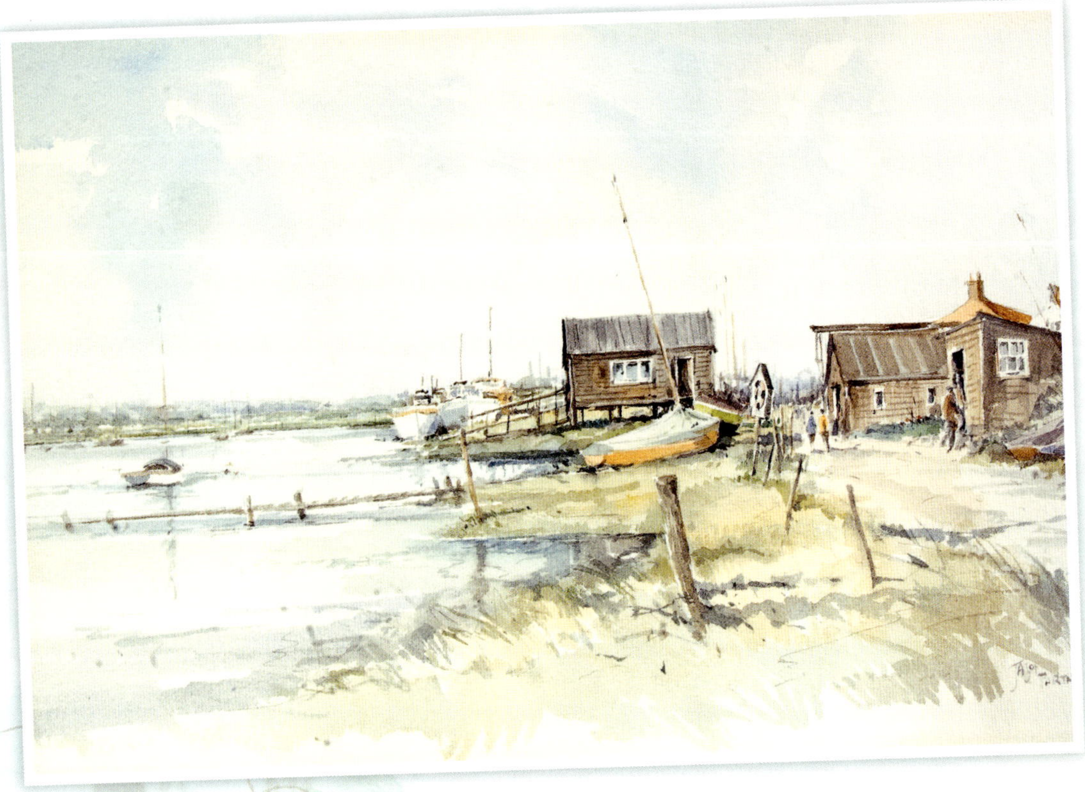

Southwold Harbour, Suffolk

© From an original watercolour by Jason Partner.

Renown for its lighthouse,
colourful beach huts and brewery,

Southwold, for many,
is certainly the place to be.

Browse among the unique shops and galleries,
along the pier take a stroll,

and you'll agree, that this seaside town
is ideal for young and old.

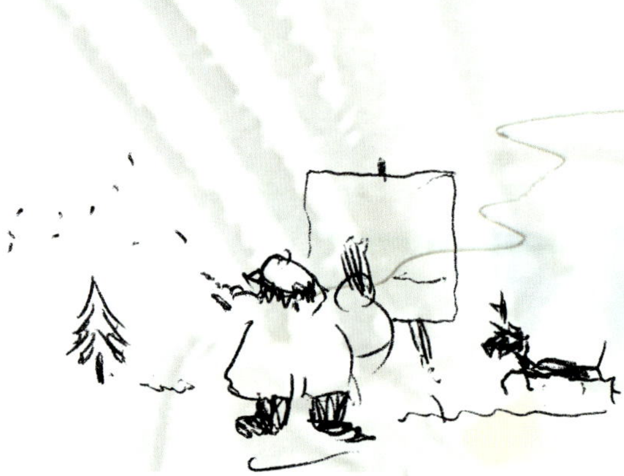

Sea Lavender, Morston, Norfolk

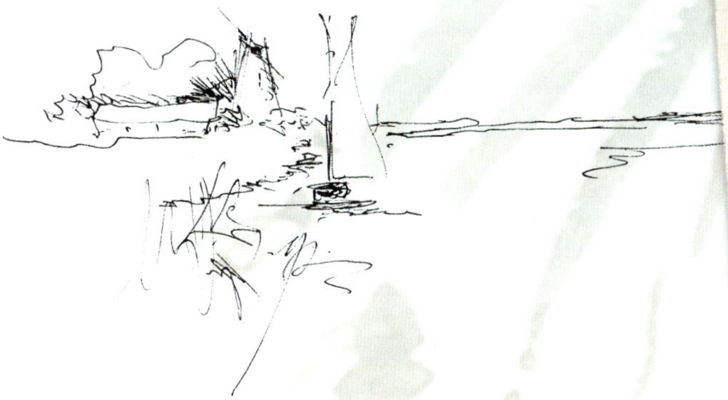

If you think that the coast
is just sea and sand,

then look beneath your feet
as you walk across the land.

Sea lavender with its lilac/pink
flowers is a delight to see,

not forgetting samphire,
which adds flavour to fish recipes.

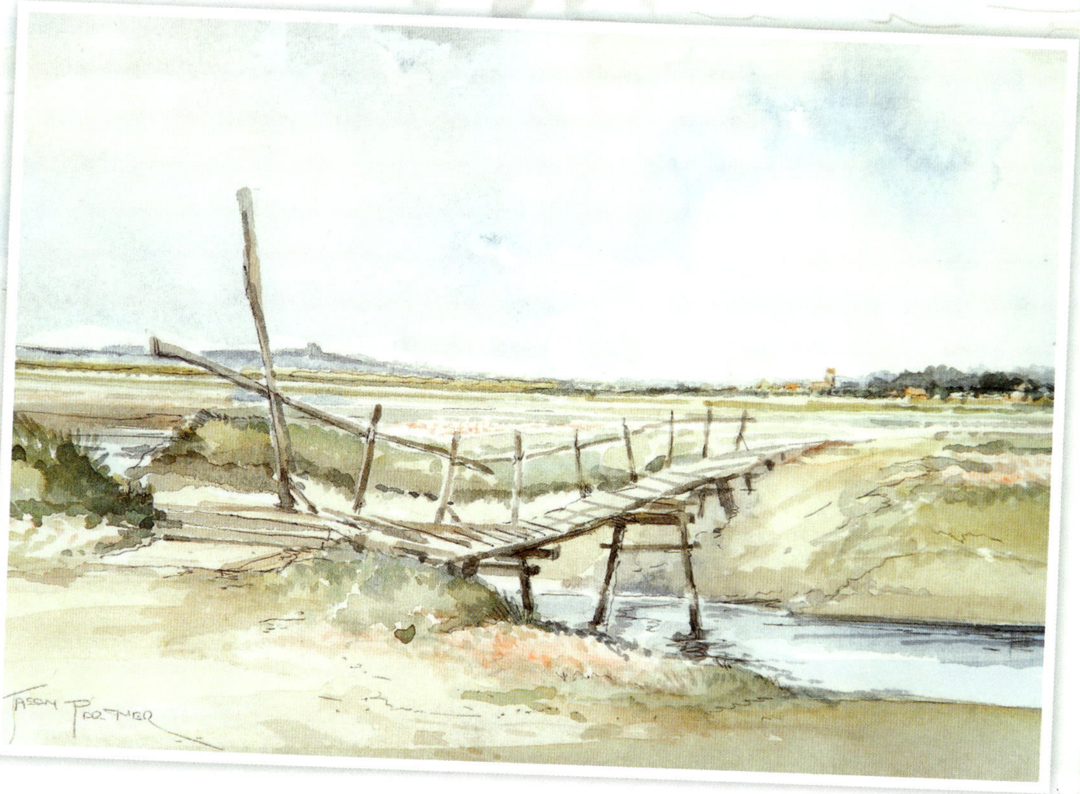

It sticks in our minds...

Jason said that if he painted the horizon 1/8 inch high - then this equated to it being 6-8 miles away.

Jason giving the 'nod of approval' to Colin and Mary's new van in 2002. He was especially proud to see his 'man and easel' painting on the side!

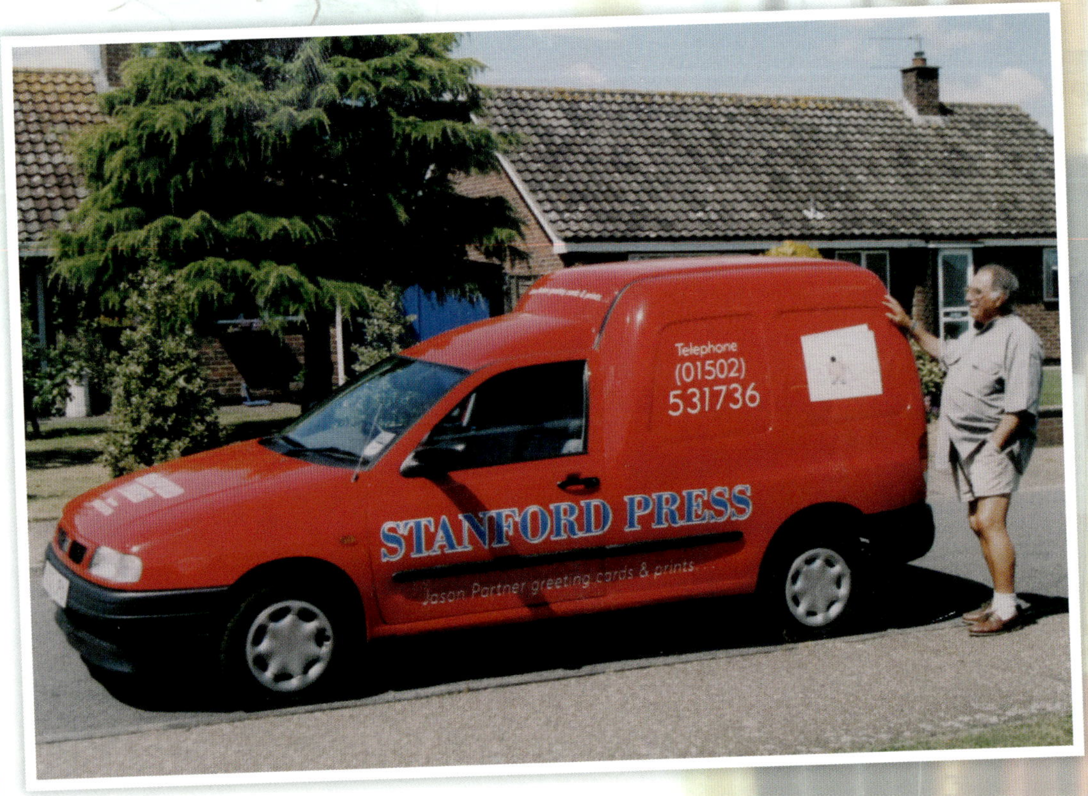

Coastal Craft

A selection of coastal craft painted by Jason.
These were mostly in and around the East Anglia region and
approximate locations are shown in the map below.

1 - Cromer, Norfolk - *see page 72*
2 - Sheringham, Norfolk - *see page 73*
3 - Walberswick, Suffolk - *see page 74*
4 - Fishermen at Blakeney, Norfolk - *see page 75*
5 - Fishermen at Blakeney, Norfolk (Oil) - *see page 76*
6 - Fisher fleet, King's Lynn, Norfolk - *see page 77*
7 - Purfleet Quay, King's Lynn, Norfolk - *see page 78*
8 - Butt and Oyster, Pin Mill, Suffolk - *see page 79*

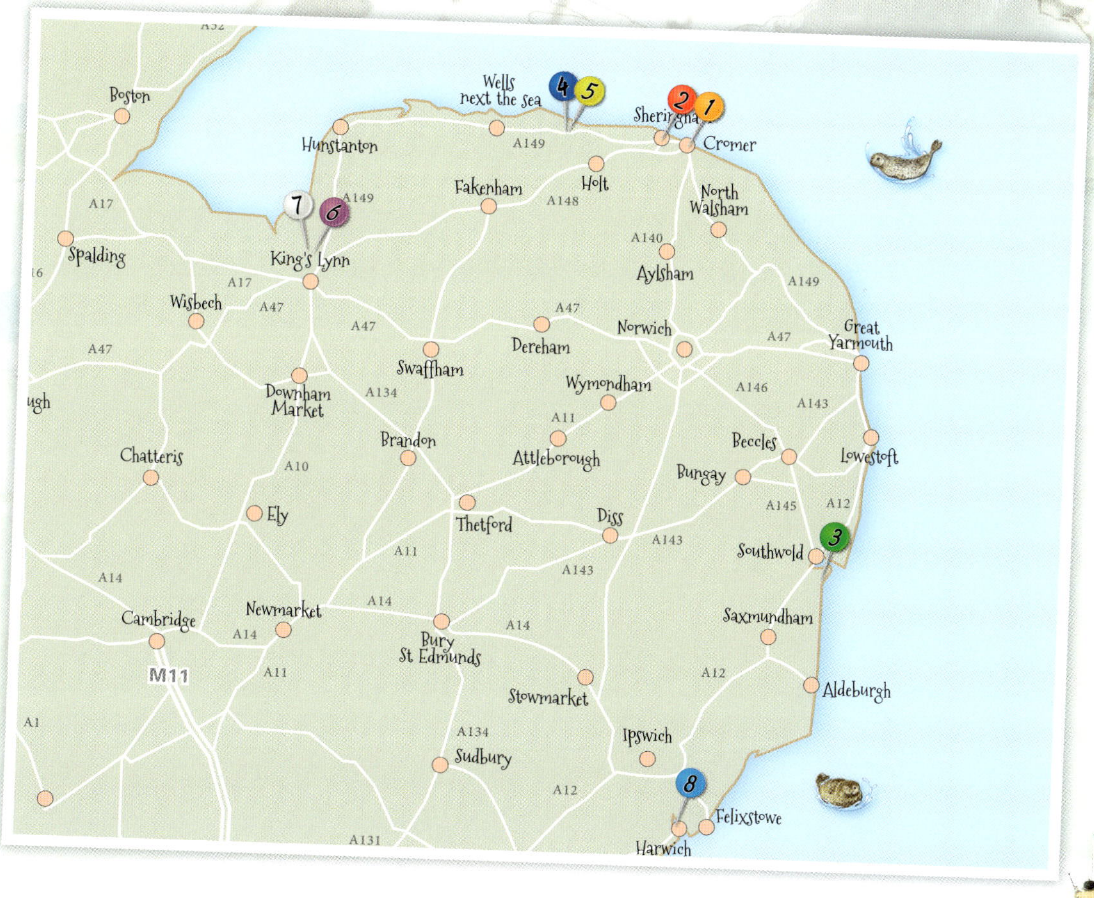

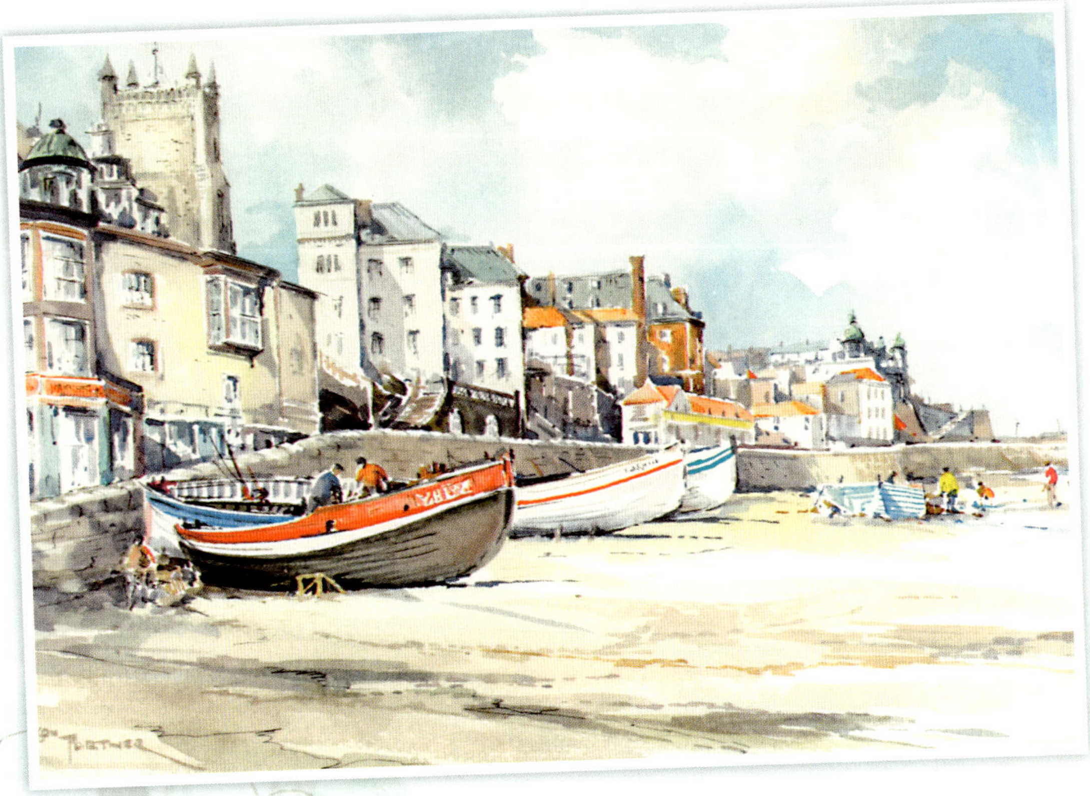

Cromer, Norfolk

© From an original watercolour by Jason Partner.

A 'Gem' of the North Norfolk coast,
That is certainly what Cromer can boast.
Known for its crabs and brave lifeboat crews,
It's also a fantastic family resort for me and you.

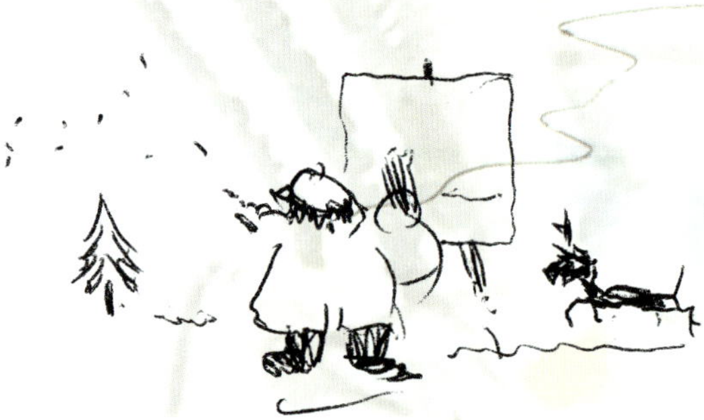

Sheringham, Norfolk

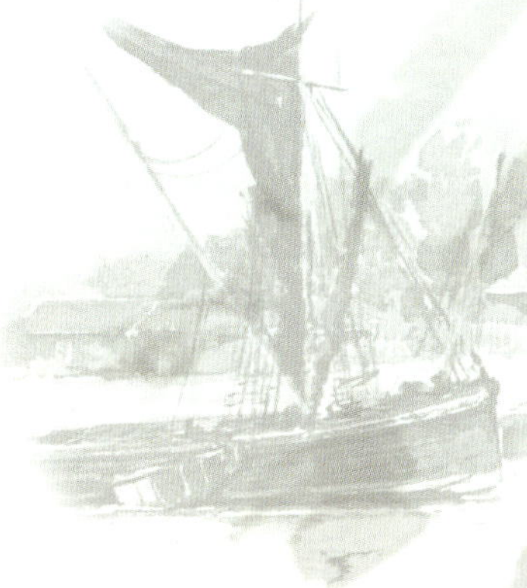

The pebbly beach stretches
from the promenade.

When the tide goes out, superb sandcastles
can be made.

There are plenty of high points from which
to admire the view,

Beeston Bump, the tower in Upper Sheringham Park,
to name but two.

At this seaside resort, young and old
enjoy a lovely time,

And their stay is made special by a ride
on the Poppy Line.

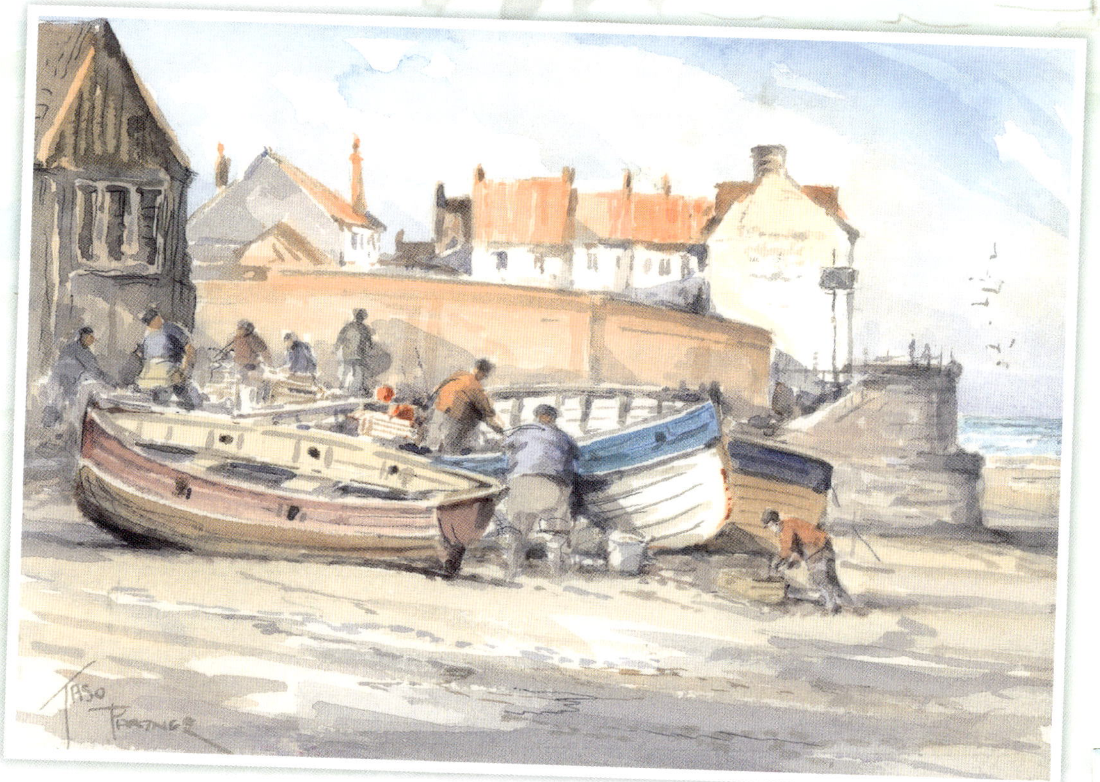

Walberswick, Suffolk

© From an original watercolour by Jason Partner.

This pretty part of Suffolk attracts people
from far and near.

Wherever you could be walking,
a famous celebrity might appear.

Along this area of coastline, there is so much
to see and do.

So instead of visiting only once,
you'll return a time or two.

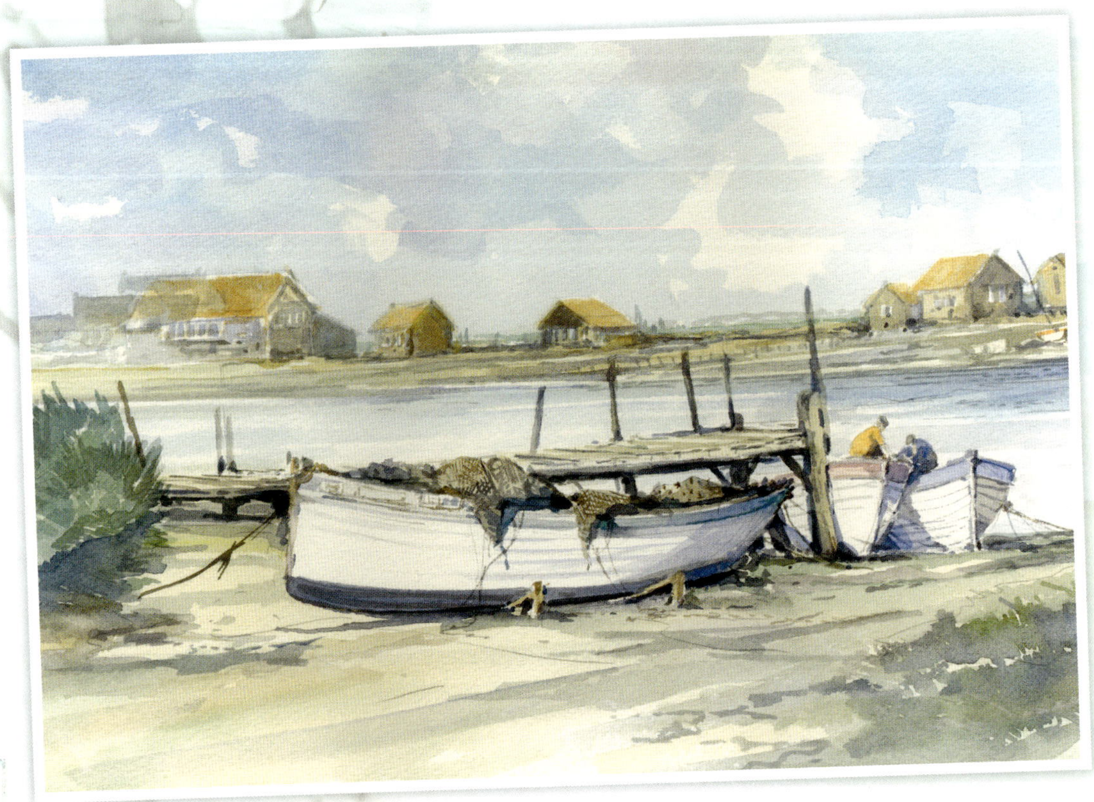

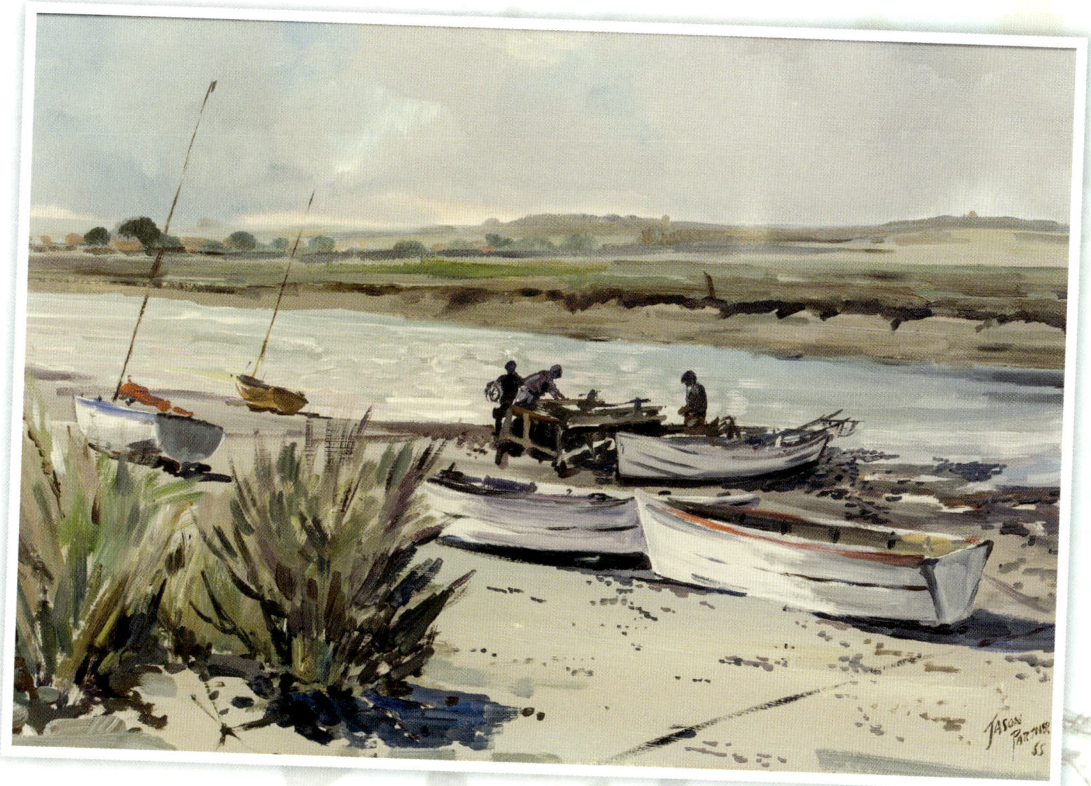

Fishermen at Blakeney Creek, Norfolk

© From an original oil on board by Jason Partner.

Watching the fishermen going about their work,
a task they do day to day.

It is hard to imagine the larger seafaring craft
which often came this way.

Packet ships from Hull and London
were frequent visitors at the quay.

However if a merchant vessel moored,
their bounty could be stolen away.

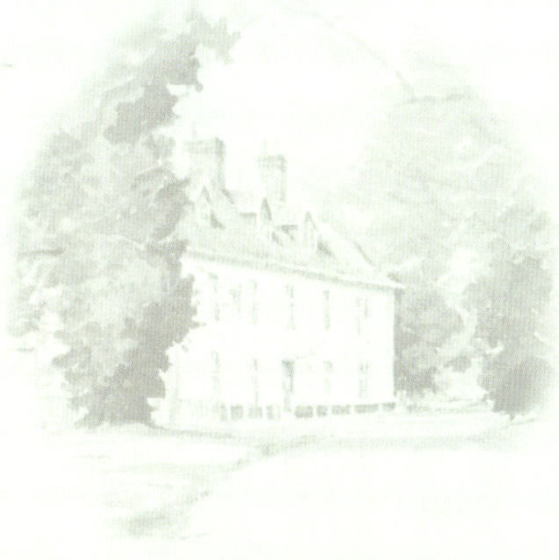

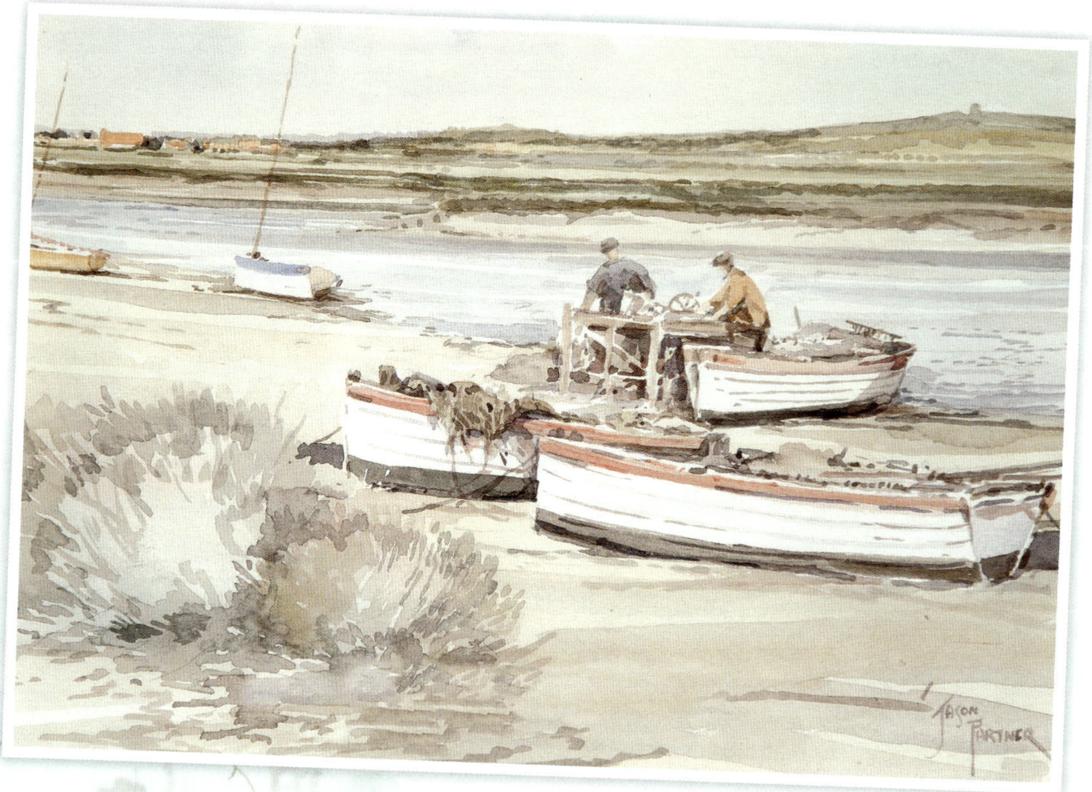

Fishermen at Blakeney Creek, Norfolk

© From an original watercolour by Jason Partner.

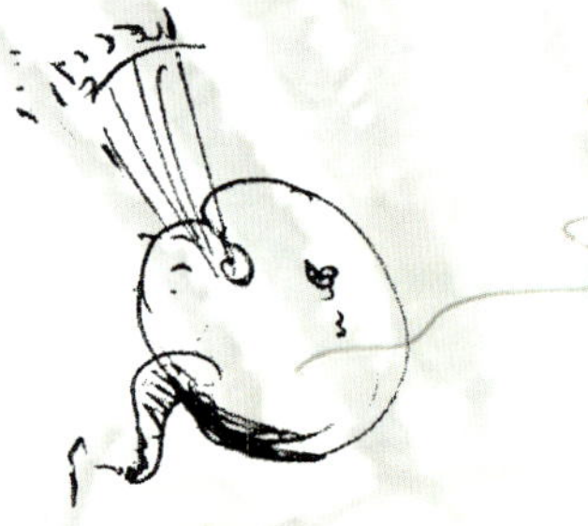

From flatfish to shellfish,
these fishermen know where to go.

A knowledge which has passed
from father to son.

When not out at sea,
checking their nets is important to do.

And coming home with a good catch
is a job well done.

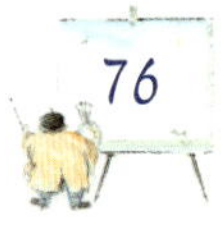

Fisher Fleet, King's Lynn, Norfolk

© From an original watercolour by Jason Partner.

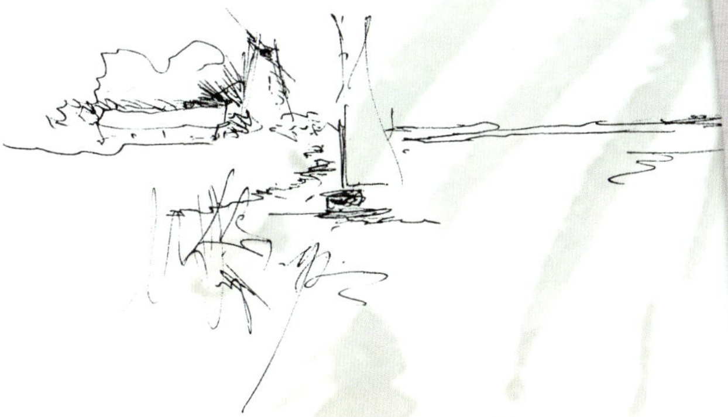

Like many a port along the Norfolk coast,
fishing played a vital role.

Along the quay or creek
the fishing craft were moored.

Whatever the weather,
the boats would head to sea,

To catch fresh fish
for people to have for their tea.

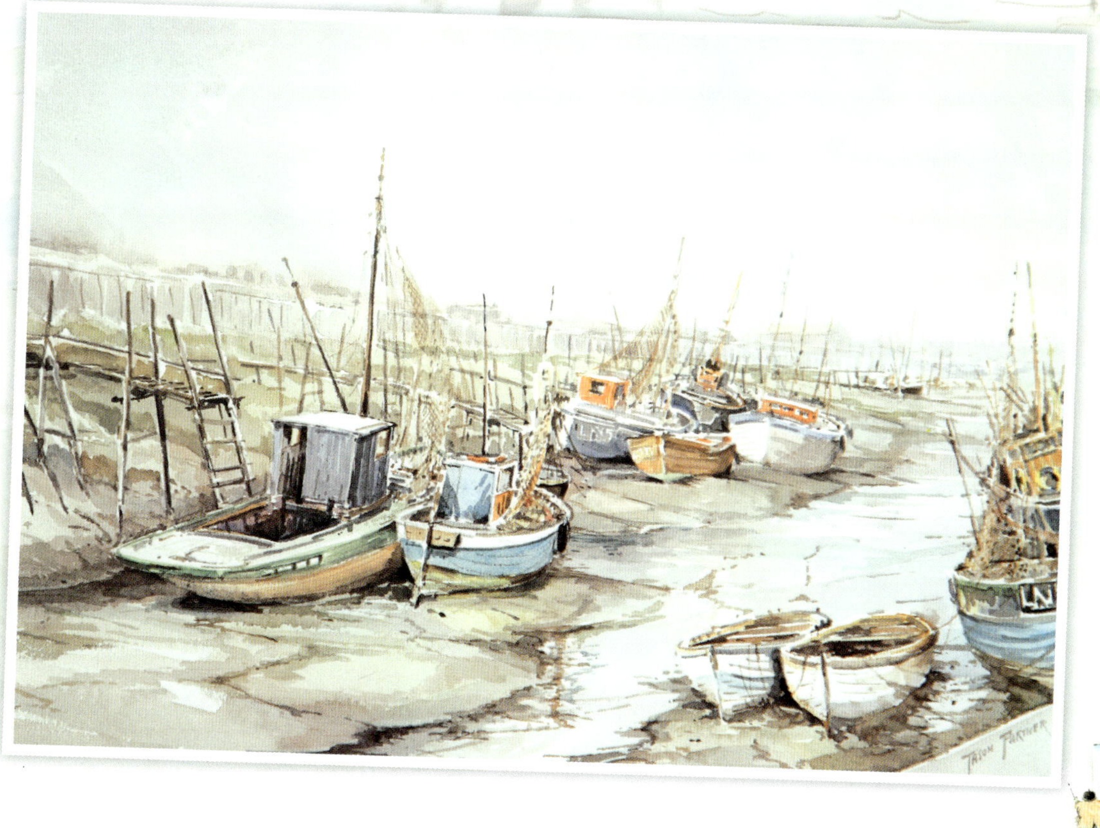

Purfleet Quay, King's Lynn, Norfolk

© From an original watercolour by Jason Partner.

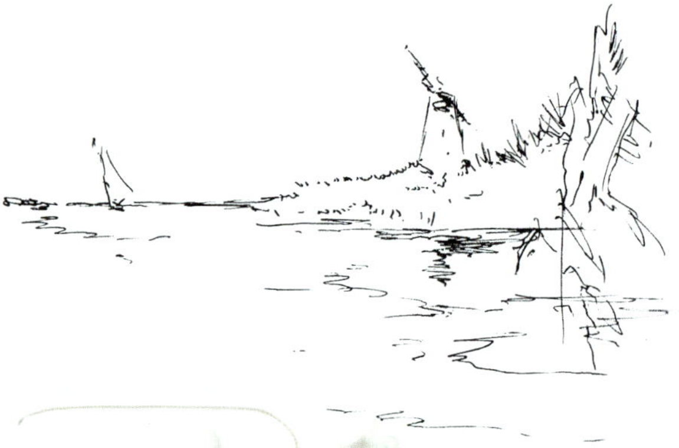

This historic maritime part of King's Lynn
was a bustling place to be,

having trade links with Europe
there were many ships to see.

Captain Vancouver began his voyage from here,
to the USA.

Charting the coastline
and territories which we know today.

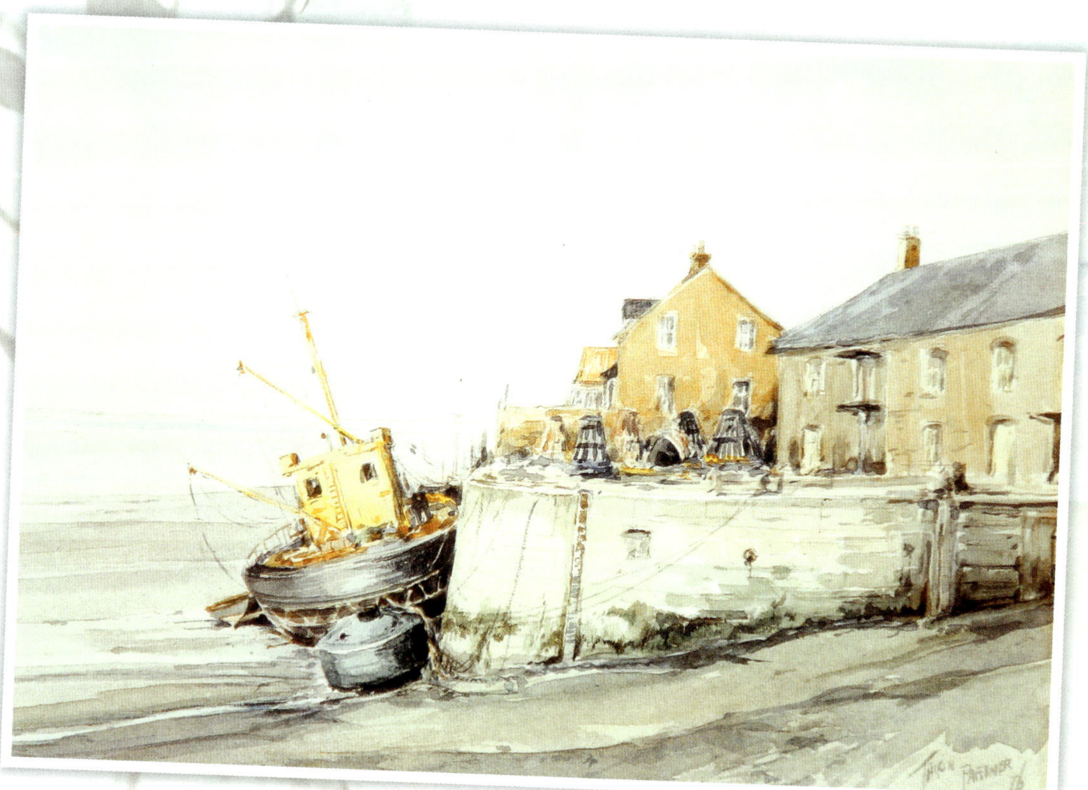

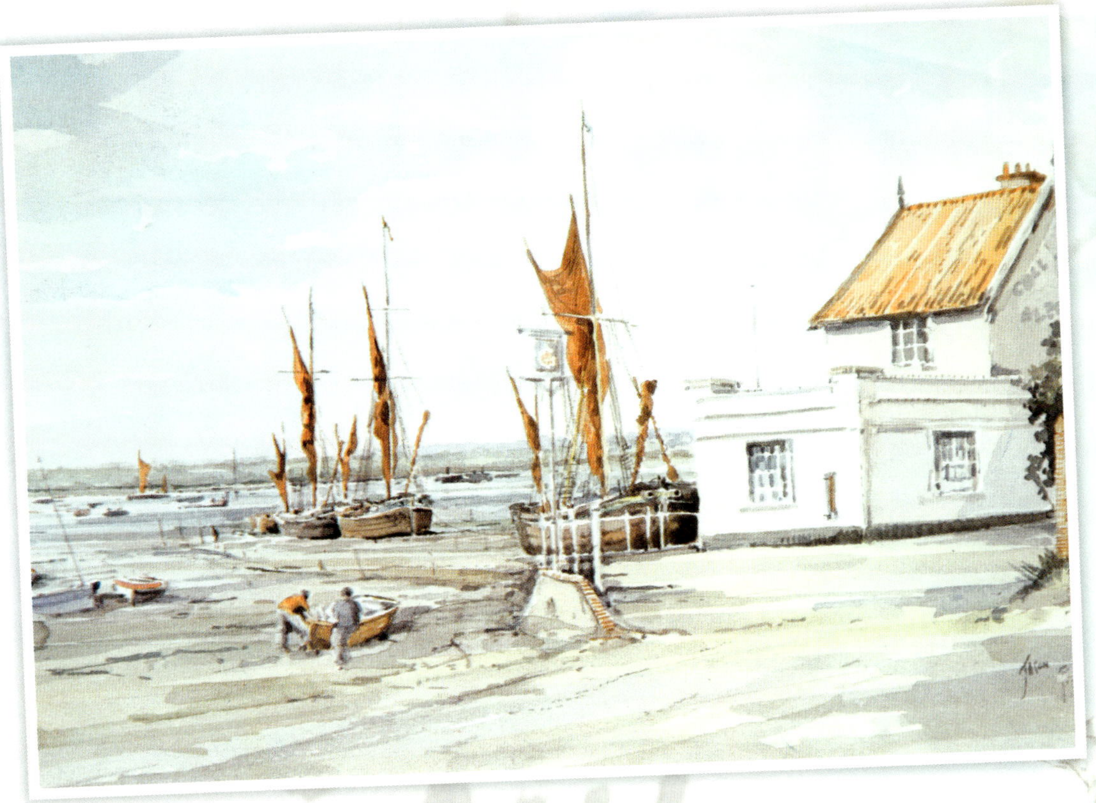

Butt and Oyster, Pin Mill, Suffolk

© From an original watercolour by Jason Partner.

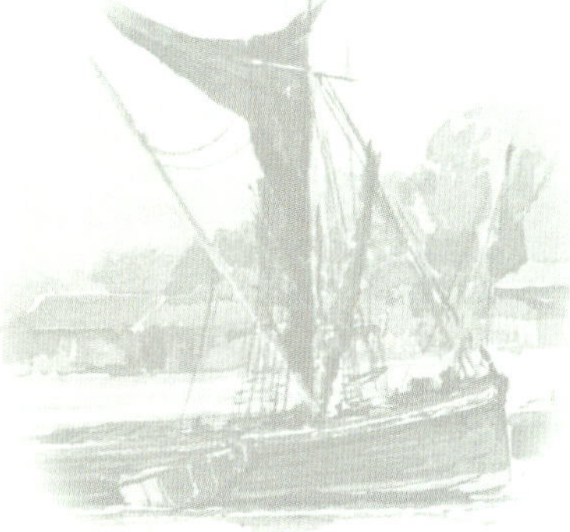

A favourite place for visitors
and artists alike, is Pin Mill.

Where the hustle and bustle
of life stands still.

During the summer,
a race of barges takes place.

Featuring iconic craft
travelling at a gentle pace.

It sticks in our minds...

Jason always preferred to have an exhibition featuring only his images as he felt that if he was joined by other artists, people visiting would make comparisons.

The art of watercolour painting was to make the paint flow rather than being too tight. The picture should not have too much detail in it either.

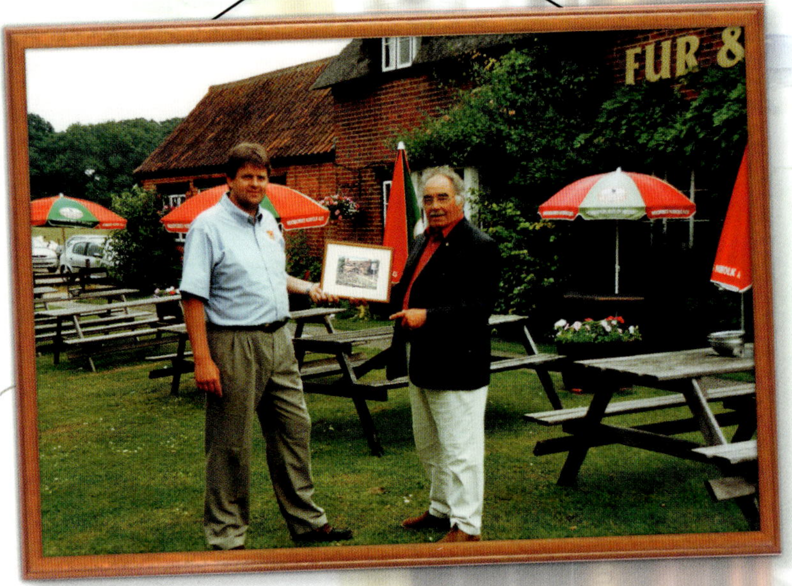

Jason proudly presenting Mr Tim Ridley of the Fur and Feather Inn, Woodbastwick, with the painting of the pub he agreed to paint after a previous visit to the village a few weeks earlier - *see page 83.*

Buildings

A selection of buildings painted by Jason.
These were mostly in and around the East Anglia region and approximate locations are shown in the map below.

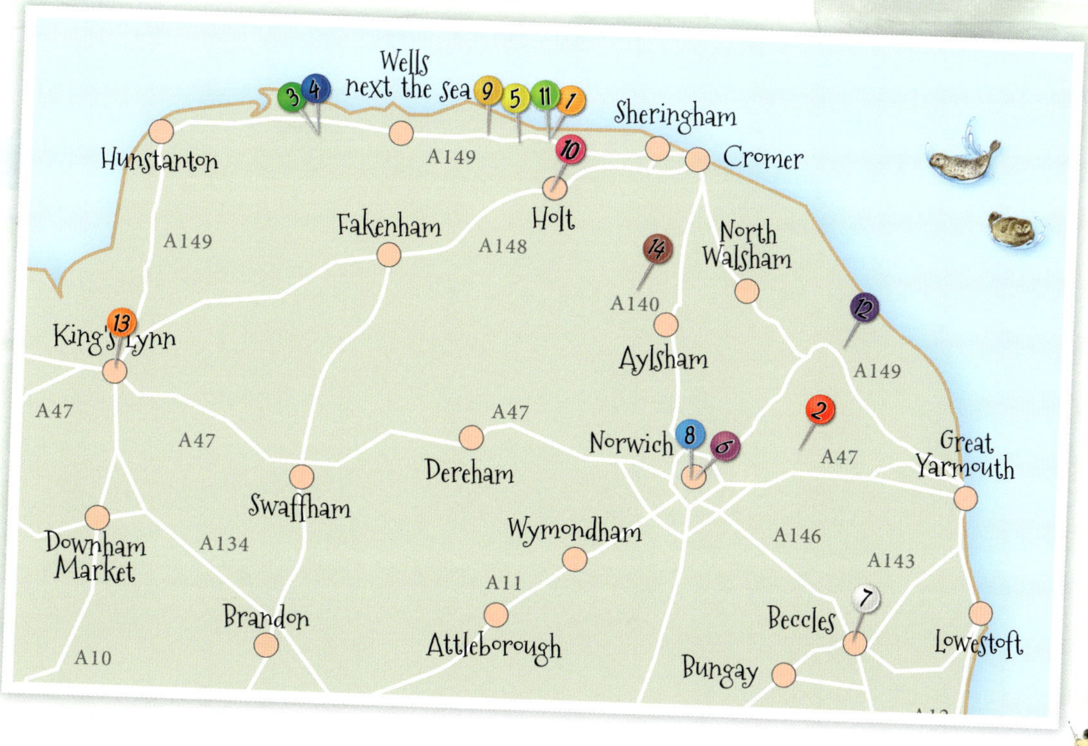

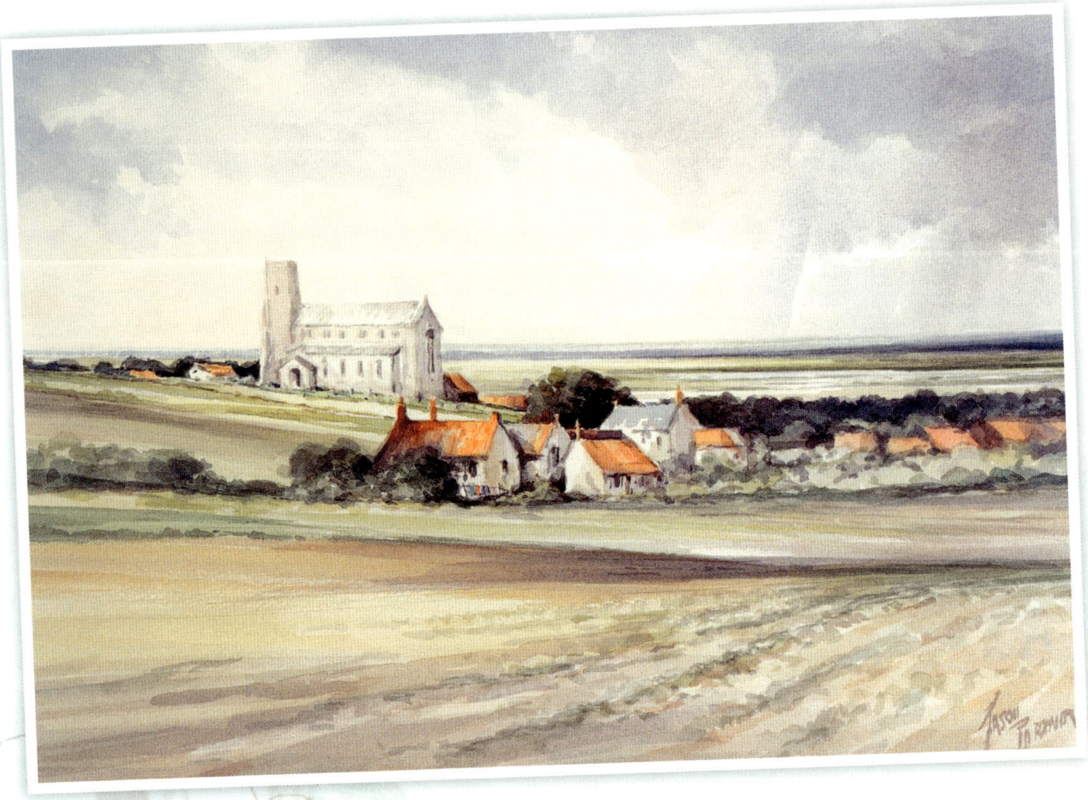

Salthouse church, Norfolk

© From an original watercolour by Jason Partner.

Overlooking the salt marshes,
Salthouse church stands tall.

From this high point,
there are marvellous views all around.

Salthouse is one of many villages
on the North Norfolk coastline,

And walkers and birdwatchers
think the area is just fine.

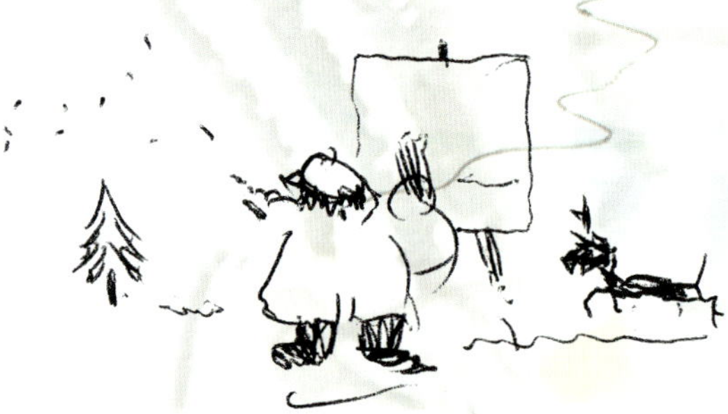

Fur and Feather Inn, Norfolk

© From an original watercolour by Jason Partner.

Norfolk can boast that it has many idyllic, picturesque villages. Woodbastwick is one of those and so Jason and I visited one day. It has an old forge, lovely thatched cottages and a very popular pub and brewery. Mr Tim Ridley, the owner of the Fur & Feather Inn, was asked if he was interested in having a picture painted which he could display in the pub. He agreed, so Jason set to work to capture the balmy summer's day with people enjoying the food and drink. A few weeks later the picture was given to Mr Ridley and afterwards there was time to visit Woodforde's brewery next door. Whilst there, one of the senior members of staff approached Jason and said that he admired his work and had one of his paintings. Being very modest, Jason said, 'I didn't pay you to say that,' but I knew how delighted Jason was to receive such praise.

In Broadland lies the village
of Woodbastwick.

A prettier place
you could not pick.

With thatched inn,
village green and smithy too.

Not forgetting local
Woodforde's brew!

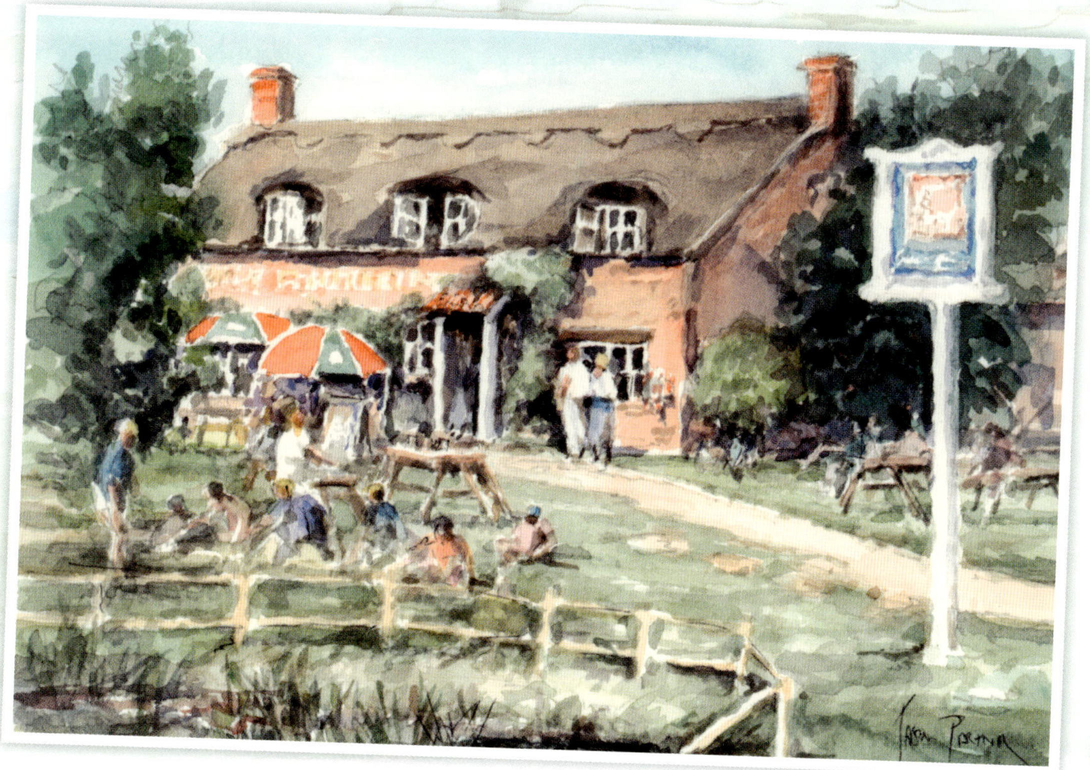

Church View, Burnham Market, Norfolk

Burnham Market is in Nelson country.
A local hero, whose ship was called *Victory*.
You'll see his name on buildings that you pass by,
This is why his memory will never die.

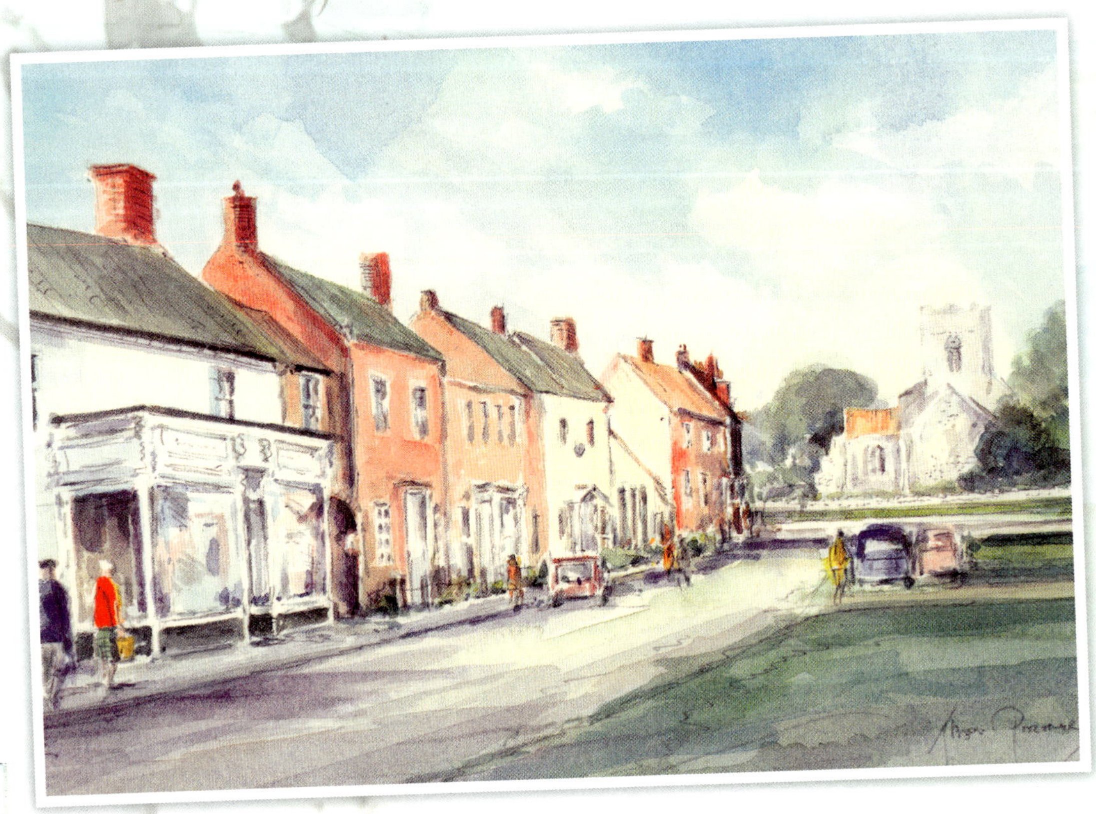

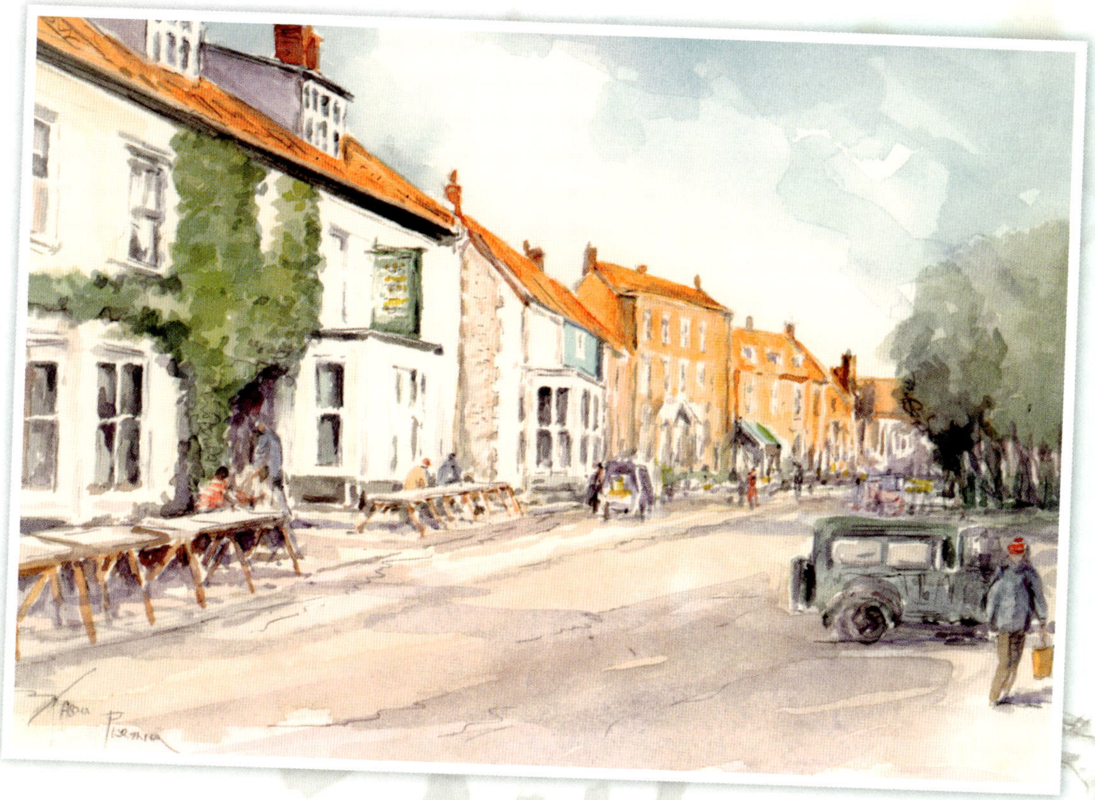

The Hoste Arms, Burnham Market, Norfolk

© From an original watercolour by Jason Partner.

A well known hotel is The Hoste Arms.

Many celebrities it welcomes, with open arms.

Although nicknamed 'Chelsea by the Sea',

Life in Burnham Market continues very quietly,

And will never lose its charm.

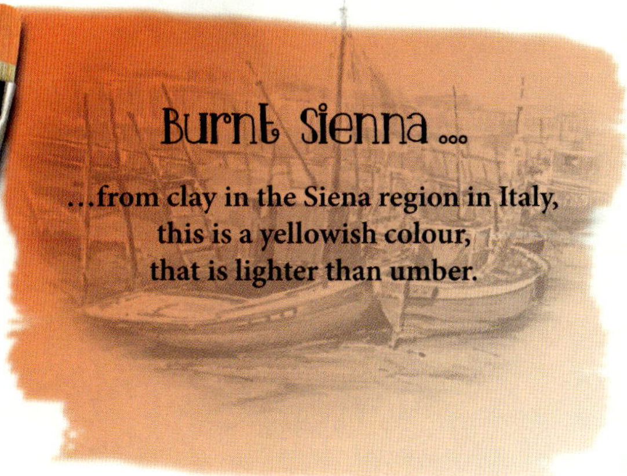

Burnt Sienna ...

...from clay in the Siena region in Italy, this is a yellowish colour, that is lighter than umber.

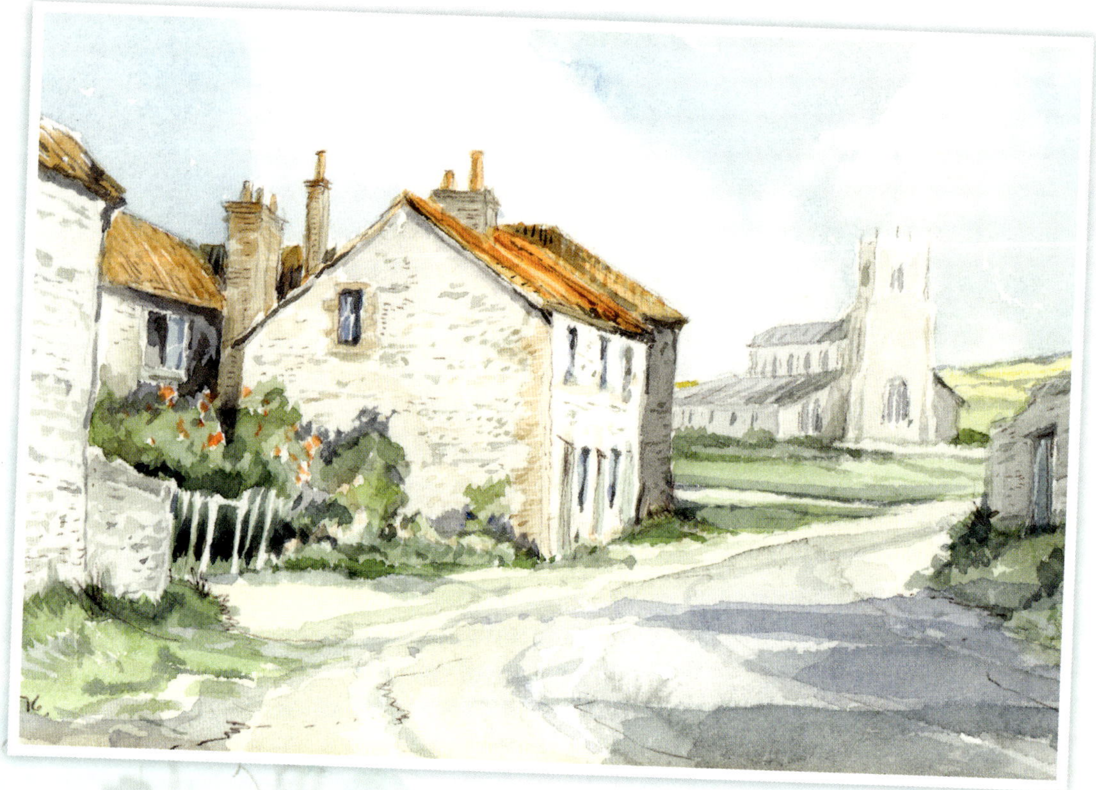

Wiveton Village, Norfolk

© From an original watercolour by Jason Partner.

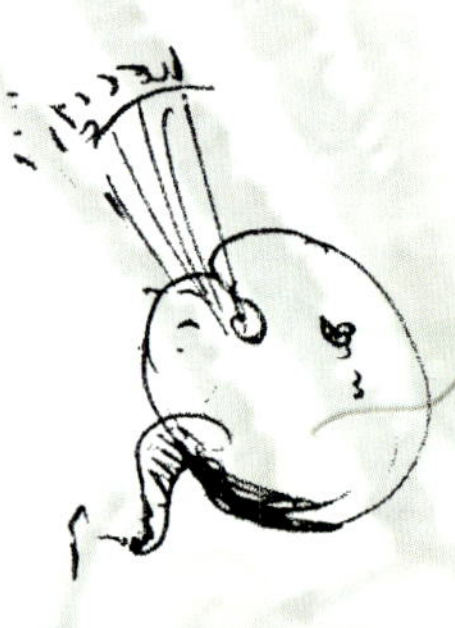

Take a step back in time with pantiles and flint,
when the sun shines they begin to glint.

The narrow winding road, buildings tight to the verge,
into the past you'll soon submerge.

Just a pebble's throw away are Blakeney and Cley,
gems of the North Norfolk coast.

And in their tranquil views,
you'll soon be lost.

Pull's Ferry, Norwich, Norfolk

© From an original watercolour by Jason Partner.

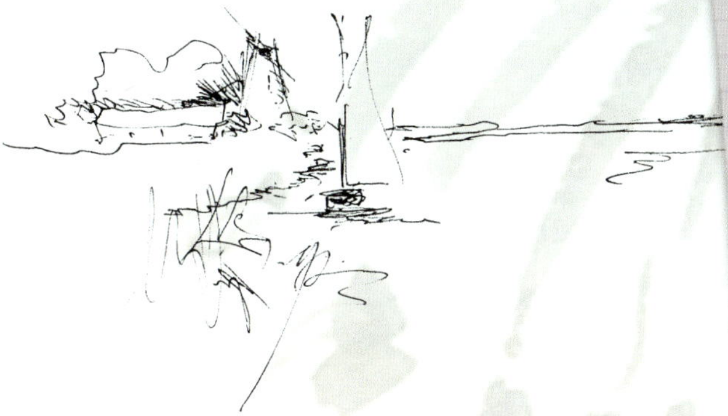

On the river bank,
Pull's Ferry stands.

With turret and archway,
it looks very commanding.

In the distance is Norwich Cathedral,
its spire hidden by trees.

Along the riverbank you can stroll,
feed the ducks or whatever you please.

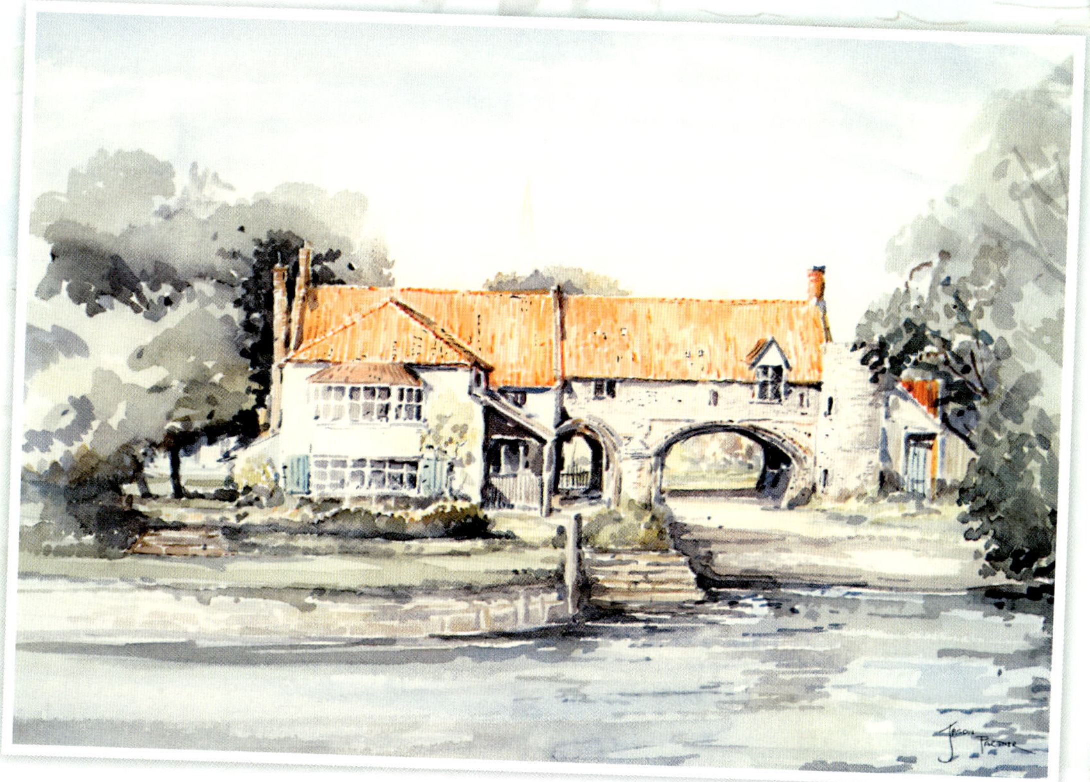

View of St Michael's Church, Beccles, Suffolk

On the Norfolk Suffolk border you will find
Beccles, a town of historical kind.
Climb St Michael's church tower and you will see
picturesque views of the River Waveney.

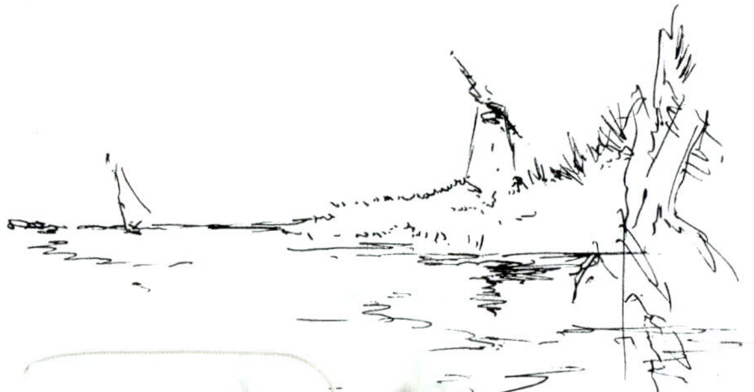

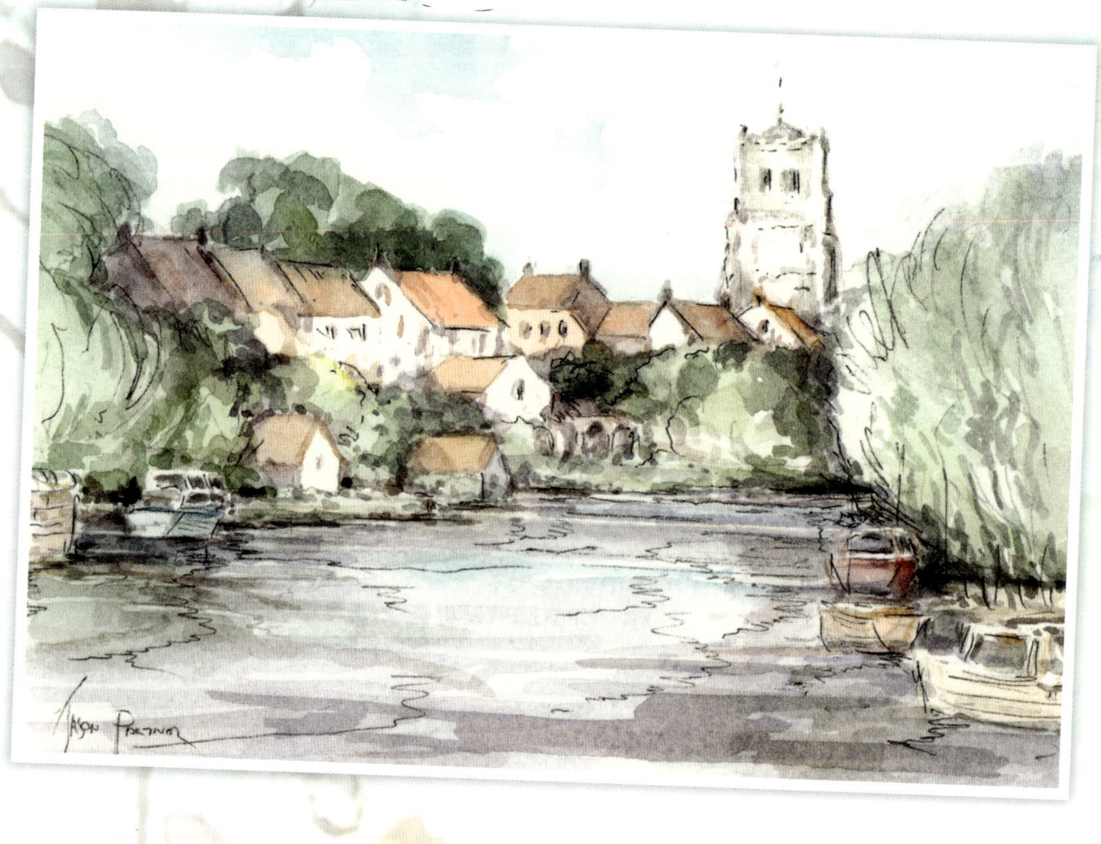

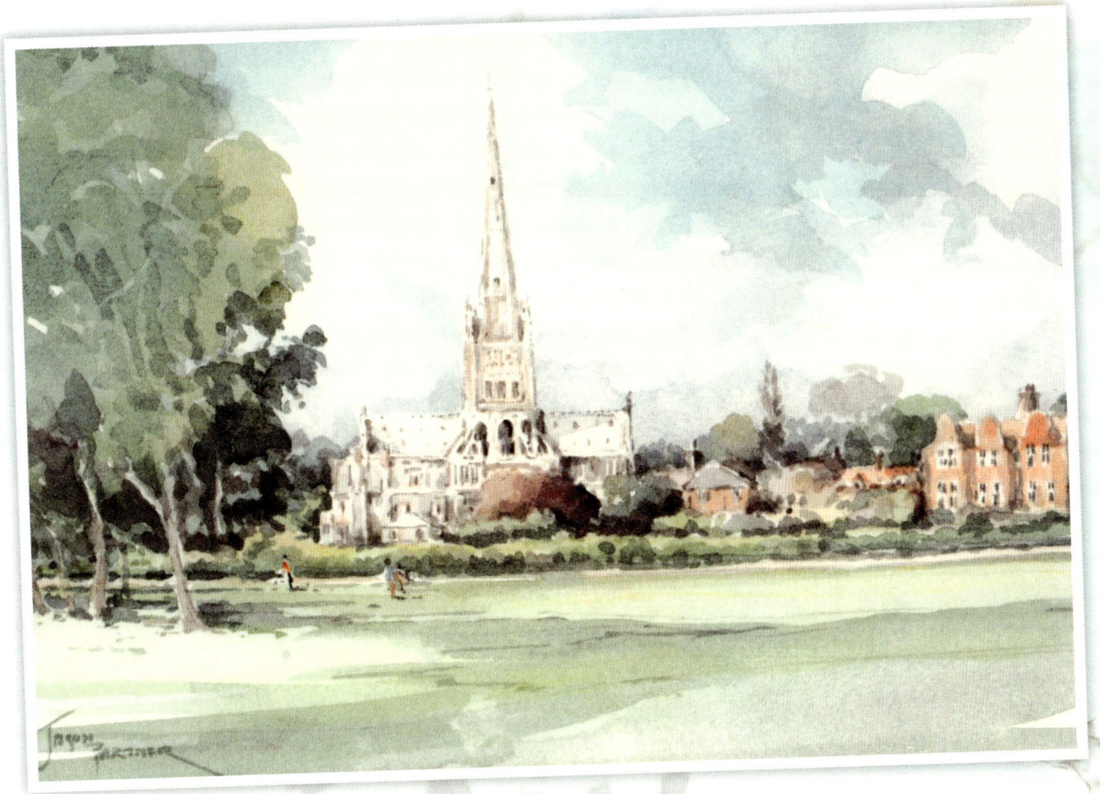

Norwich Cathedral, Norfolk

This Norman built cathedral
is one of the delights to see,

when visiting Norwich's
fine historic city.

Admiral Lord Nelson
went to school in the grounds,

And in the close, statues of Wellington
and him can be found.

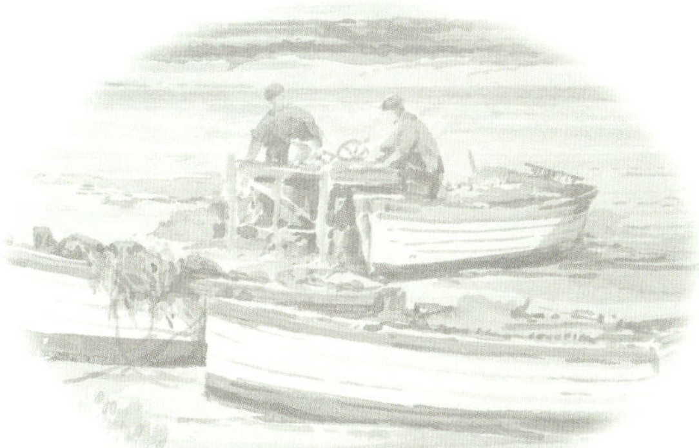

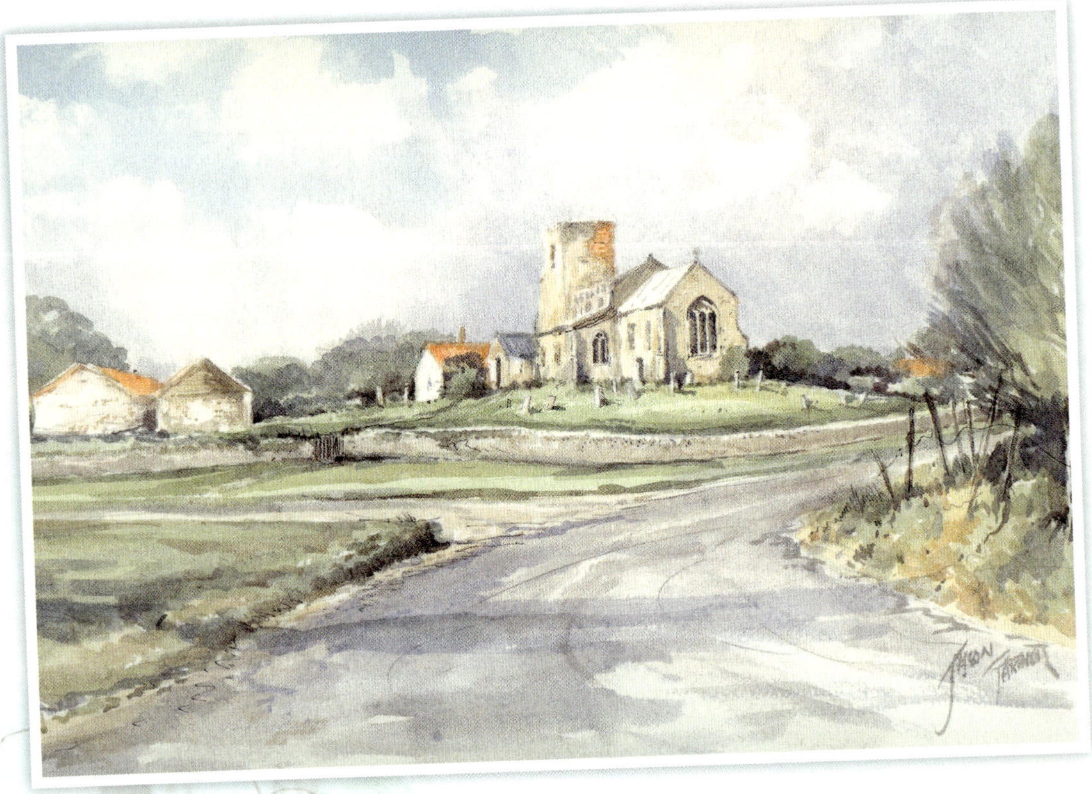

Morston Church, Morston, Norfolk

© From an original watercolour by Jason Partner.

All Saints Church, Morston,
on the Blakeney coast road, lies;

a famous artist and author
with its peacefulness were beguiled.

Known for its octagonal font
and wonderful rood screen,

this picturesque church
is a 'must see'.

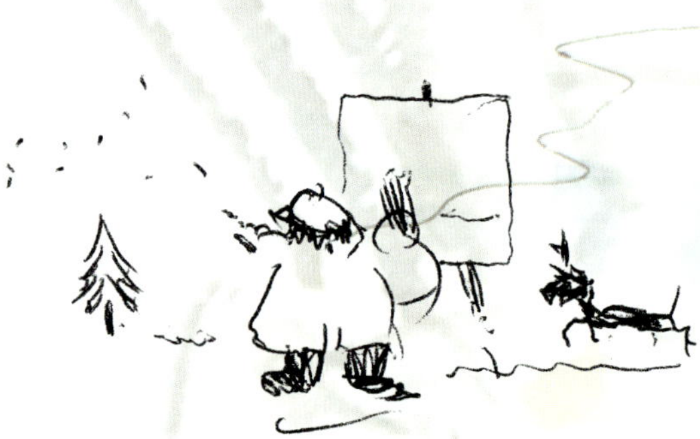

Holt town centre, Norfolk

© From an original watercolour by Jason Partner.

Whether you arrive by road or rail,
the delights of Holt never fail.
With its independent shops and courtyards galore,
there is plenty for shoppers to explore.

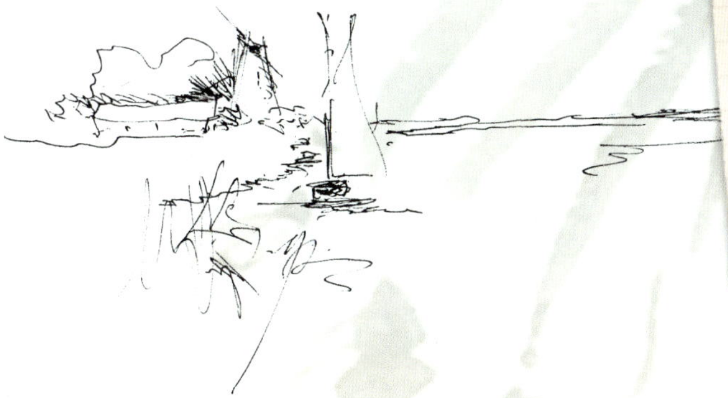

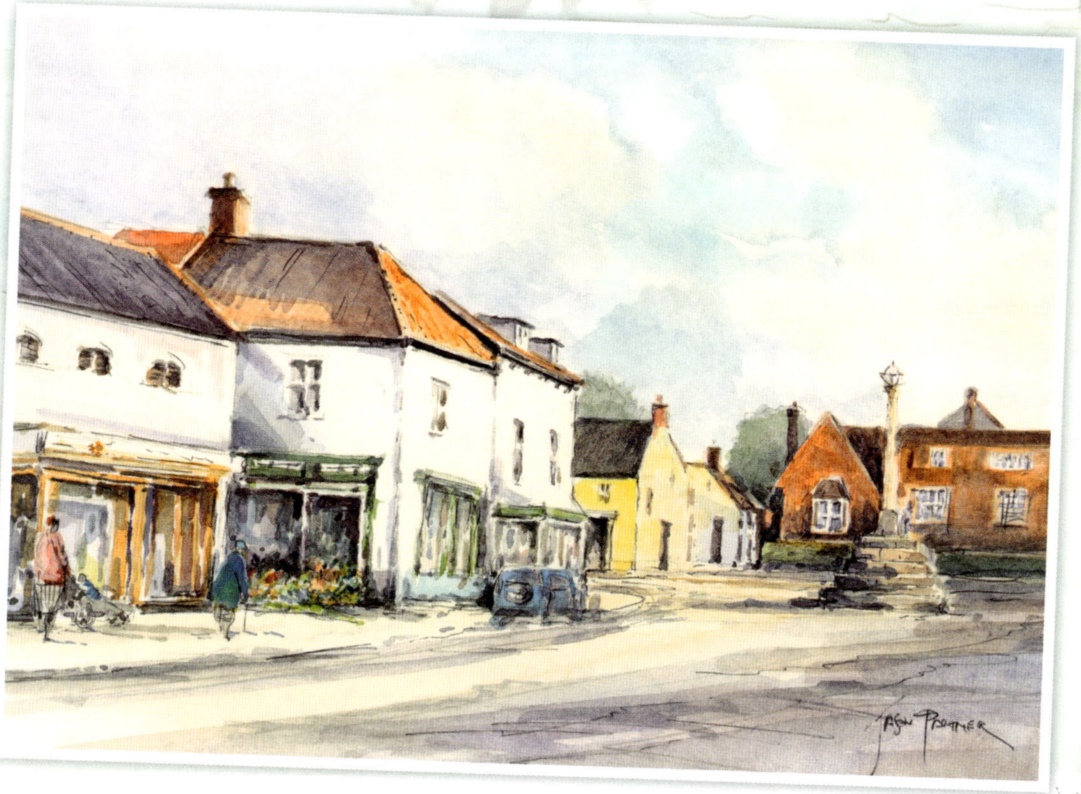

Salthouse marshes, Norfolk

Salthouse residents are always prepared
in case of high tides.

The sea can envelope the saltmarsh so quickly,
washing everything aside.

This NWT area is carefully managed,
and by many people loved.

Making it possible for every feathered visitor
to be safely observed.

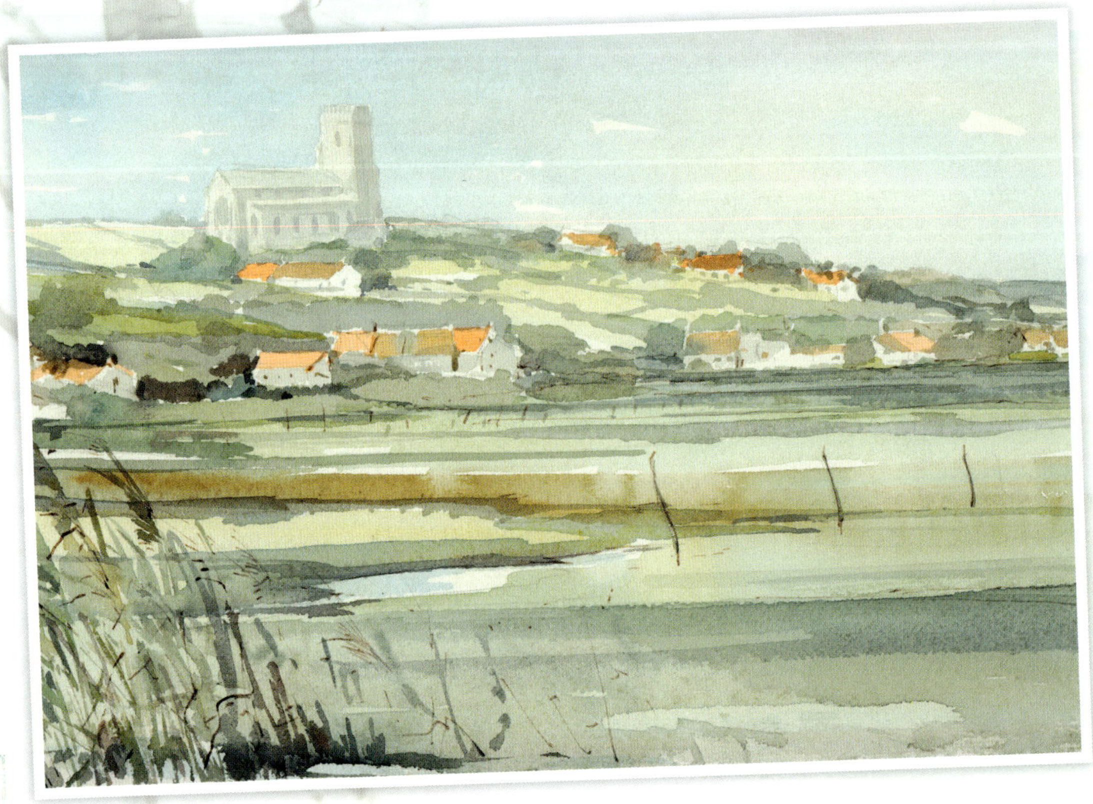

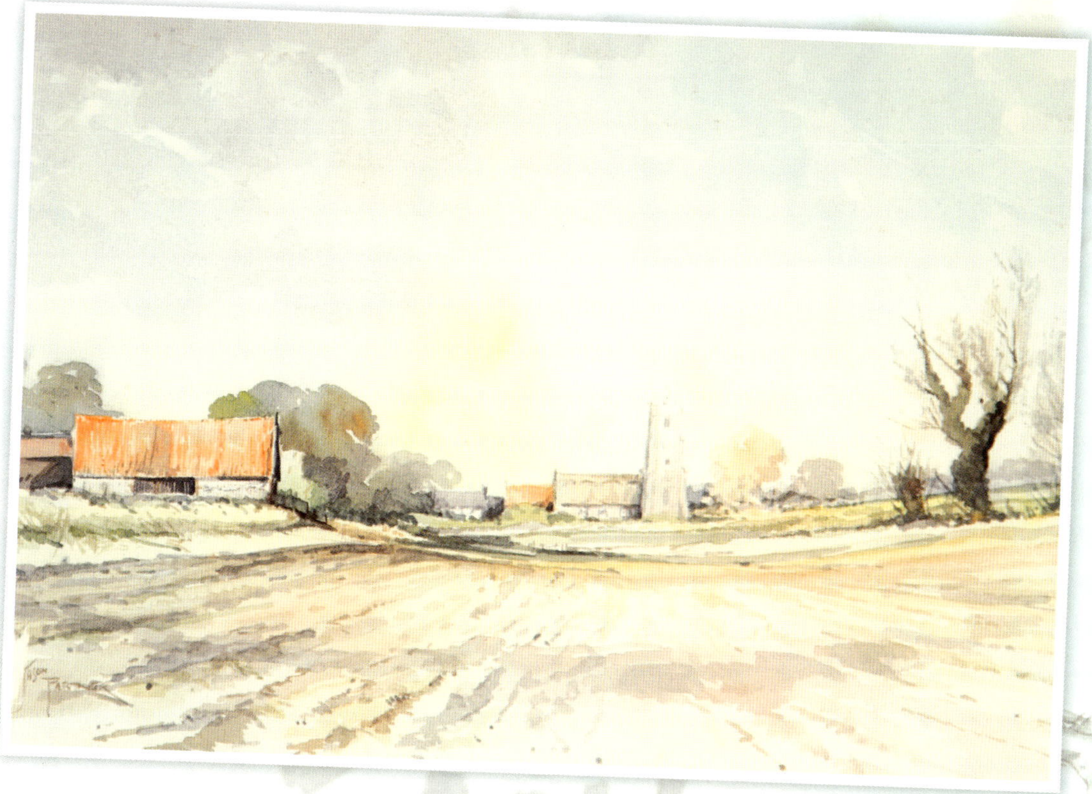

Stalham Green, Norfolk

Over the last hundred years villages
in Norfolk have changed.

The movement of workers
from land to city played a hand.

One thing which remains constant,
a land mark for all to see,

Is the village church,
a source of local history.

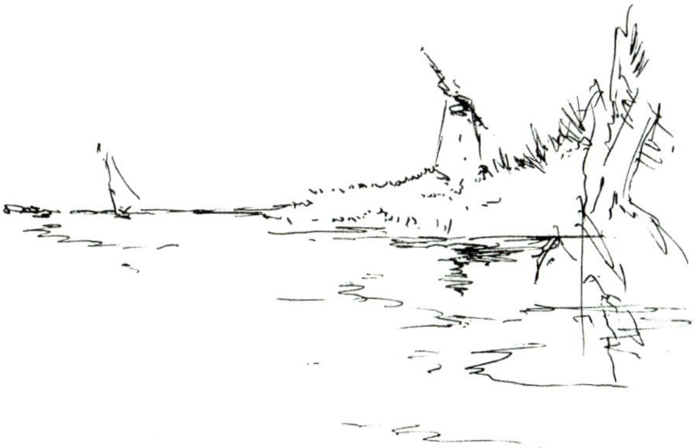

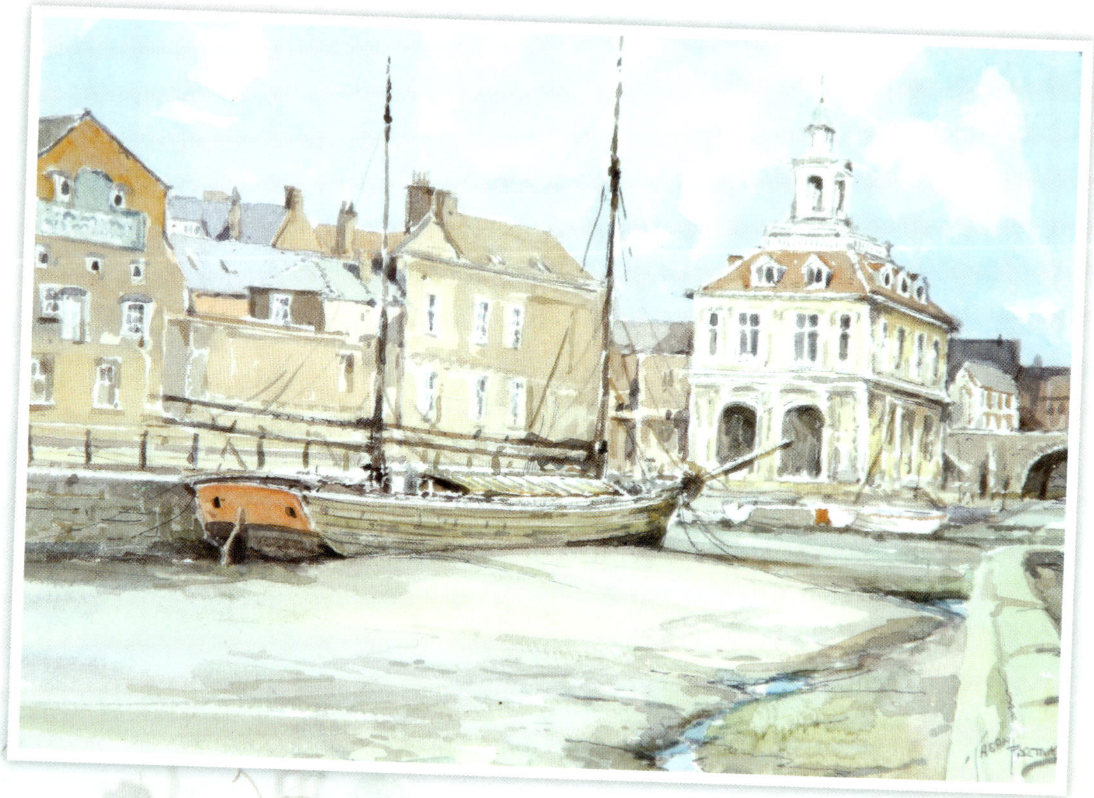

Custom House, King's Lynn, Norfolk

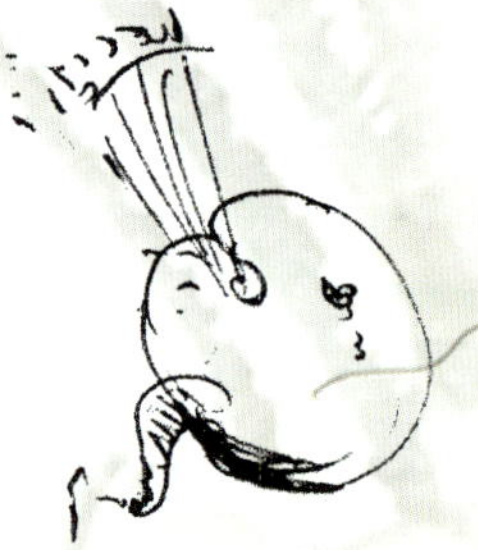

King's Lynn has a history
as long as your arm.

And through the years
has not lost its charm.

The yearly Mart
and world renowned festivals, too.

For visitors
there is much to see and do.

Buckinghamshire Arms, Blickling, Norfolk

© From an original watercolour by Jason Partner.

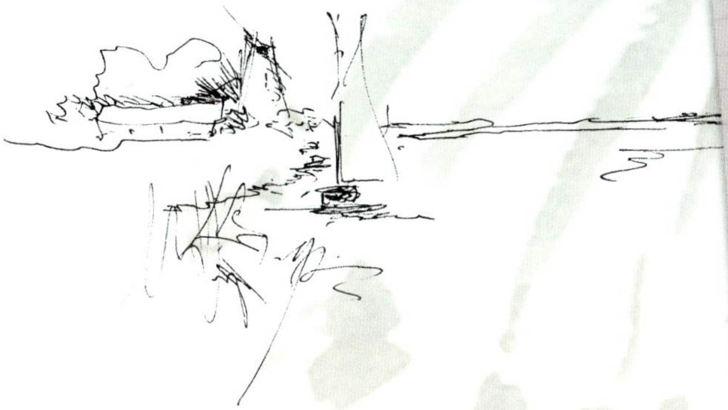

Situated close to Blickling Hall,
this hostelry is ideally placed

For visitors from the countryside
or nearby coast.

Delicious meals are available,
to suit all tastes.

That is why many awards
they can boast.

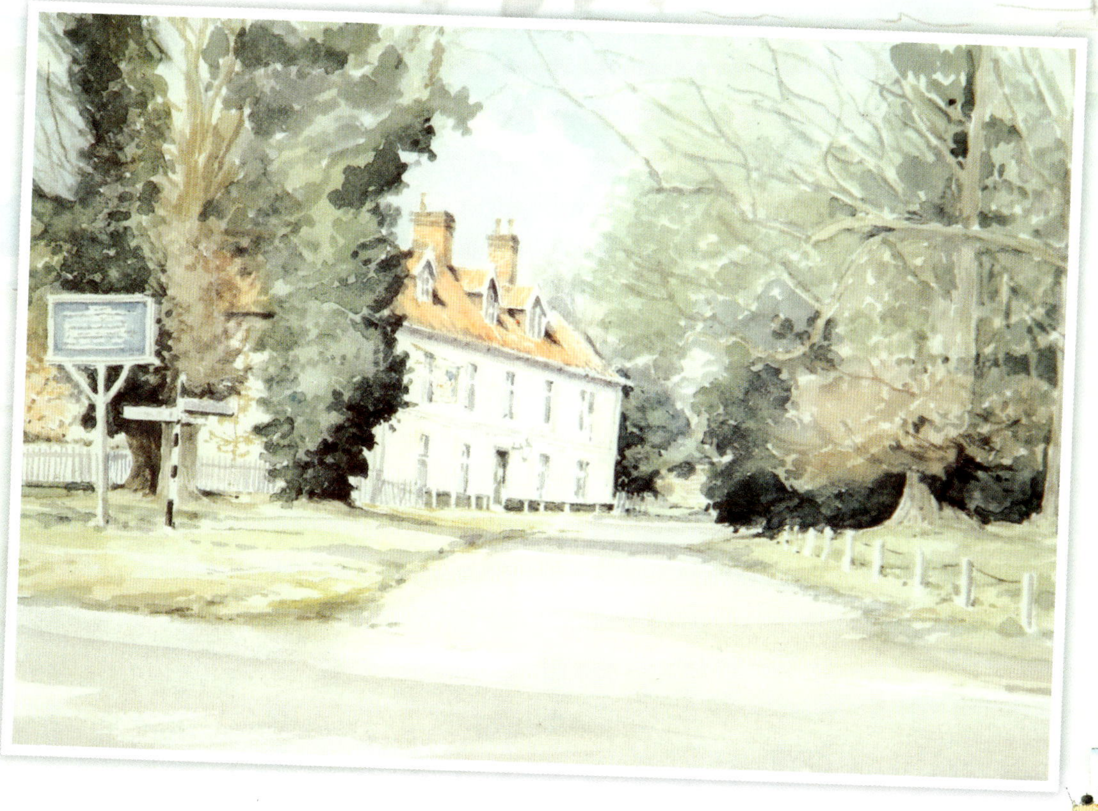

It sticks in our minds…

Whenever I got the chance to visit Jason, he was always pleased to impart his knowledge of the Old English style of watercolour painting.
The art of watercolour painting is knowing the correct amount of water and colour, the use of subtle shading and minimal detail.
His philosophy was, 'a watercolour is more about what you leave out, rather than what you put in.'

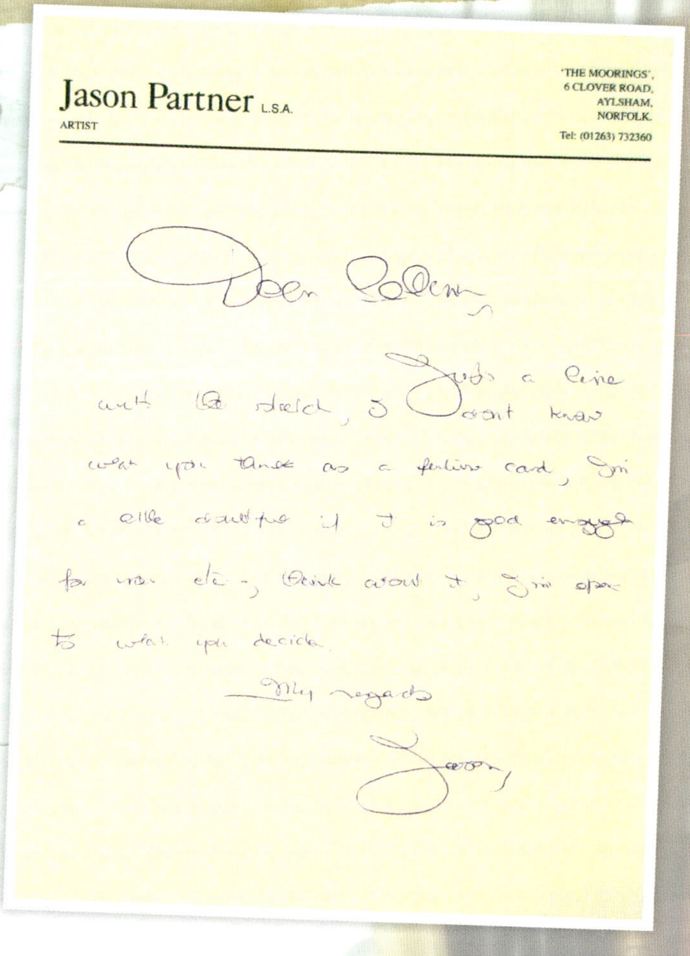

Jason Partner L.S.A.
ARTIST

'THE MOORINGS',
6 CLOVER ROAD,
AYLSHAM,
NORFOLK.
Tel: (01263) 732360

Dear Colin,

Just a line with the sketch, I dont know what you think as a festive card, I'm a little doubtful if it is good enough for [illegible] etc., think about it, I'm open to what you decide.

My regards

Jason

A letter from Jason
to me (Colin),
asking my opinion as to
whether I thought one of his
original sketches was good
enough to become a future
greetings card…
…as if!

Wildlife

A selection of wildlife painted by Jason.
These were mostly in and around the East Anglia region.

East Anglia is an area which can boast a varied selection of wildlife due mostly to its diverse habitats. Some include winter visitors like geese and swans. Whilst others spend all year along the coast, marshland and in gardens.

The otter, once persecuted and nearly extinct, was saved by the late Philip Ware and his wife who realised that they needed protection and founded the Otter Trust. Thanks to their care, the otter now thrives in rivers and streams.

The common and grey seals live along the coastline and in various resorts like Hunstanton, Blakeney and Morston; daily seal trips are available to visitors and are a popular attraction. At Horsey, near Great Yarmouth, a large colony of seals and pups can be seen during the winter months.

On a winter's morning, there is nothing more special than to see a flock of geese flying in formation over the fields searching for food, whilst many people flock to Welney to feed the swans which over-winter there year after year.

There is no need to travel far to see a blue tit or wren as they visit many gardens in their hunt for food, whereas the marsh tit much prefers the reeds and vegetation.

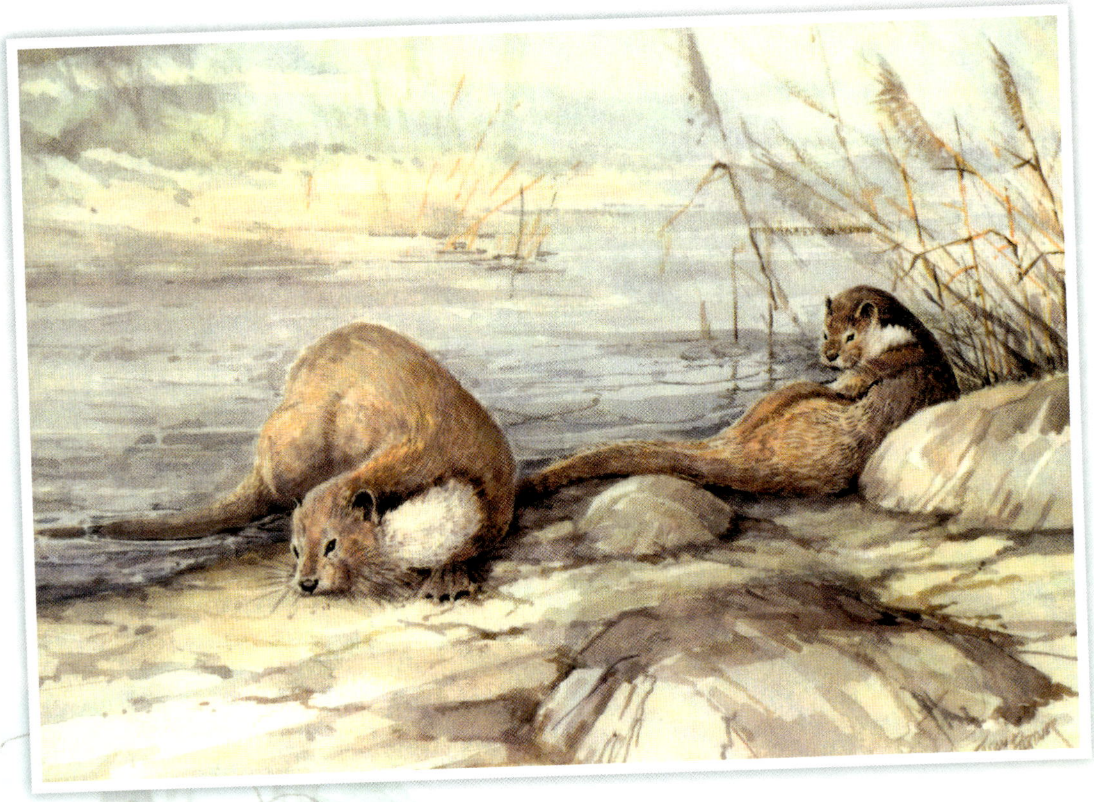

Otters on the riverbank

© From an original watercolour by Jason Partner.

These creatures are agile and swift,
as through the water they dart.
Hope they are brought back to life
through the work of art.

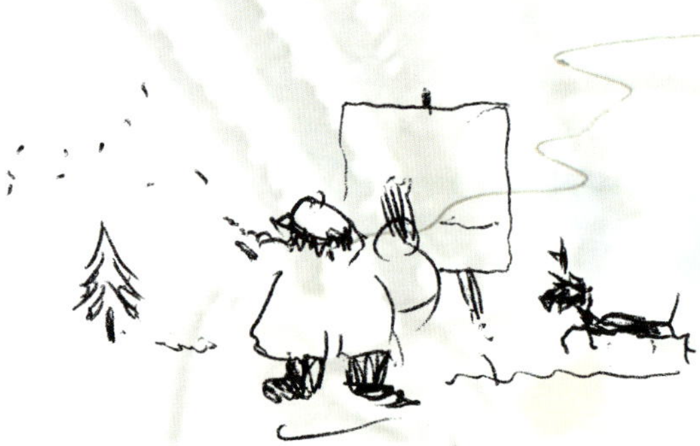

East coast seals

© From an original watercolour by Jason Partner.

Bobbing around in the sea, they float,
watched by people on a boat.
They are agile and sleek amongst the waves,
but look quite different when on sand they bathe.
With their big brown eyes, it's no surprise
that east coast seals have lots of appeal.

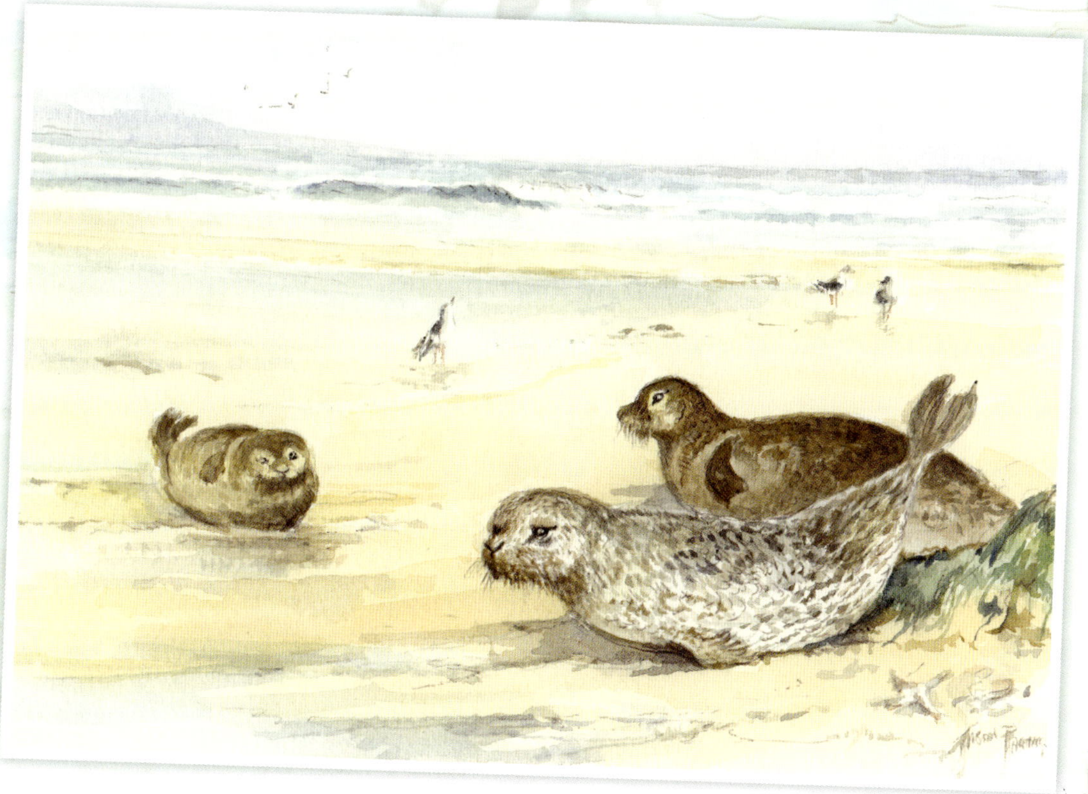

Canada geese on the wing

© From an original watercolour by Jason Partner.

These brown and grey birds
have been on our shores

For over a quarter
of a millennium.

As ornamental fowl
the county they've adorned

From coast to inland there's always
a chance to see them.

Whether you're a keen bird spotter
or like the wildlife to watch,

Canada geese never fail your heartbeat
to raise a notch.

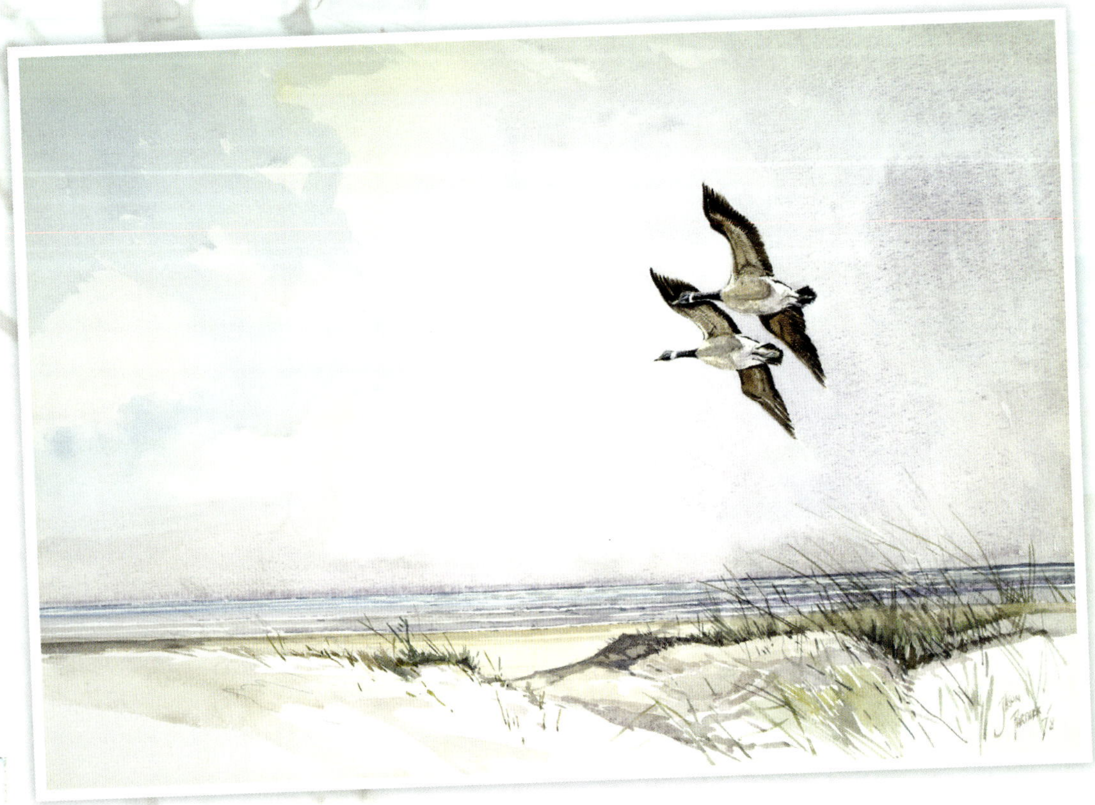

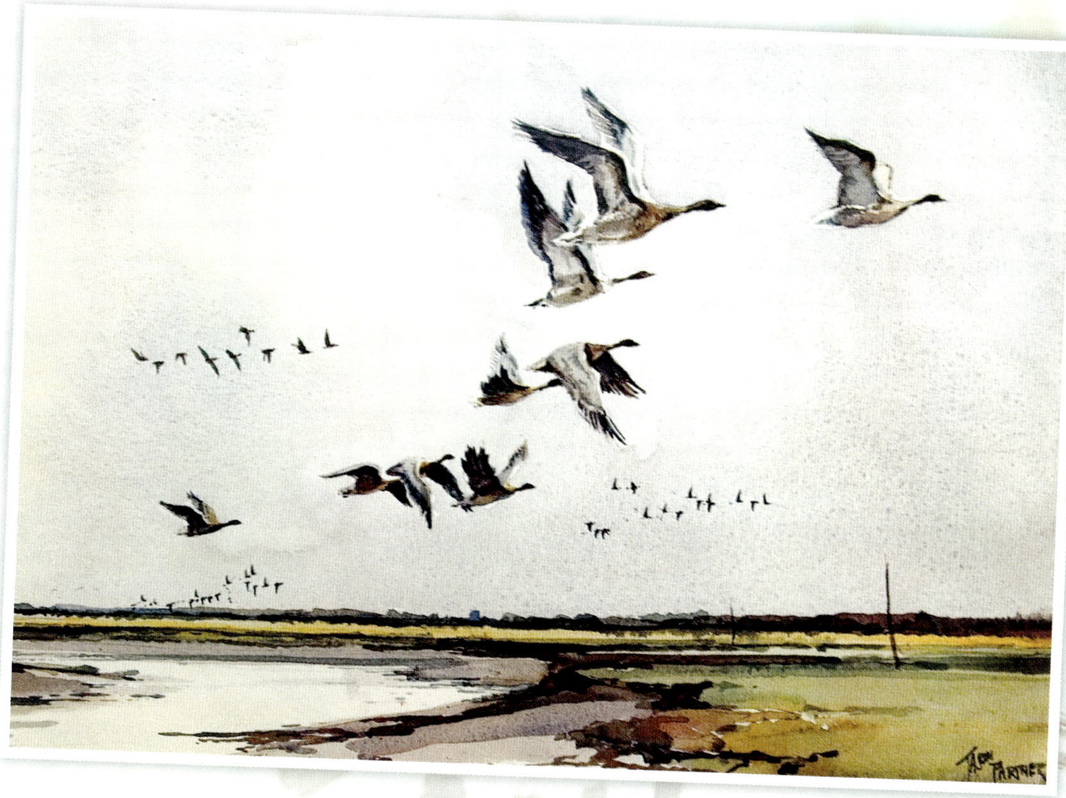

Geese Leaving the marshes

© From an original watercolour by Jason Partner.

These winter visitors come from far and wide,
And are closely governed by the tide.
You will see an abundance of these geese,
As on nearby fields they go to feast.

Ultramarine ...

...this violet-blue is derived from the semi-precious stone Lapis lazuli.

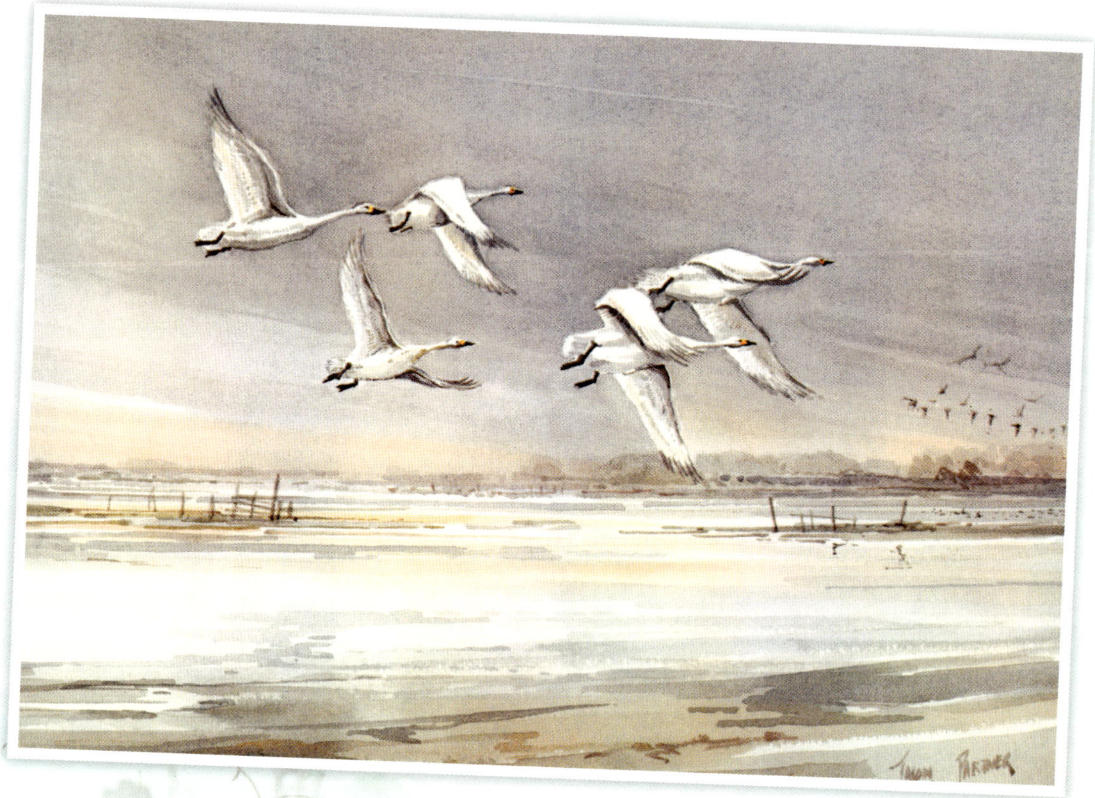

Bewick's swans over the marshes

© From an original watercolour by Jason Partner.

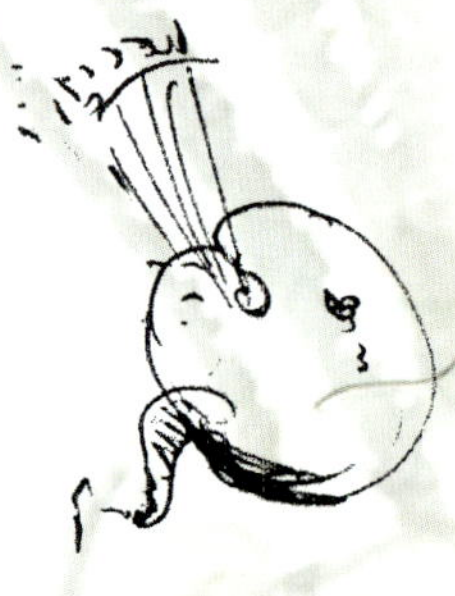

Majestically floating, not a water splash,
Even on the wing, swans certainly look dashing.
These elegant birds of water and sky command,
But do not look so steady when coming in to land.

Blue tit

© From an original watercolour by Jason Partner.

This colourful bird is a popular garden visitor.

It may be small in size but is big in colour,

And quite an acrobat when feeding.

It is easy to see why blue tits are appealing.

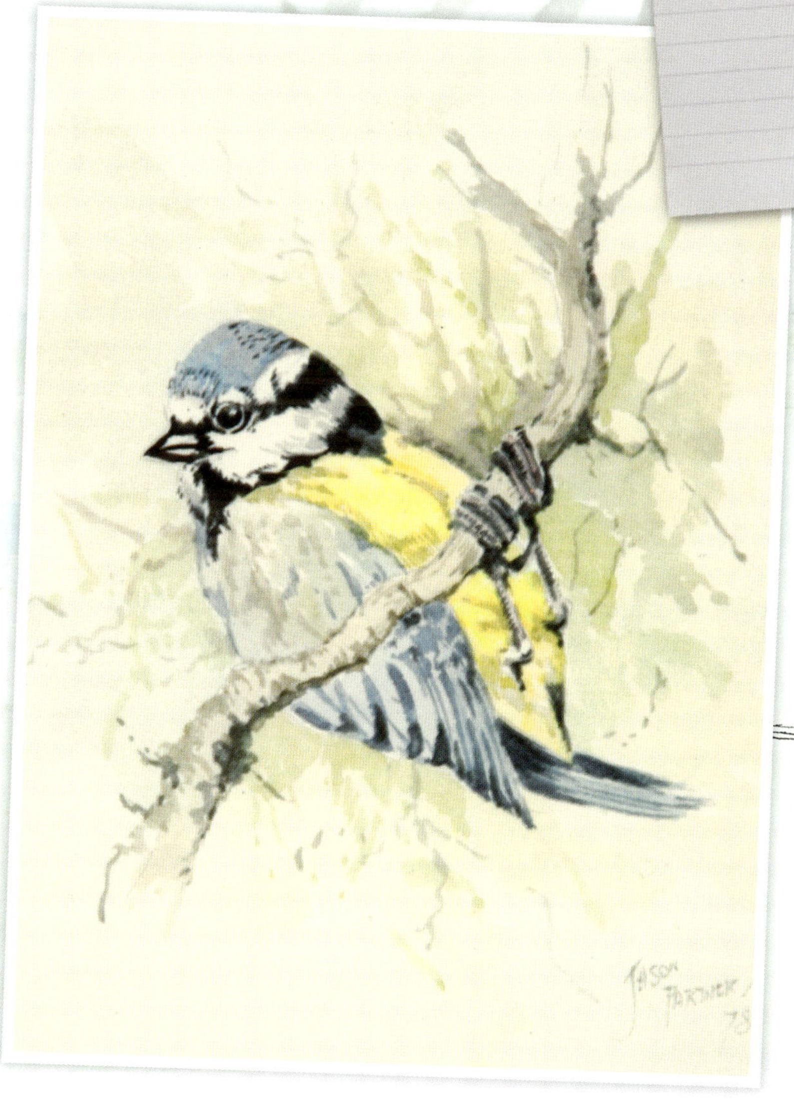

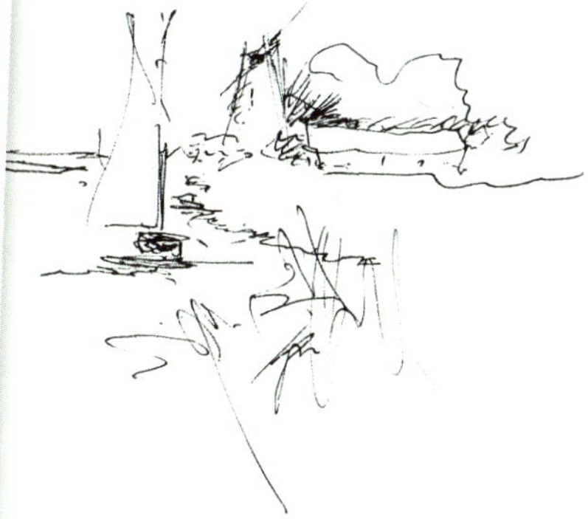

Wrens

Being small and brown, wrens may be
bottom of the list

Amongst the larger blackbird,
song thrush and all.

But one thing you certainly cannot miss

Is the shrill noise of their call.

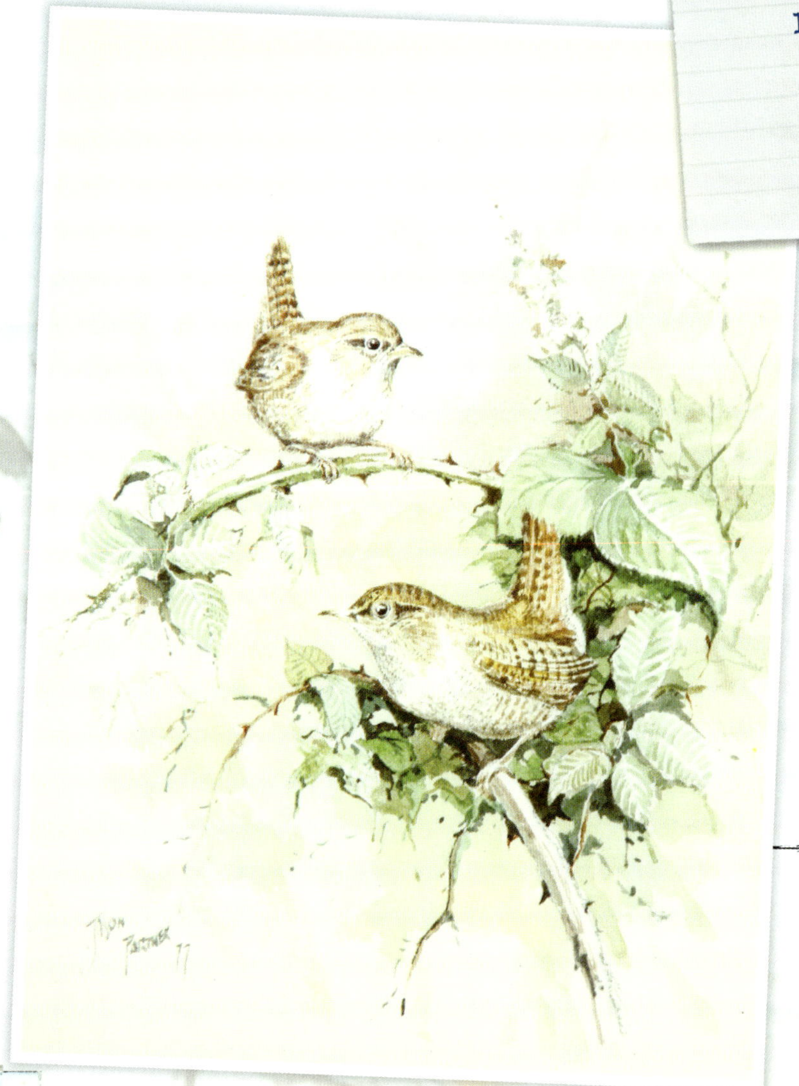

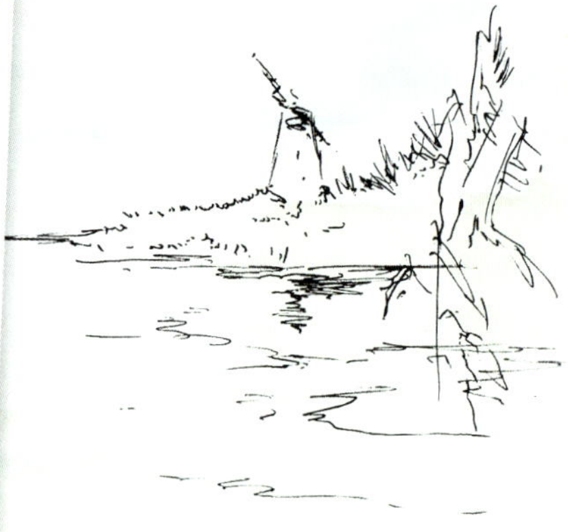

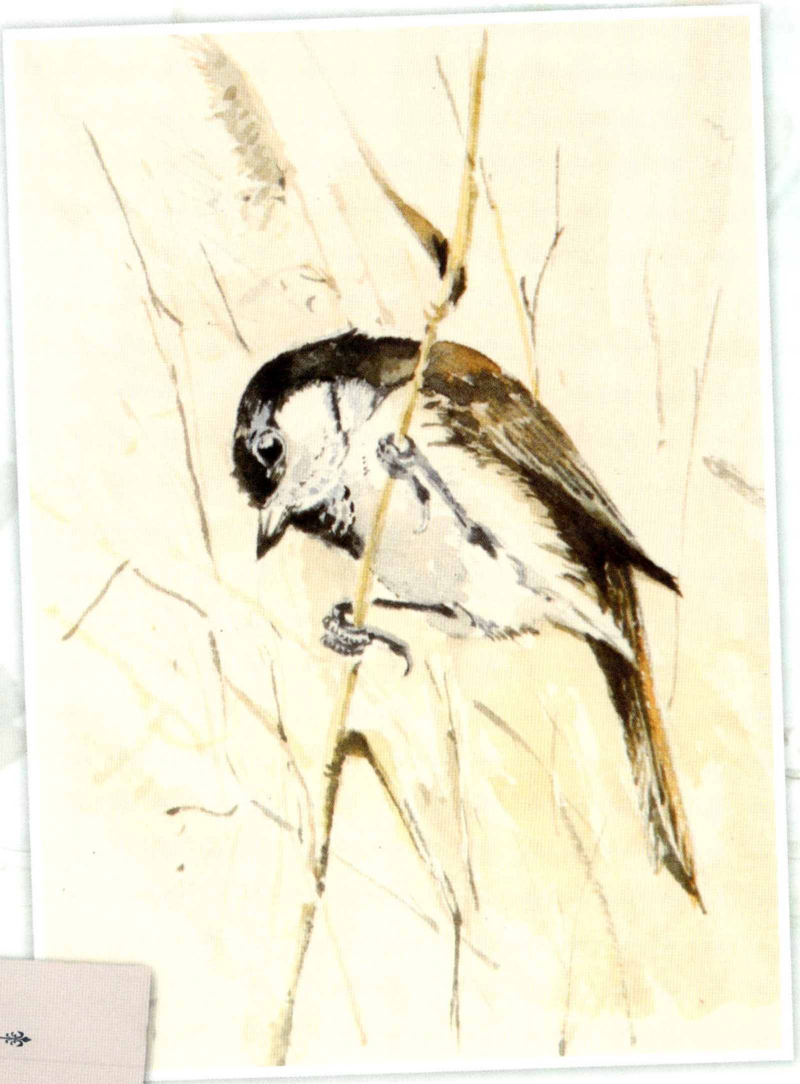

Whilst marsh tits have rather a muted hue,
The reason being the habitat they choose.
Their call sounds very much like a sneeze,
And they enjoy eating insects and seeds.

Marsh tit

It sticks in our minds...

Over the years Jason built up a large following of his work through his popular exhibitions, which usually sold out in the first day, and his art demonstrations in Norfolk and Suffolk.

Working with the National Trust he held one-day workshops; in the morning the amateur artists would paint under the direction and encouragement of Jason, followed by lunch. Then in the afternoons he would often sell any paintings he had with him.

There was nothing he liked more than to give art lovers the benefit of his wealth of knowledge.

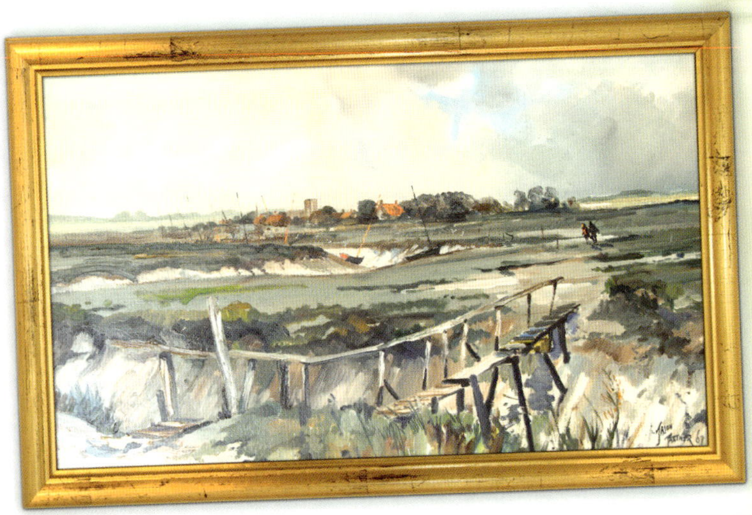

OIL OF RICKETY BRIDGE BETWEEN MORSTON AND BLAKENEY

Although Jason was living in Leicestershire during the early 1960s, he enjoyed visiting Norfolk and painting local images.

On several occasions he would have travelled to Norfolk by bus, either with his sketch book or bringing the finished paintings with him, and this image could have been one of those. Over the course of a year he sold many pictures at hotels etc, building up a good reputation, and was able to buy a car with the proceeds.

Original oil on board © Jason Partner.
By kind permission of Colin and Mary Nelson.

Pastoral

A selection of pastoral scenes painted by Jason.
These were mostly in and around the East Anglia region.

For those who are lucky to live in the eastern region of the UK, there are many outdoor pursuits to take part in and enjoy throughout the year.

Walking is one which is popular, especially along country lanes where you may catch sight of pheasants strutting across the track from one field to another, maybe a solitary horse quietly grazing in a field, or even a rare glimpse of a gypsy caravan.

From August onwards landowners and farmers hold shoots for people to take part in, either as beaters or those with their trusty dog and gun.

Whatever your preference, there is so much that the countryside has to offer.

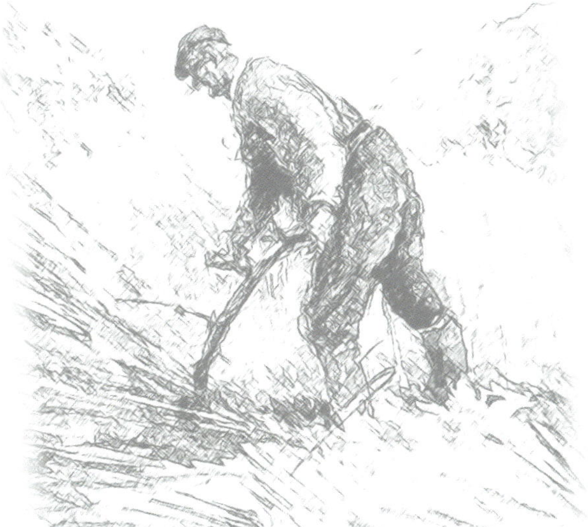

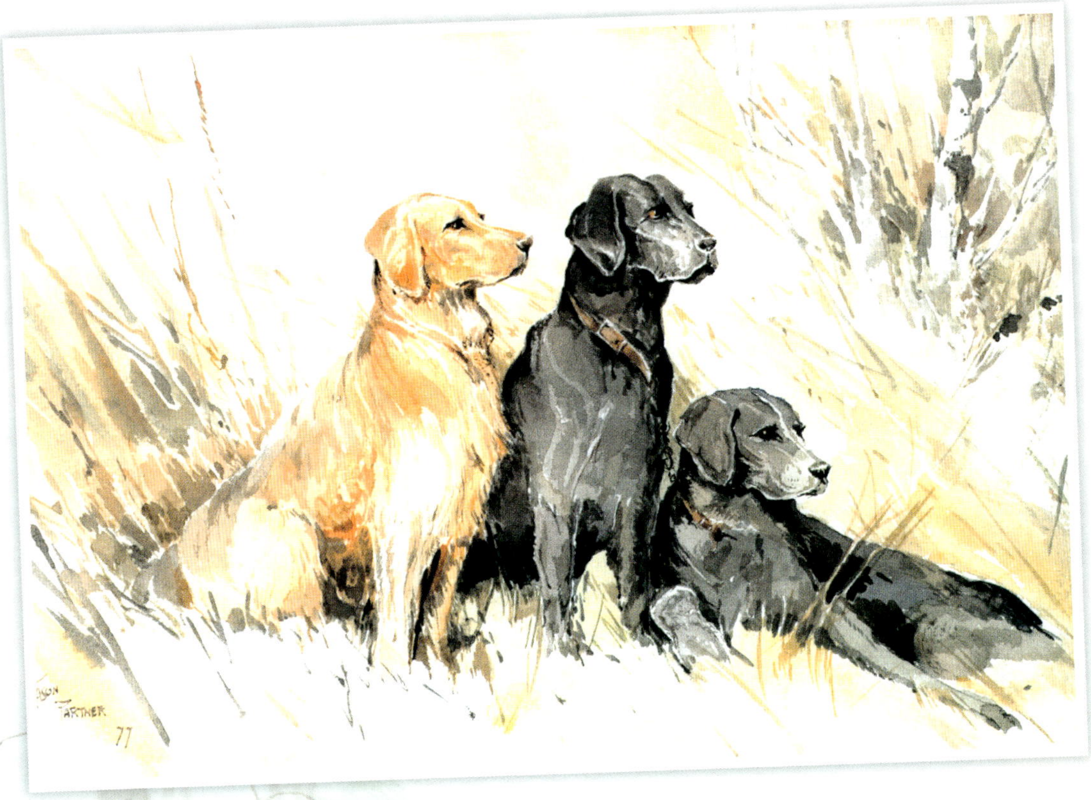

Gun dogs

© From an original watercolour by Jason Partner.

Jason always loved relating stories to me during my visits to him. One being of his dog, Sheba.

She was bred from local gun dogs and had a lovely nature. She liked being taken for walks and was befriended by adults and children alike. During the shooting season, Jason and Sheba were invited to watch. So off they went and joined the group of people and gun dogs. All was going well, until the guns began to fire, at which point Sheba took fright and ran off. Jason went to catch her and felt very embarrassed. From then onwards, if Jason was invited to join the shoot again, he made polite excuses.

It was on one of the walks with Sheba that Jason may have first heard the Norfolk dialect. A gentleman walking along the road happened to call out, 'How yer gittin' on, ole partner?' Not realising that this was a form of greeting, Jason wondered how this stranger knew his surname.

Waiting patiently, keeping still and
quiet is part of the job

for gun dogs like Sheba, Ollie and Bob.

Listening intently for the command,

bringing the game to their owner's hand.

Whether they're in the rough or near water side,

from these dogs, nothing can hide.

A near thing

© From an original watercolour by Jason Partner.

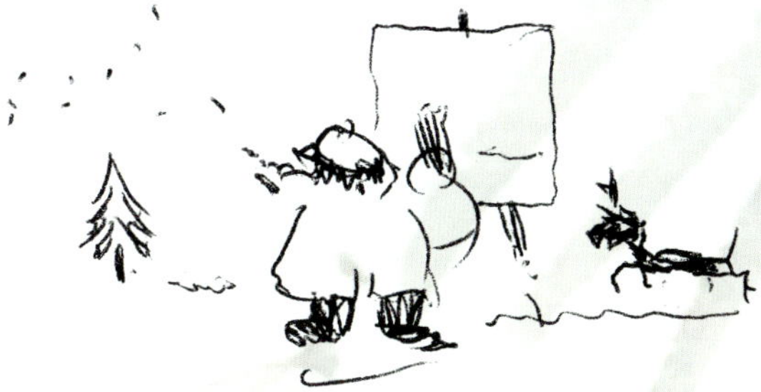

Silently, through undergrowth
creep two gun dogs.

Over ferns and bracken
and small pieces of logs.

Ahead stands a pheasant,
without a care.

But it soon takes flight,
when the dogs appear.

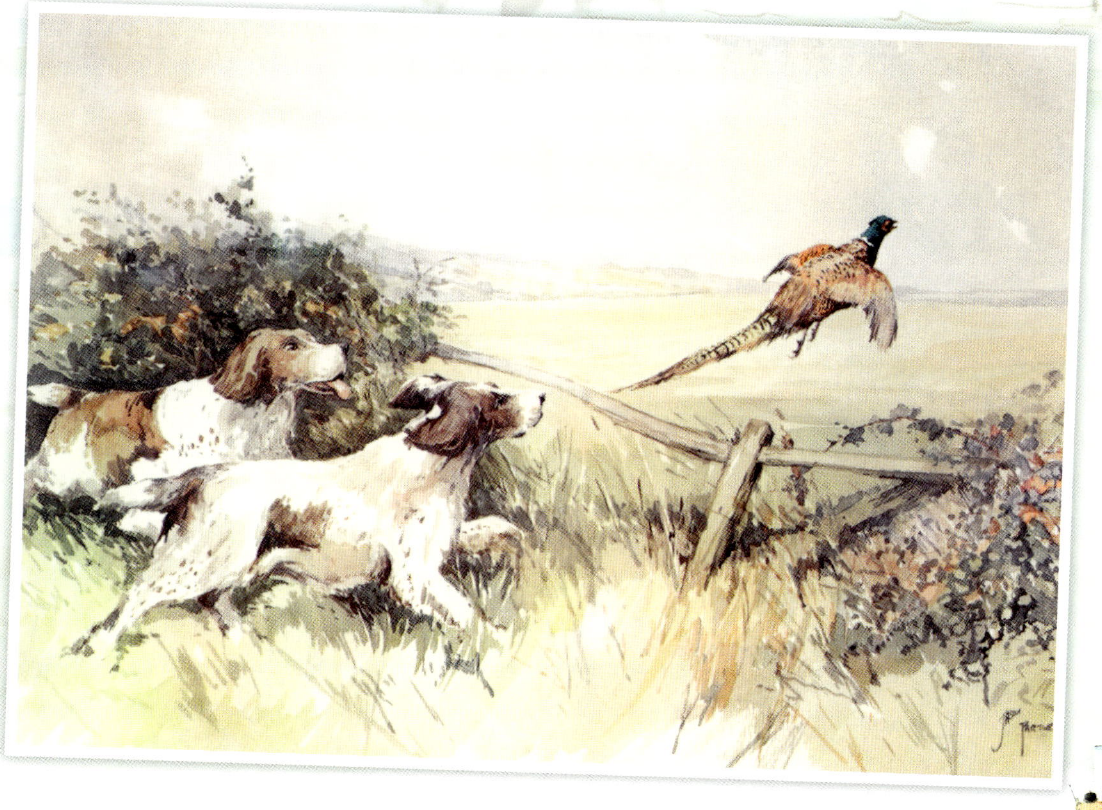

Grazing horse

On this hill top I graze alone,
just behind the church is my stable home.

Being on my own does not trouble me,
I can munch on this delicious grass quite happily.

Occasionally I stop to admire the view,
amble around the field a time or two.

I wander down to the gate
when the church clock chimes three,
as I know my owner will be waiting there for me.

I'll have a saddle and reins attached, ready to ride,
and together we'll canter through the countryside.

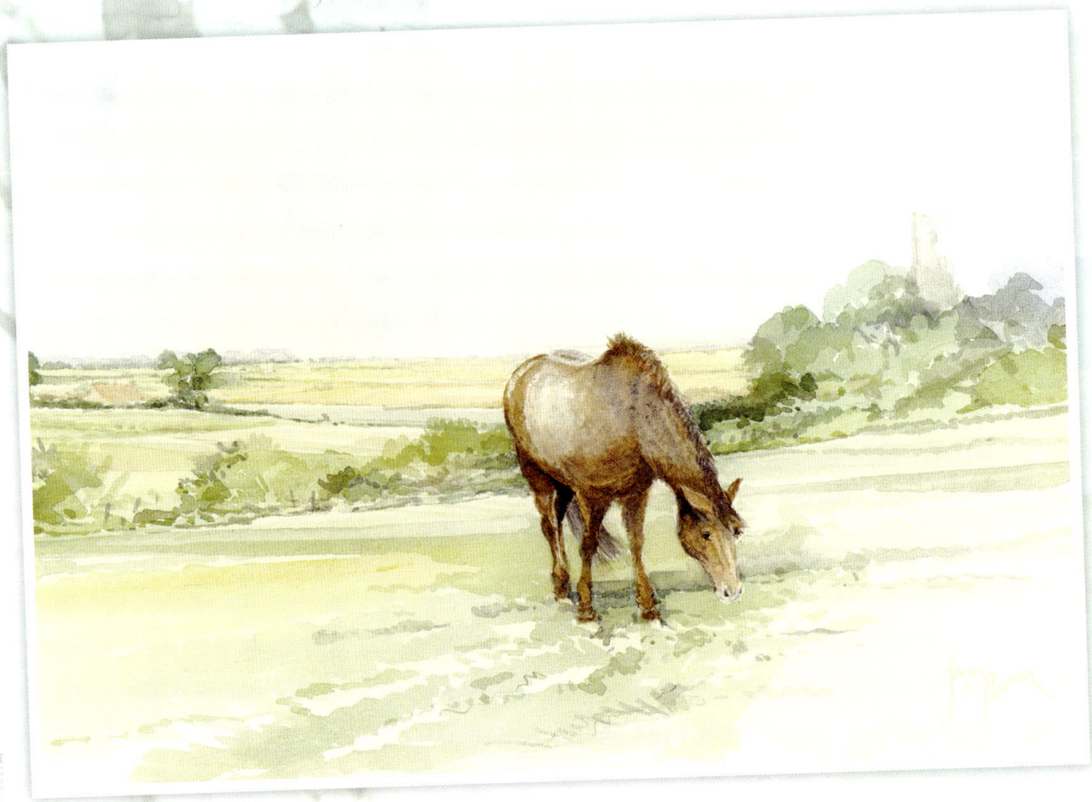

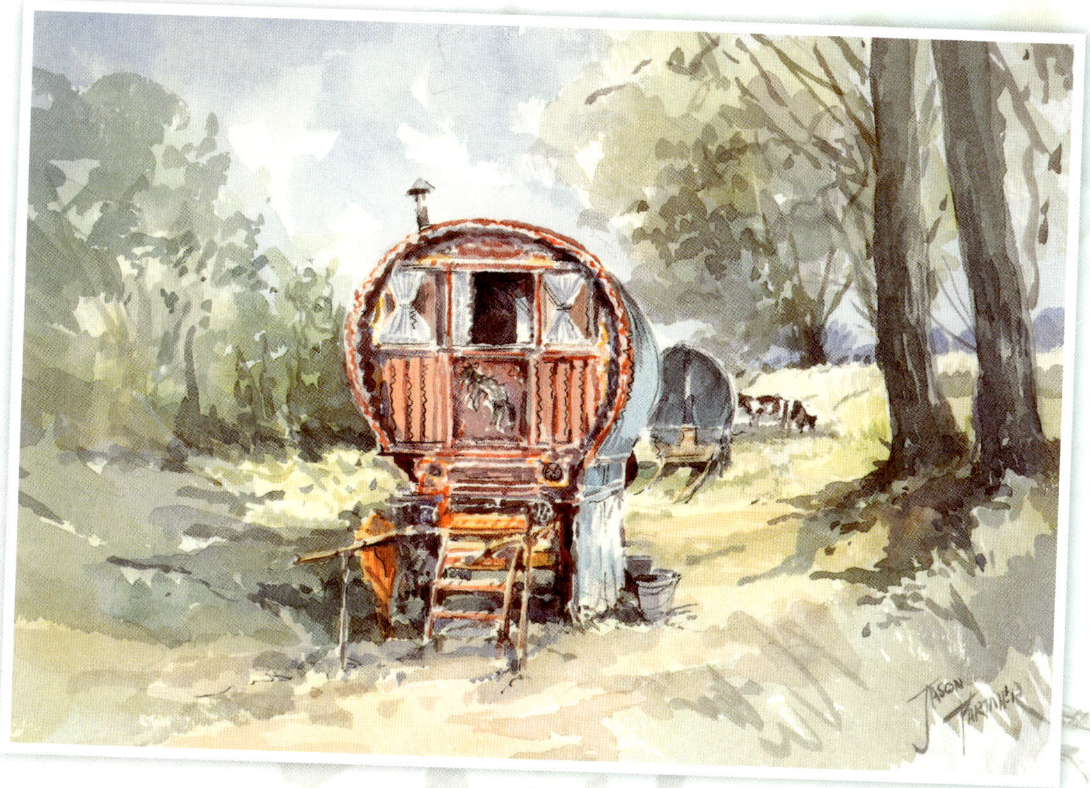

Gypsy caravan

© From an original watercolour by Jason Partner.

This colourful form of transport
is on the wane.

You'll not see many now,
which is a shame.

Driven by horses
along country lanes.

Travellers only stayed awhile,
before moving on again.

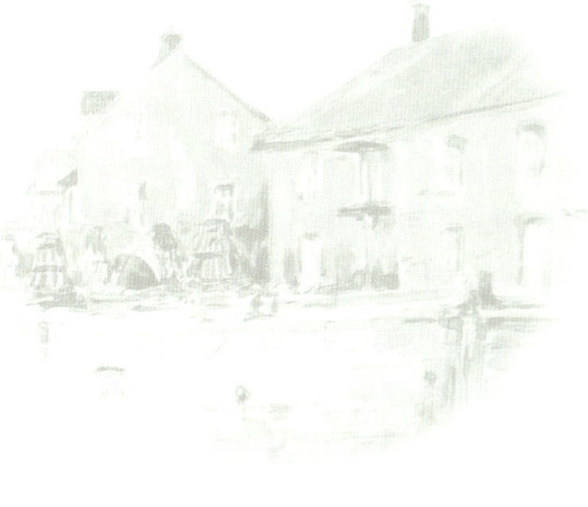

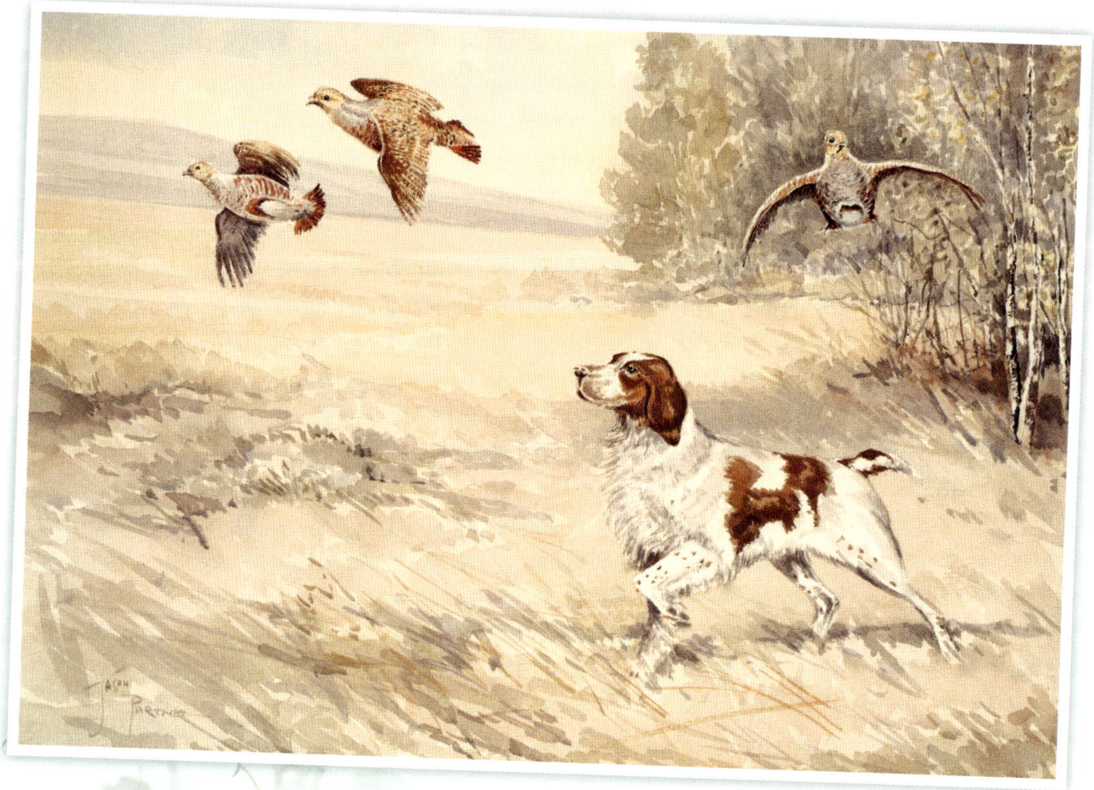

Flushing partridges

© From an original watercolour by Jason Partner.

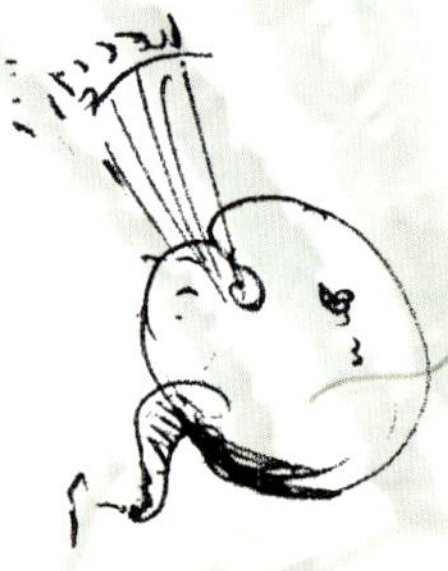

Flushing the partridges away from safe cover,
owners and dogs in the woodland hover.
But, as the pointer draws near to the prey,
the partridges take flight and get clean away.

Breaking cover

© From an original watercolour by Jason Partner.

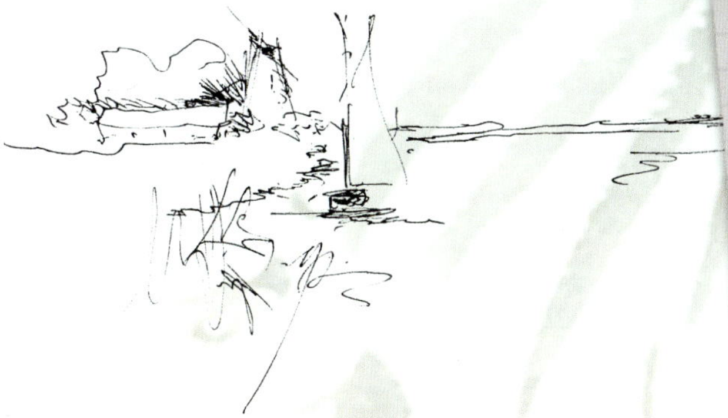

In the early morning,
just as the sun rises in the east,

the pheasants can break cover,
to start their feast.

It's the perfect place to stay awhile,
under the cover of trees,

and these game birds
can do whatever they please.

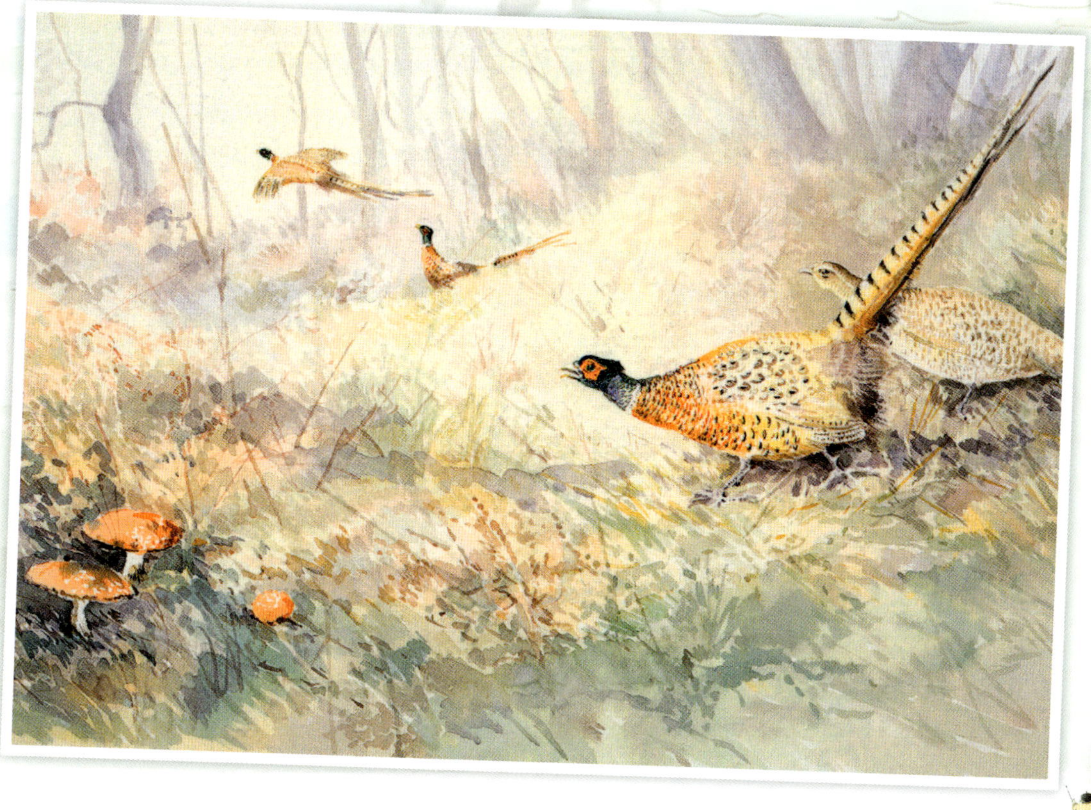

Jan makes a retrieve

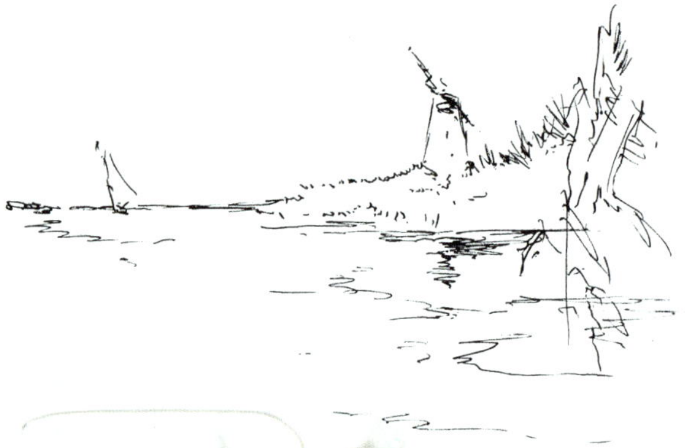

It's great being a gun dog
and I love the outdoors.

I do not mind getting wet
and having muddy paws.

There are times when I sit by my master's side,
listen for orders which I must abide by.

My duty is to wait until I get the command
to retrieve the game bird for my master's hand.

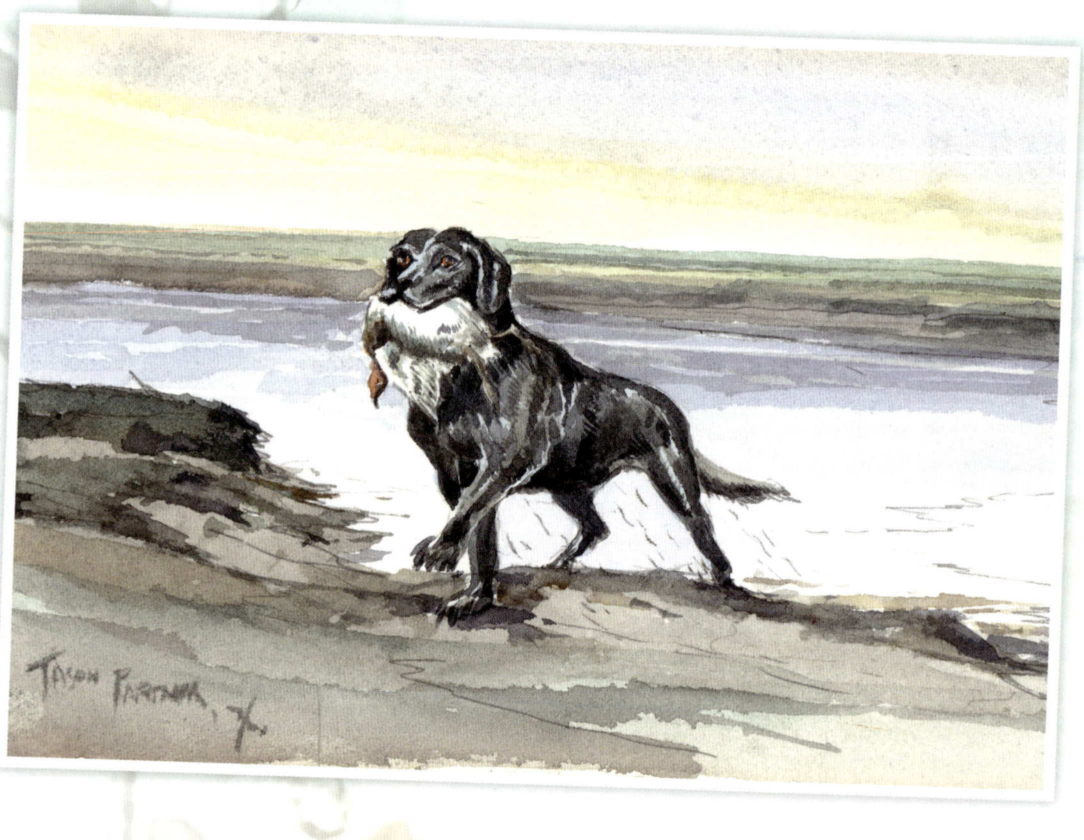

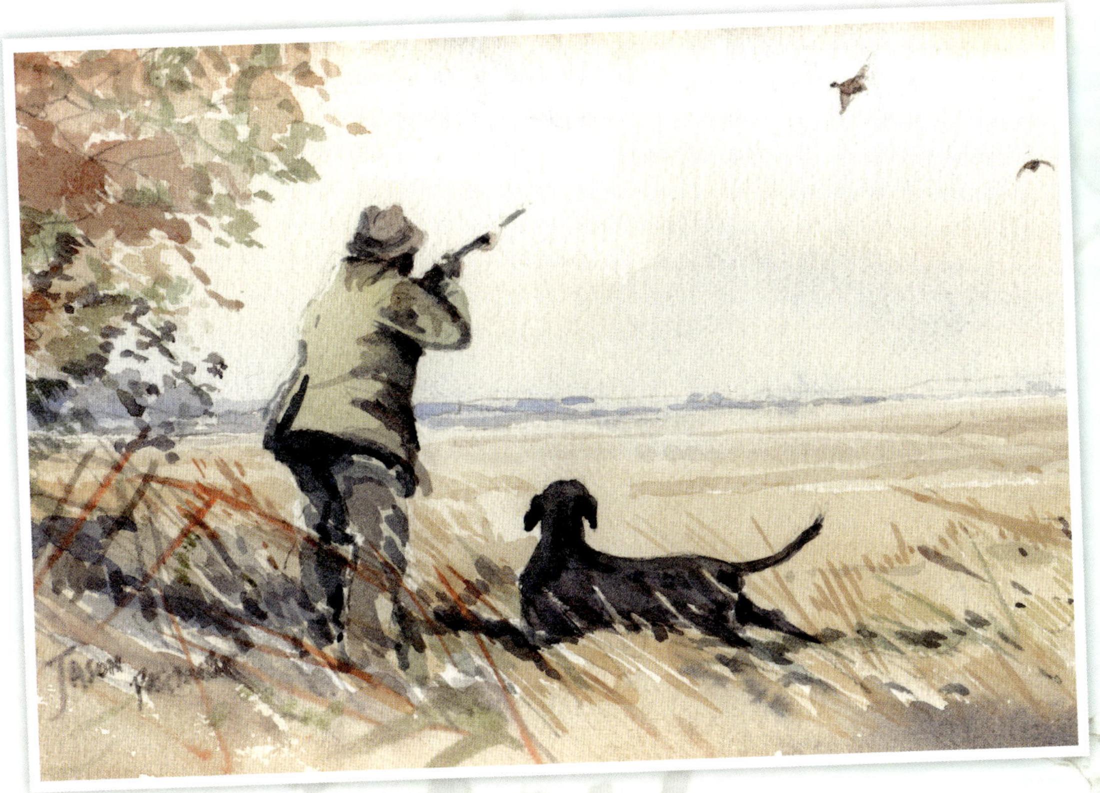

Biding our time

© From an original watercolour by Jason Partner.

We're hiding just in the cover of trees,
so our quarry cannot see us.

The perfect place to bide our time.

It won't be long before the birds
from the fields will be disturbed.

I hope that they'll be in my eye line!

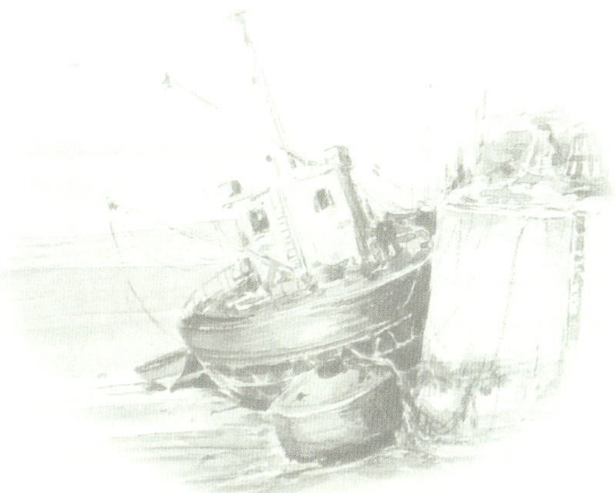

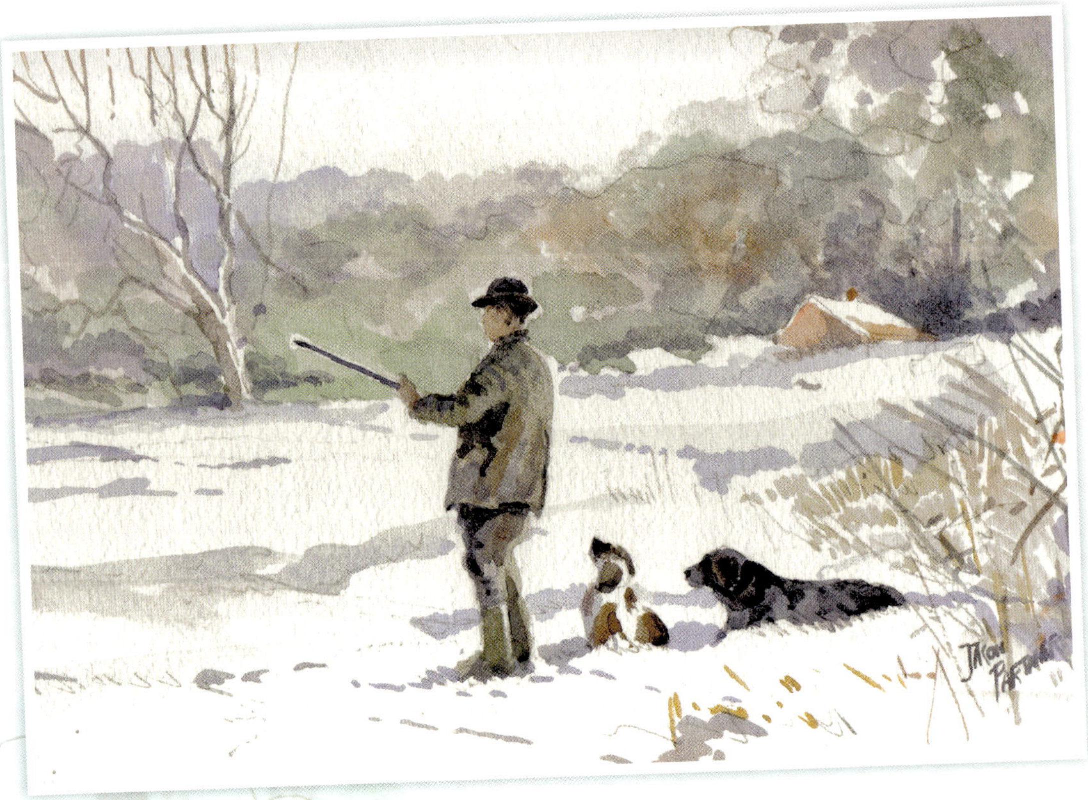

Waiting for the drive

© From an original watercolour by Jason Partner.

How long do we have to wait
for the call to come?

We could be snuggly tucked up
in our beds at home.

Our owner has told us
to lay quiet and still.

We haven't seen any game birds
and doubt we ever will.

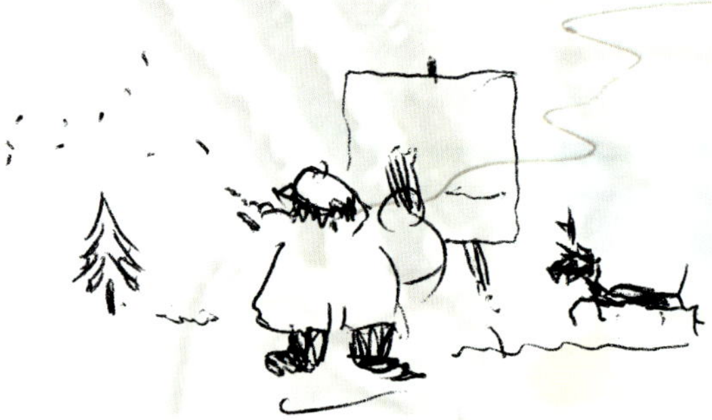

Taking aim

© From an original watercolour by Jason Partner.

From late summer onwards,
on farmland low or high,
you may see a row of people,
with their heads to the skies.

Standing in line,
guns at the ready
and a few feet apart,
waiting for birds
from the scrubland to dart.

Whether you're on target
or the birds get clean away,
it's all part of the experience
on a game shooting day.

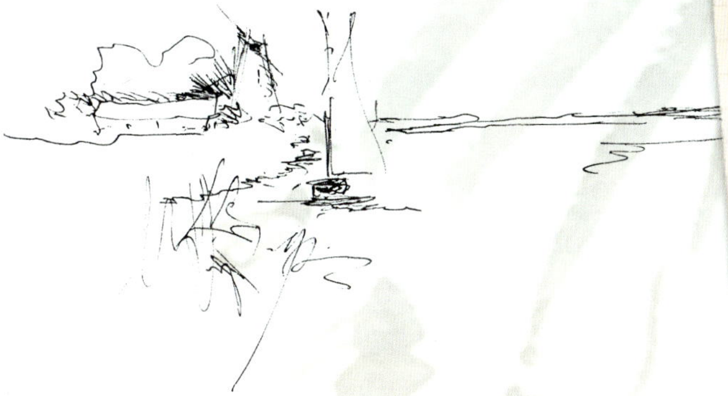

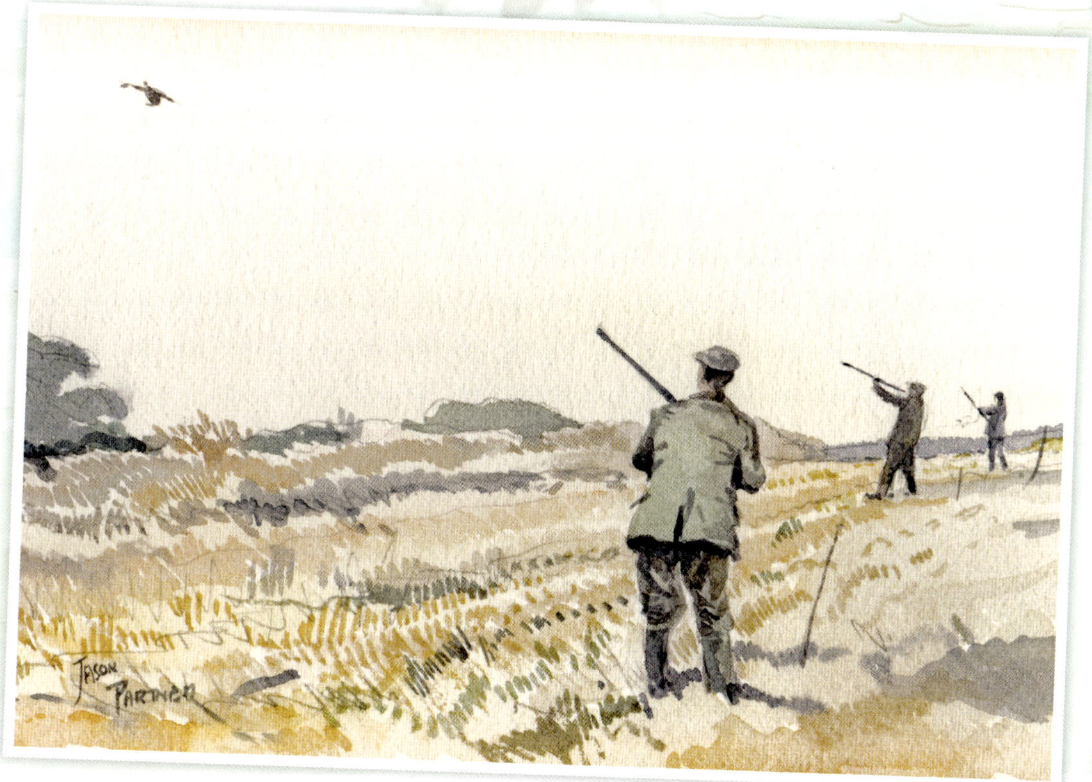

Memories of Jason...

Joe Crowfoot, *well known Suffolk artist.*

My first meeting of Jason Partner was in 1978 at the Beccles Art Society. Jason had come to speak and do a demonstration of his work, to encourage others to draw and paint. The evening was filled with his warmth, humour and art style was first class, making painting look so easy. Another thing I remembered was his large plate he used to mix the paints, rather than a traditional pallet.

During the break I managed to have a quiet word with Jason regarding my future as an artist. I had been thinking about changing my career and becoming a professional artist. Jason's advice to me was so positive, telling me to 'go for it', to believe in my ability and that he was sure I would be all right. These kind words became instrumental in my life and I have never looked back. Jason's legacy will be with us forever.

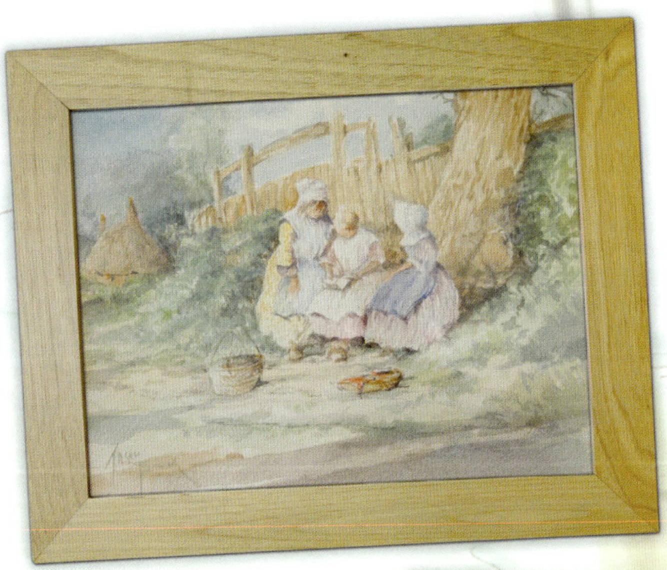

Reading Lesson

Jason painted this image of three small children, titled 'The Reading Lesson'.

He also painted four other pictures in the style of Myles Birkett Foster and this image has certainly caught the feeling of Victorian times.

Original watercolour © Jason Partner.
By kind permission of Colin and Mary Nelson.

Summer meadows

Living so close to vast areas of countryside, Jason was fortunate enough to paint images of the changing seasons and how they affected the area he lived in.

The image of lush growth with stream running through the meadow and cattle grazing is a rural scene still seen today.

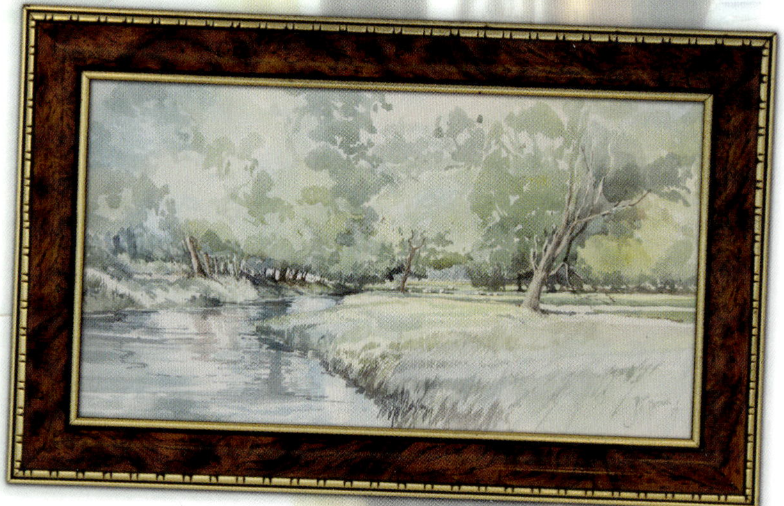

Original watercolour © Jason Partner.
By kind permission of Colin and Mary Nelson.

Winter Landscapes

A selection of winter landscapes painted by Jason.
These were mostly in and around the East Anglia region.

Jason loved painting winter scenes and many of the following images were painted especially for his wife and family. He thought, that with the changing light, the use of subtle shading, dark silhouettes of bare trees made the images more intense and dramatic.

He chose places close to his home, country lanes, landmarks, buildings and wild birds to feature in the paintings.

They show the beauty of winter time.

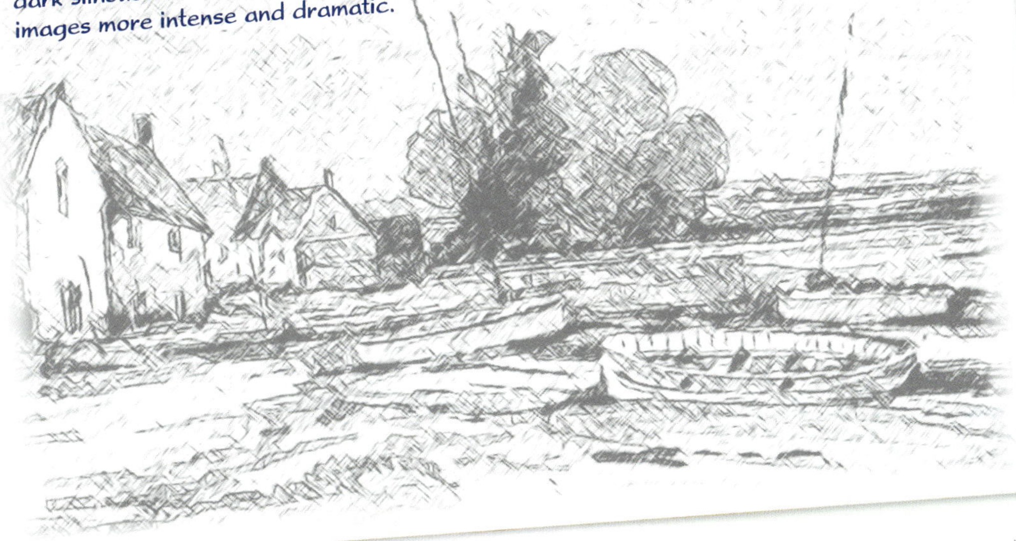

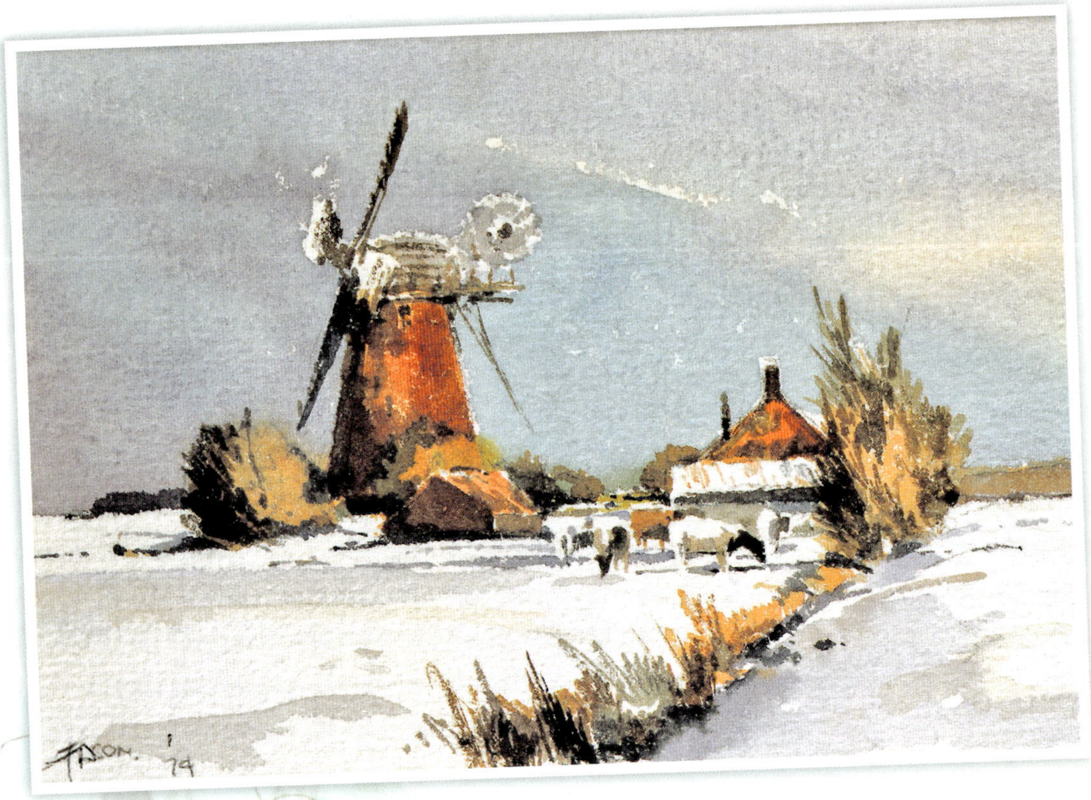

Snowy pastures

© From an original watercolour by Jason Partner.

The wind may be blowing a gale,

Snow is mixed in with hail.

The cattle in the pasture
are keeping snug,

Under their deep winter coat
as thick as a rug.

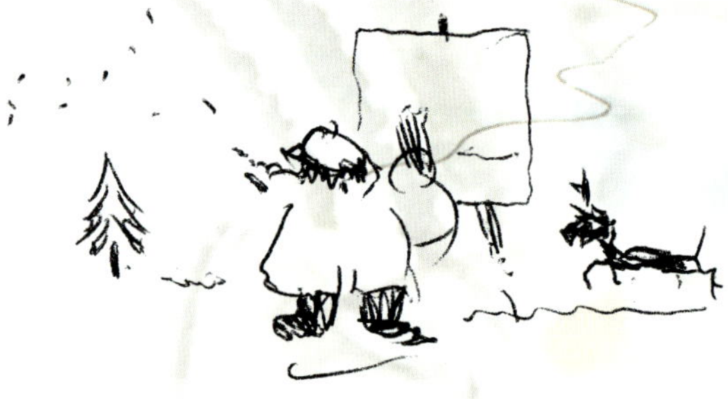

Winter's morning

© From an original watercolour by Jason Partner.

If the temperature falls below zero
and icicles begin to form.

On the roof tops,
dense layers of snow adorn.

Vegetables, cereal crops and garden plants
are covered too.

Spring is around the corner and new growth
will soon start to show.

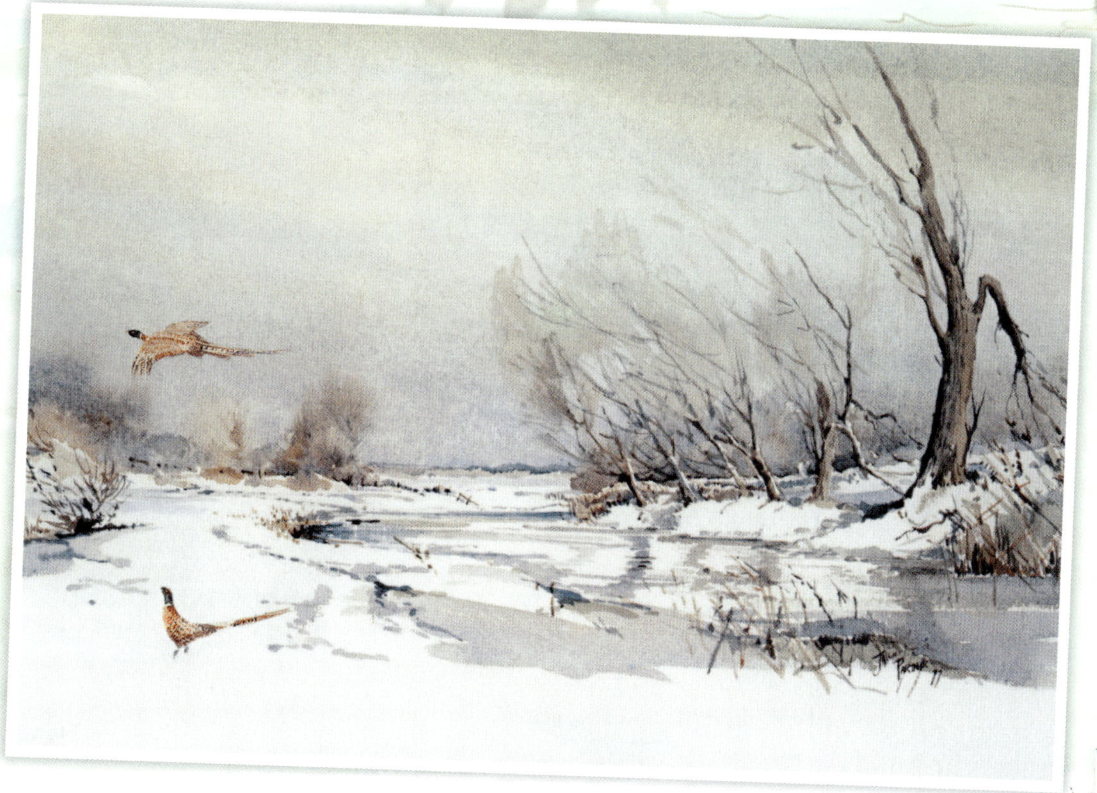

A new winter's day

© From an original watercolour by Jason Partner.

If you're a child
the first glimpse of snow can excite,

It's a chance to build snowmen
and such like.

Kitted out with coat, hat
and scarves,

Using spades and hands,
ice sculptures they carve,

And then finish with
a snowball fight.

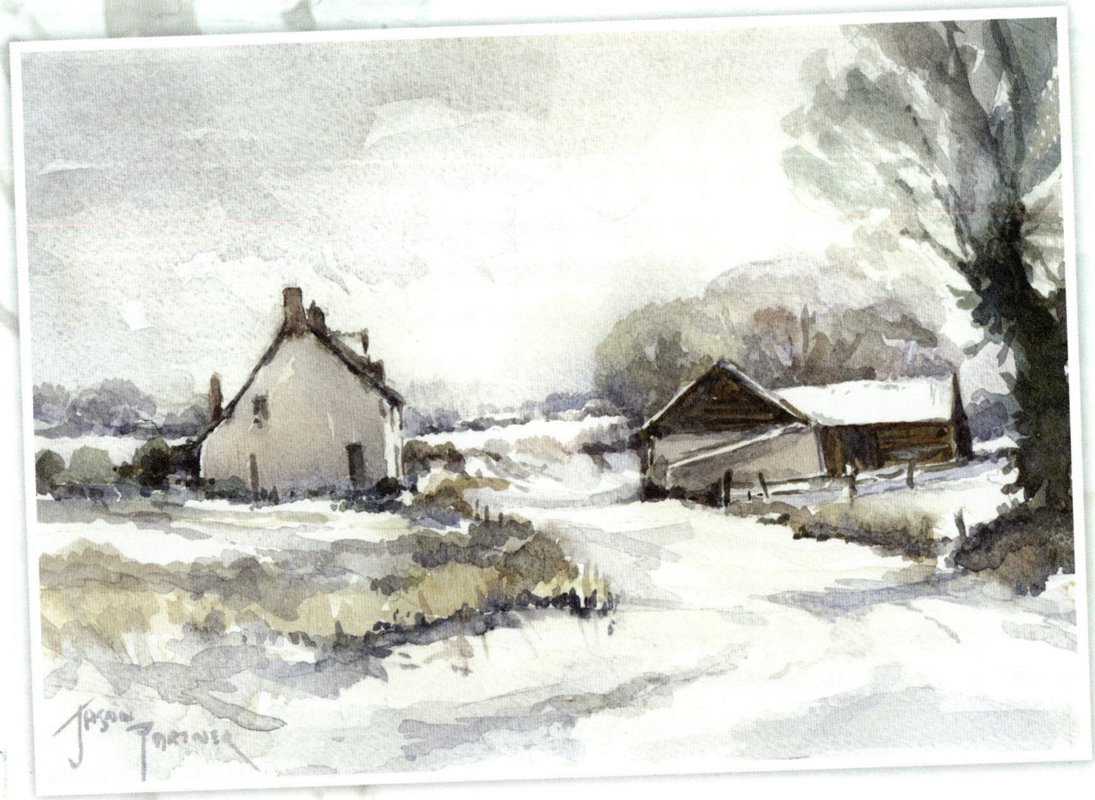

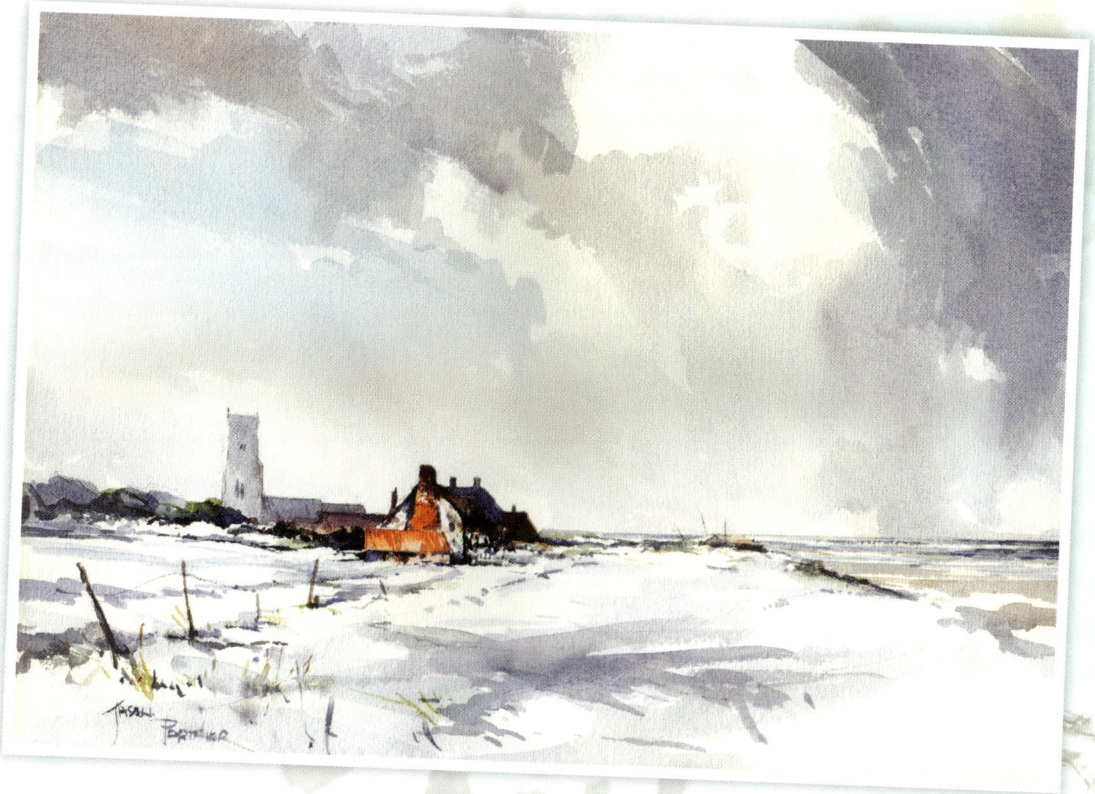

The first snowfall

© From an original watercolour by Jason Partner.

When it's the first heavy snowfall
of the year,

Traffic can come to a halt,
until roads are cleared.

Although we may have food and heat,

Animals and birds
still want something to eat.

Many look after them until
the snow disappears.

Scarlet Red ...

...has a slight orange tinge.

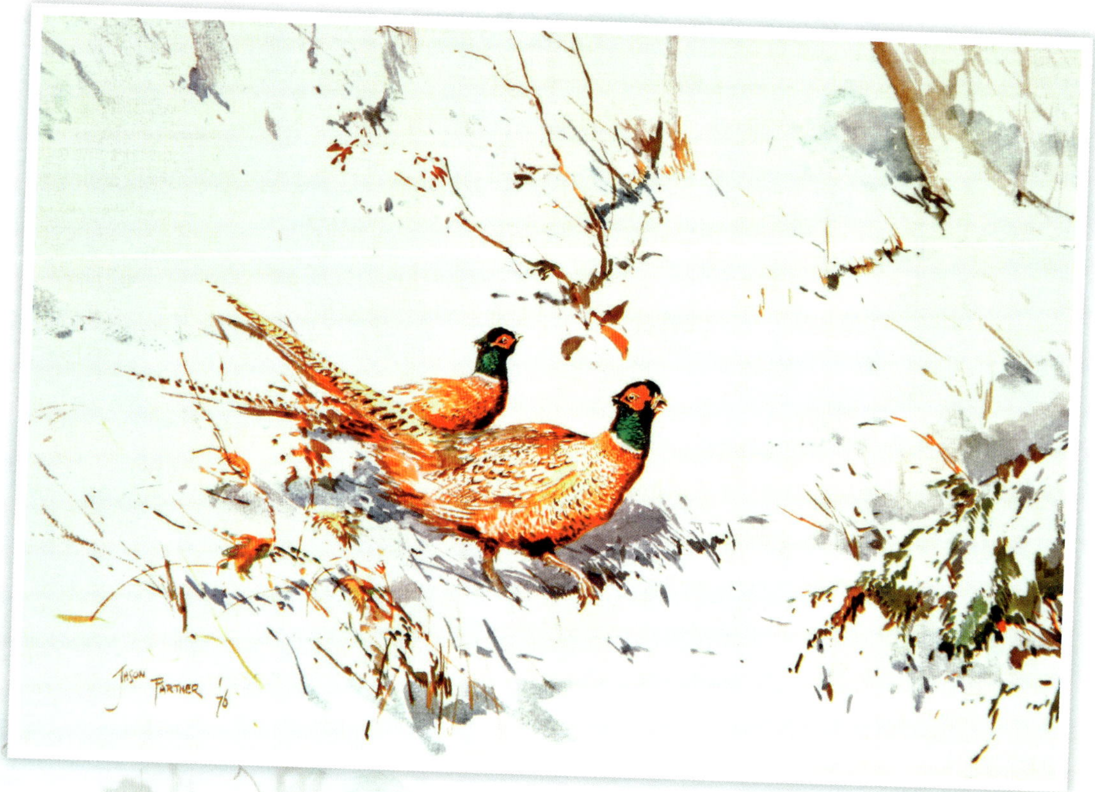

Pheasants in the snow

© From an original watercolour by Jason Partner.

When the only colour you can see is white,
A pheasant can seem really bright.
Hunting for food in fields and hedgerows,
How it keeps warm, no one knows.

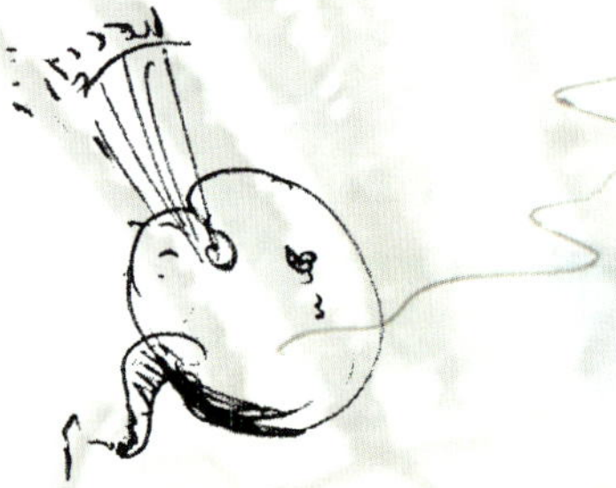

Winter scene, Loddon

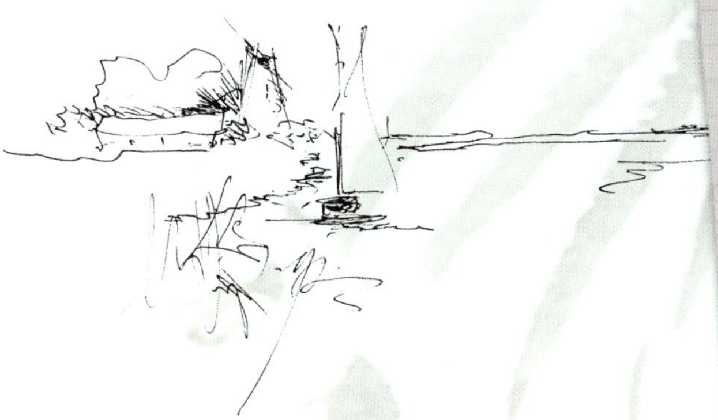

After a heavy snowfall
the landscape looks serene.

The sun now lower in the sky
sheds a watery beam.

Many may prefer to keep warm
and stay indoors.

But for some they cannot wait
to have fun outdoors.

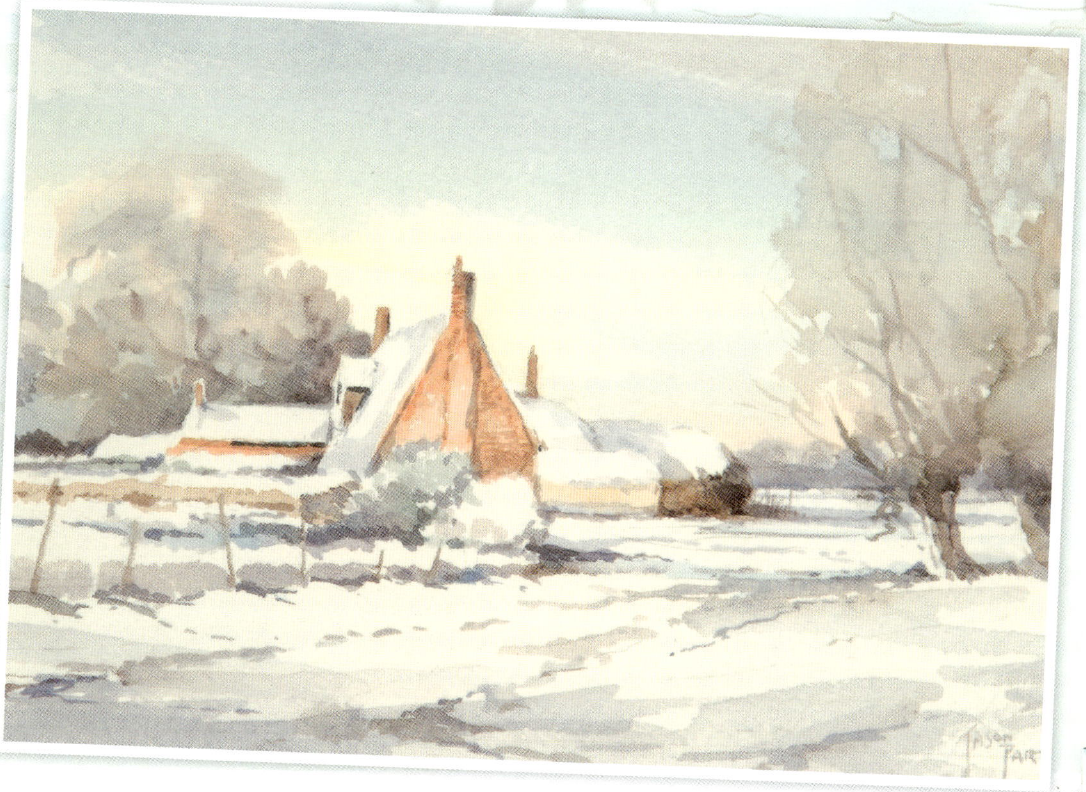

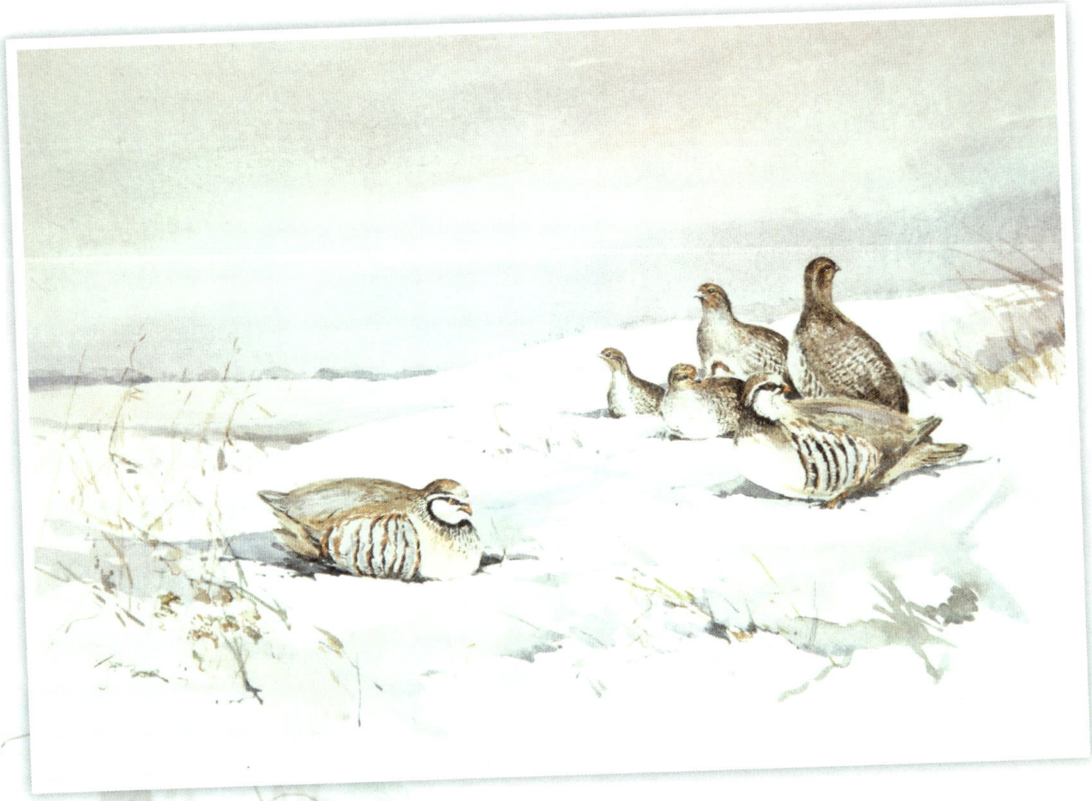

Partridges in winter

© From an original watercolour by Jason Partner.

When the air turns colder
and the nights draw in,

All creatures know
that winter has begun.

Keeping warm and safe
in the bitter chill,

And any available food,
they'll have their fill.

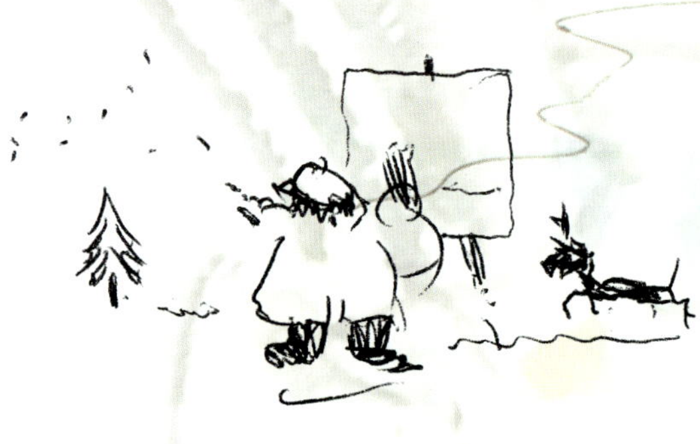

Victorian scenes

A selection of Victorian scenes painted by Jason
in the style of Myles Birkett Foster.

Children at play - *see page 128*
Stepping stones - *see page 129*
The shepherd boy - *see page 130*
Blackberry picking - *see page 131*

As an artist, Jason was interested in trying different techniques and he liked the 'chocolate box' work of Miles Birkett Foster and Helen Allingham at the turn of the last century.

Using a similar series of small paint strokes rather than his usual broad and flowing ones, he produced this selection of four images which he presented to family and friends.

The four images of children at play, stepping stones, blackberry picking and shepherd boy recount times past.

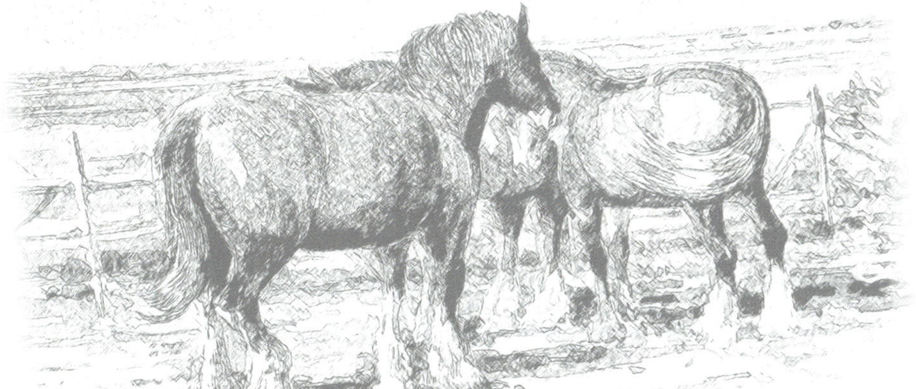

Children at play

Down the hill, hand in hand,
the girls skip along.

The little boy pulls on his kite,
while his faithful dog looks on.

When they reach the rippling brook,
they'll bathe their aching feet.

Then they'll make their way back home,
another day complete.

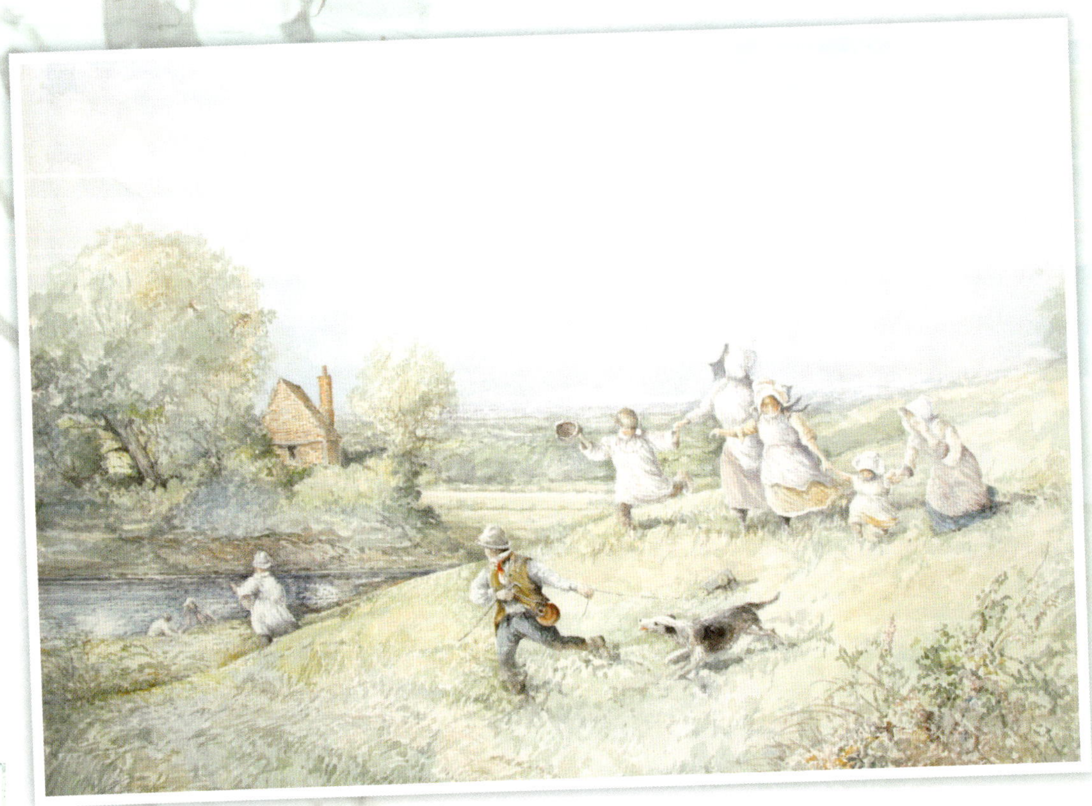

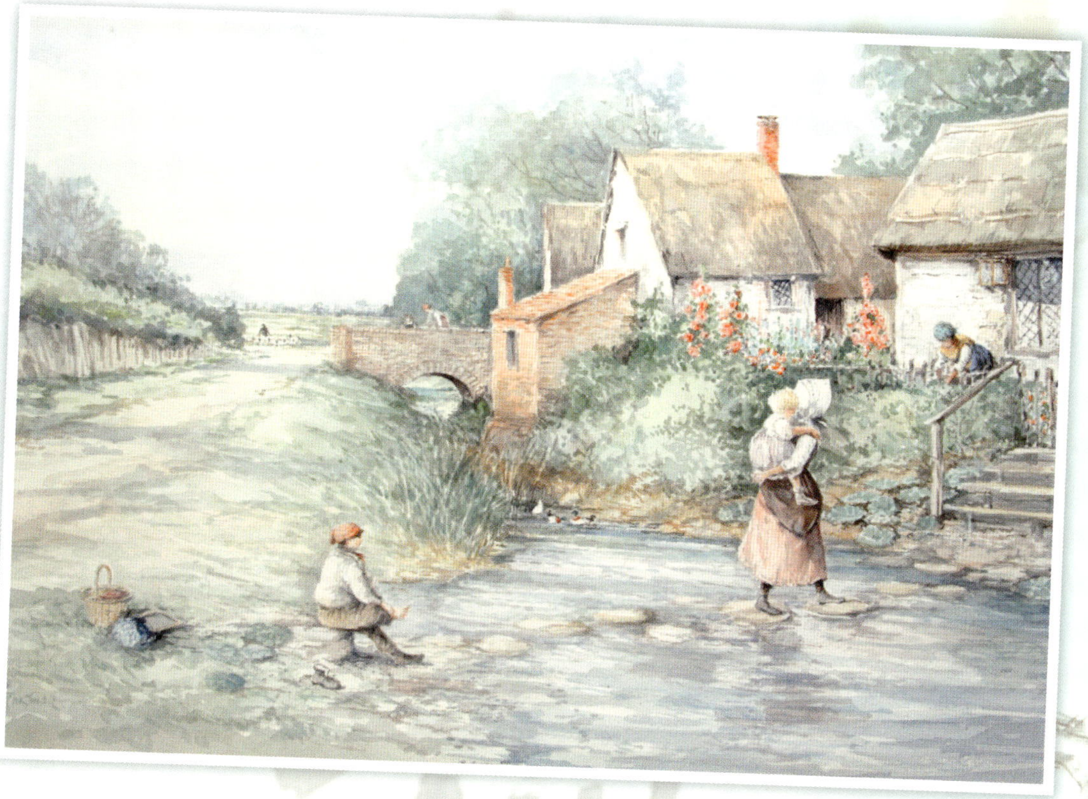

Stepping stones

© From an original watercolour by Jason Partner.

Carefully stepping
from stone to stone,
the children make their way back home.

Whilst boys on the bridge
gaze into the stream,
watching its passage, so calm and serene.

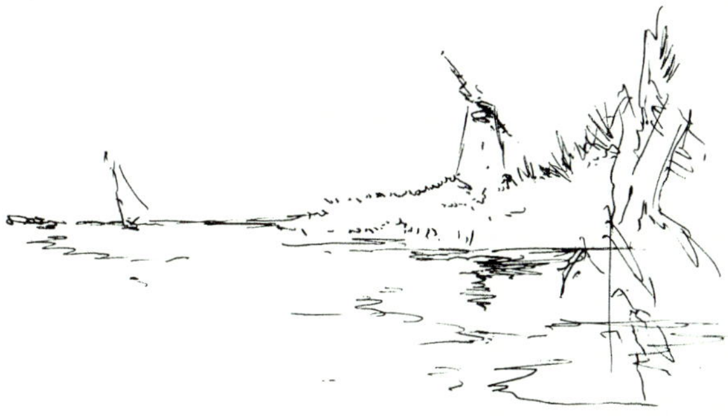

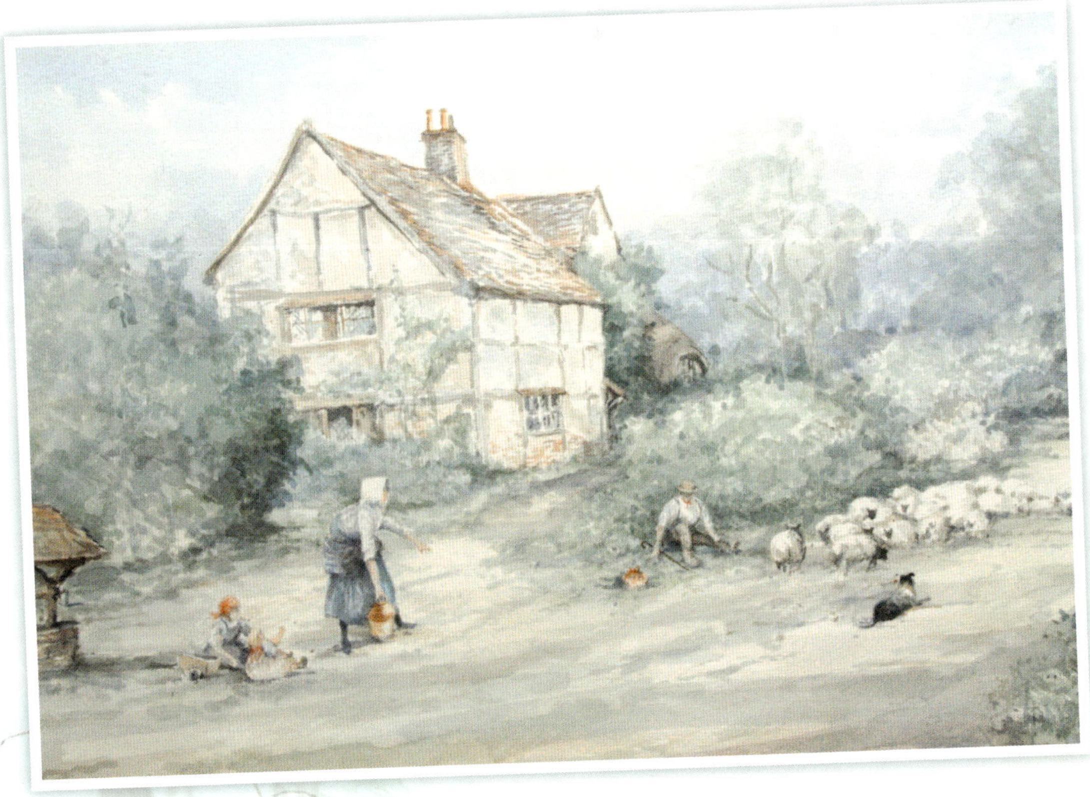

The shepherd boy

© From an original watercolour by Jason Partner.

It's a long, long day
for boy and dog.

When I get home,
I'll sleep like a log.

Up to the pasture and back,
in time for tea.

Keeping watch over sheep
is hard work for Bob and me!

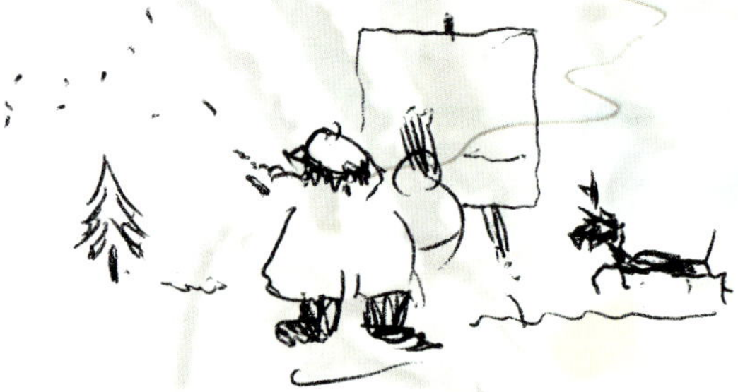

Blackberry picking

© From an original watercolour by Jason Partner.

As Autumn approaches,
these juicy fruits appear.

Be wary how you pick,
as those thorns your skin can tear.

One for the basket
and one for me to eat.

Then a blackberry pie -
what a wonderful treat!

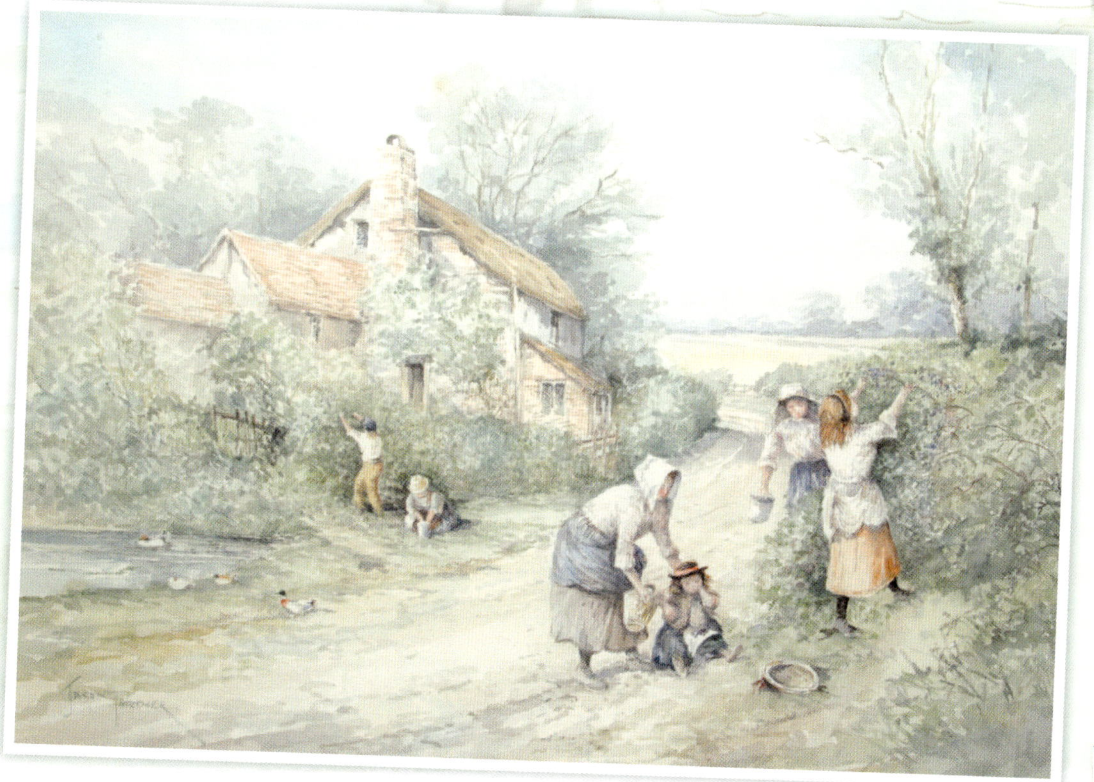

Memories of Jason...

Pamela Dickerson, *artist and owner of Tudor Galleries, Norwich.*

As a fellow artist I first met Jason in the early 1970s when I showed my work at the Aylsham Rotary Club in Aylsham which he had organised. He was generous with his time and became a favourite speaker at many organisations including art groups and the WI.

It was soon after that Jason invited me to exhibit some of my work at the very first art exhibition at the Royal Norfolk Show and I was delighted to take part. Alongside Jason were many friends and helpers who set out the display, but as there was no security, Jason decided to camp in the marquee overnight. He was always full of ideas in respect of promoting Norfolk artists.

In 1994 I was interested in raising funds for the Quidenham Hospice, known as EACH. I approached Wallace Kings furniture store, which was situated in Prince of Wales Road, Norwich, to ask if they would let me use their front windows to display an art exhibition. They were happy to assist, local businesses provided raffle prizes, including Wallace Kings. Many artists in the area brought along their work to be sold including Jason. He was delighted to paint an image of 'Children Playing' which was to be the main prize, saying that he was fortunate to have healthy grandchildren. The exhibition lasted two weeks and the total raised was over £3,000.

We kept in touch over the years, either at the Assembly Rooms in Norwich where he filled two rooms with his work, or Southwold where he took part in my exhibition. My memory of Jason is that he is a true watercolourist, adding his own style: 'A man on his own.'

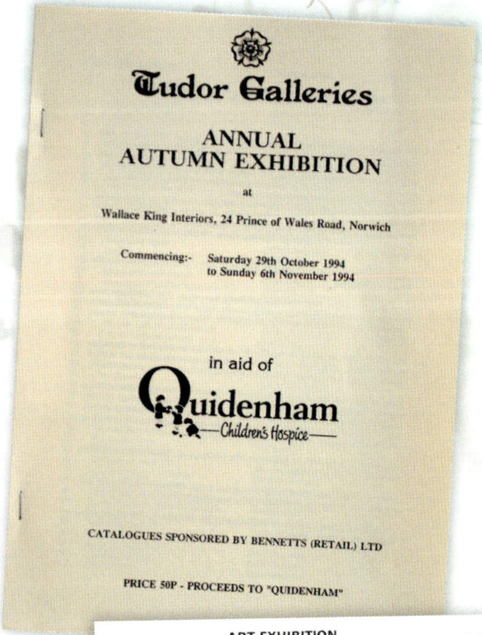
Tudor Galleries

ANNUAL AUTUMN EXHIBITION

at

Wallace King Interiors, 24 Prince of Wales Road, Norwich

Commencing:- Saturday 29th October 1994 to Sunday 6th November 1994

in aid of

Quidenham Children's Hospice

CATALOGUES SPONSORED BY BENNETTS (RETAIL) LTD

PRICE 50P - PROCEEDS TO "QUIDENHAM"

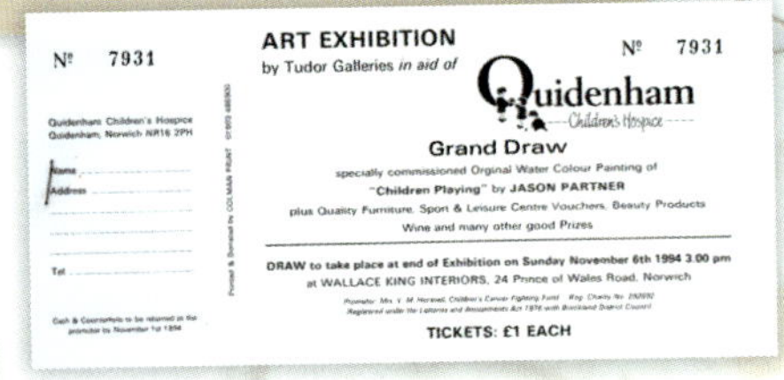
Nº 7931

Quidenham Children's Hospice
Quidenham, Norwich NR16 2PH

Name

Address

Tel

ART EXHIBITION

by Tudor Galleries *in aid of* Quidenham Children's Hospice

Nº 7931

Grand Draw

specially commissioned Orginal Water Colour Painting of "Children Playing" by JASON PARTNER

plus Quality Furniture, Sport & Leisure Centre Vouchers, Beauty Products Wine and many other good Prizes

DRAW to take place at end of Exhibition on Sunday November 6th 1994 3.00 pm at WALLACE KING INTERIORS, 24 Prince of Wales Road, Norwich

TICKETS: £1 EACH

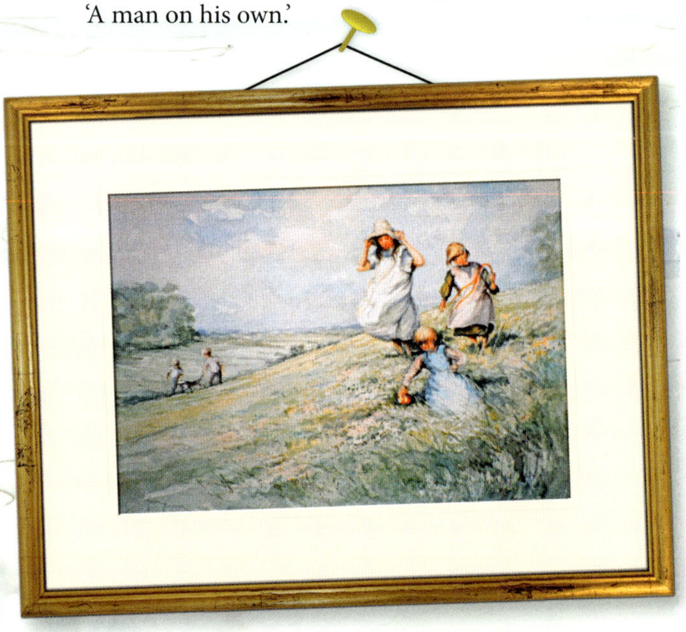

Children playing

© From an original watercolour by Jason Partner.

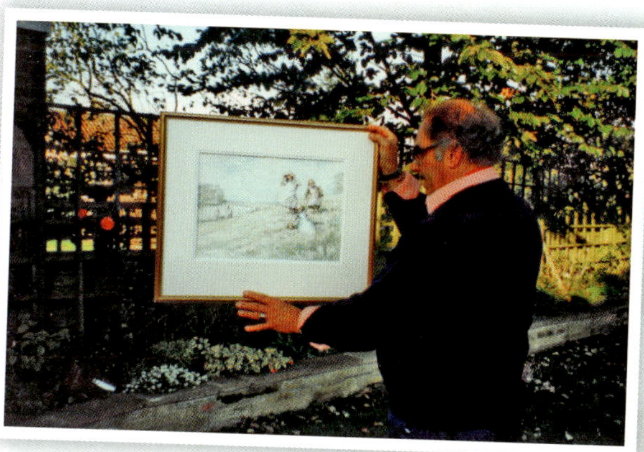

TUDOR GALLERIES
SUPPORTS
QUIDENHAM CHILDRENS HOSPICE

THE AUTUMN EXHIBITION
IN
WALLACE KING INTERIORS
RAISED
£3024.00
FOR THE HOSPICE

WITH GRATEFUL THANKS
TO ALL THOSE WHO
CONTRIBUTED AND HELPED

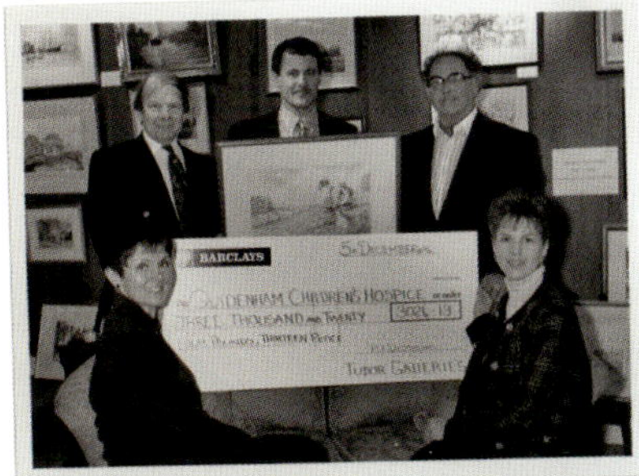

JASON PARTNER
1922 – 2005

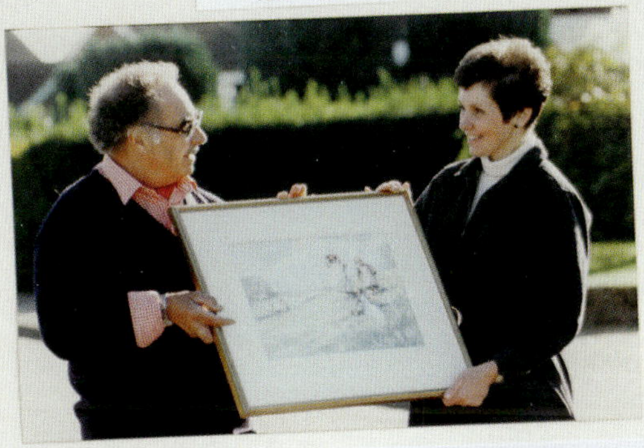

In 1994 Tudor Galleries staged a major art exhibition in aid of 'Quidenham', East Anglia's Children's Hospice and, through a long association with the Gallery, Jason painted a special watercolour of children running down a hill flying their kites which was donated as the main raffle prize raising a considerable sum for the children's charity.

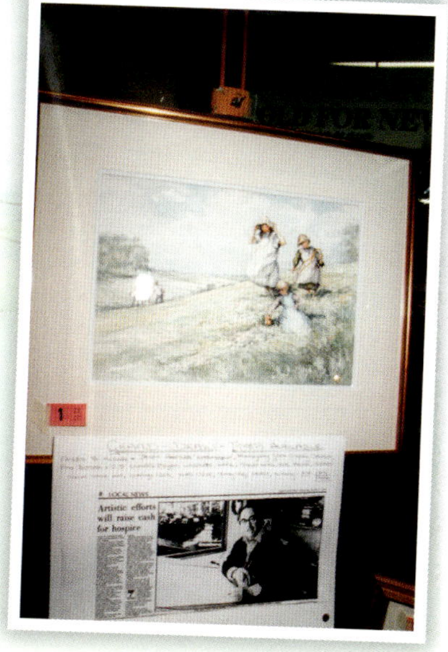

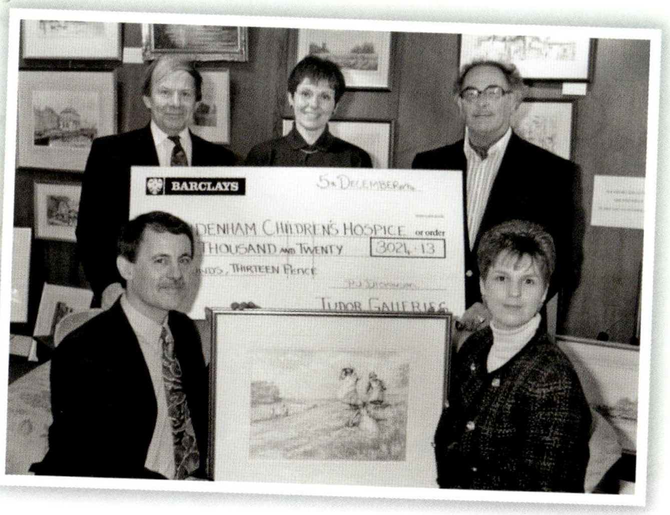

The Annual Autumn Exhibition and the Raffle proved very successful - a cheque for £3024.13 was proudly presented to Quidenham Children's Hospice.

Pamela Dickerson is pictured top middle, Jason is pictured top right and bottom left is the lucky winner of the painting, Richard Clover.

Winter 1995

The Quidenham Quarterly

Children's Hospice Newsletter

Art for our Sake!

In October Pamela Dickerson of Tudor Galleries held an Art Exhibition at Wallace King Interiors which was supported by many art lovers who saw a wide range of paintings and drawings by local artists. With many superb gifts, donated by local companies for the grand draw, together with a magnificent watercolour donated by Jason Partner this popular event raised £3034.13. (We are currently persuading Pamela to do the same again in 1995!)

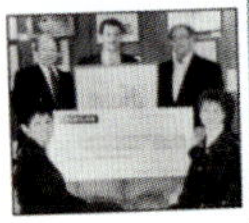

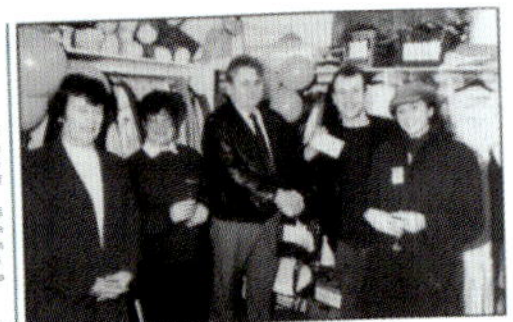

Theatre Stars Open Shop

Christmas Revelry

New Outreach Service

Schools Schools Schools

EDP Monday, October 24, 1994

What's On 2

Arts

Welsh singing superstar in city

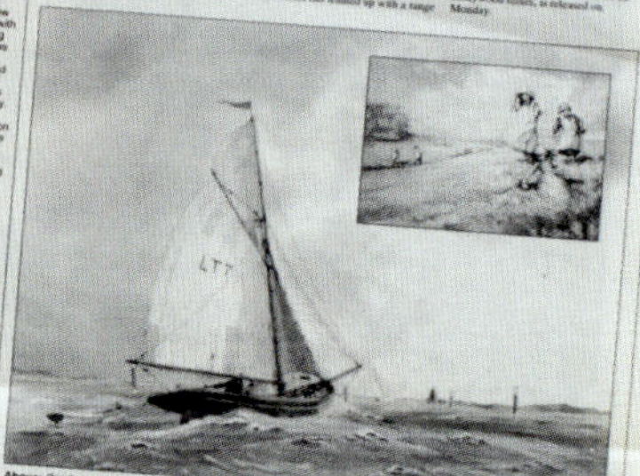

Above: *Old Smack on Breydon Water* by Robert Horne, and, **top inset**, *Children Playing* by Jason Partner

Charity exhibition

A visit to Quidenham Children's Hospice in south Norfolk so moved gallery owner Pamela Dickerson that she decided to turn her annual autumn exhibition into a fund-raiser.

Norwich furniture store Wallace King Interiors offered support, and the use of a large area on the ground floor of its Prince of Wales Road premises.

Norfolk artist Jason Partner contributed as a raffle prize a specially-painted picture of Victorian children at play in the countryside. Many more gifts were contributed by local businesses.

And more than 50 artists, showing 250 canvases between them, will take part in the exhibition, which opens to the public on Saturday, to November 6. On the final day, BBC East television presenter Kim Riley will make the draw.

All proceeds from the preview on Friday evening, and from the draw, will go to the hospice, together with a percentage on any pictures sold.

Pamela Dickerson, who owns Tudor Galleries at Brundall, says that the idea was spurred by a visit to Quidenham, which cares for children who are terminally ill or who have life-threatening diseases.

She was filled with admiration for the nursing staff and helpers, and for the warm and friendly environment in which children find an abundance of love and happiness while their parents are given a respite.

For draw and private view tickets, call Pamela Dickerson on Norwich (01603) 713356.

What's on MAGAZINE

COVER STORY

Editor: Tim Petzold

Assistant editors: Keith Morris, David Wakefield

Writer: Sarah Hardy

Listings: Vince Yallop

Advertisement sales manager: Marie Barnes

0603 628311

Contents

The Annual Autumn Exhibition held at Tudor Galleries proved very newsworthy and Jason's contribution made it into the Quidenham Quarterly magazine and the *Eastern Daily Press* - you can't beat good publicity!

8 LOCAL NEWS

Eastern Daily Press, Wednesday, October 5, 1994

Artistic efforts will raise cash for hospice

Artists are brushing up their money-spinning power to help sick children.

A major art show in Norwich this month will raise cash for Quidenham Children's Hospice in South Norfolk.

And a painting by a North Norfolk artist will be one of the main prizes helping to boost funds.

Popular watercolour landscape painter Jason Partner has donated a picture of Victorian children playing in the countryside.

He is pleased to help the hospice, which cares for children with life-threatening and serious illnesses and gives support to their families.

"I have three grandchildren, and when I sit them on my knee I am grateful for their good health," said Mr Partner of Aylsham.

He lost his brother and father with cancer and says: "It stays with you. I have had a wonderful life, with pictures collected by the Queen Mother, and I want to give something back."

The art exhibition, which is being staged at Wallace King's furniture shop in Prince of Wales Road, Norwich, is the brainchild of Brundall artist and gallery owner Pamela Dickerson.

She knows a five-year-old boy who gets help from the hospice.

"He goes there three or four times a year while his parents have a respite break, and he has a marvellous time.

"The hospice has the warm cosy feeling of a farmhouse, and is full of fantastic play rooms," said Mrs Dickerson.

Quidenham Children's Hospice has helped 100 families in the region since September 1991 but its intensive operation costs £1 a minute to run, every day of the year.

The art show, which runs from October 29, will be open from 9.30am to 5.30pm daily and 11am to 4pm on Sunday.

Money will be raised from painting sales, collection boxes, catalogues, and a private viewing.

A draw, which includes Mr Partner's painting, will be carried out on the final day, November 6, by BBC East television presenter Kim Riley.

Hospice appeals officer Alison Lanchester said the six-bed unit costs £500,000 a year to run, mostly from public donations, so efforts such as the art exhibition were always welcome.

Anyone else with money-raising ideas for the hospice should contact its appeal office on 0953 498404.

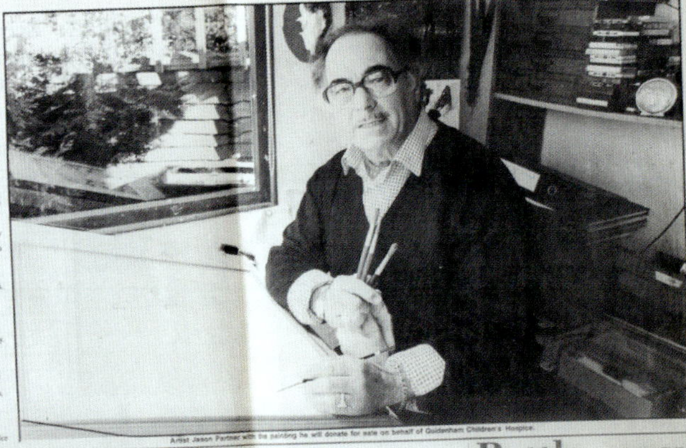

Artist Jason Partner with the painting he will donate for sale on behalf of Quidenham Children's Hospice.

Tepid on twinning

Building society to

Battle over prime site

Memories of Jason...

Hazel Ashley, *artist and owner of Ashley Studios, Wells-next-the-Sea.*

I first got to meet Jason in the early 1960s. He took evening classes at Aylsham Secondary School. When I opened my art shop, he was very encouraging.

Over the years I got to know him and his wife, Jo, becoming good friends.

I found Jason to be a very generous and charming man who, with his great skill and knowledge of art, was always ready to give advice and help to everyone.

Staff at *Barnwells Shop and Barnwell Print, Aylsham.*

As Jason Partner lived in Aylsham, he often called into the shop in the Market Place and got to know Gwen Wright and the staff. He also knew the staff at the printers too, having had his greeting cards printed there.

His patronage and friendliness were always sincere, while his greeting cards and paintings were a pleasure to behold.

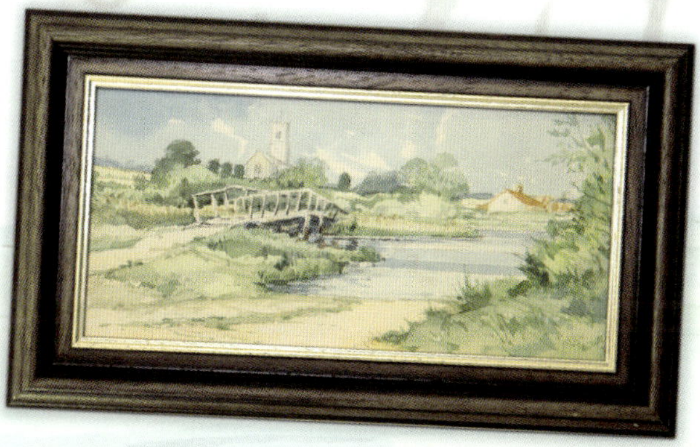

Glandford

This north Norfolk village on the River Glaven is picture postcard perfect.

It lies close to Cley-next-the-Sea so can sometimes be overlooked by tourists and visitors.

Original watercolour © Jason Partner.
By kind permission of Colin and Mary Nelson.

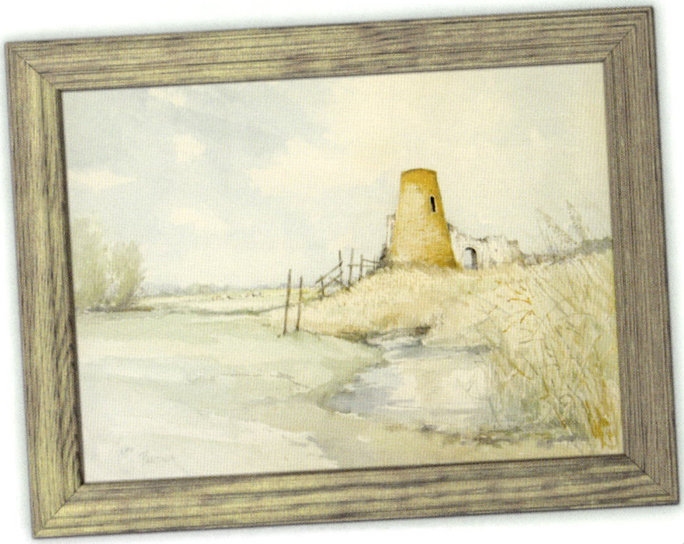

St Benet's Abbey

Nestled in Broadland this ancient abbey is situated, surrounded by marshland.

A magical, historical place which can be accessed either by boat, footpath or vehicle.

Original watercolour © Jason Partner.
By kind permission of Colin and Mary Nelson.

Jason's Last Commission

In 2004 plans were taking place to celebrate the bi-centenary of the Battle of Trafalgar which would take place the following year. A flotilla of navy ships and other seafaring craft was to take place in Portsmouth presided over by The Queen. As Norfolk was Nelson's birthplace the county was to hold special events too. Bernard Matthews had organised that every Norfolk boundary sign should have 'Nelson's County' displayed on it.

I asked Jason if he would be interested in painting a commemorative piece for the celebrations. He was very excited about the project and set to work. It was agreed that the montage should include an image of young Nelson, the Battle of Trafalgar, and with his connections with Great Yarmouth, their coat of arms plus the monument which was central to the original racecourse used by the military. Jason set to work with great enthusiasm.

Once the montage was completed, Jason said that I should give a framed signed print to Bernard Matthews. He was very surprised and delighted when I presented the picture to him.

As the Lord Nelson Grandstand was celebrating its first year at the Great Yarmouth racecourse, together with the bicentenary of the Battle of Trafalgar, it was arranged that Jason Partner, his wife Jo, together with us, would meet with members of the Royal Navy and the owner of the racecourse. The date set for the presentation of the Nelson montage painting would be May 2005. Sadly, a couple of weeks before the presentation was to be held, Jason died. He was not able to see his final commission hanging in the Trafalgar Lounge where it remains to this day. A fitting tribute to a well loved and respected artist and gentleman.

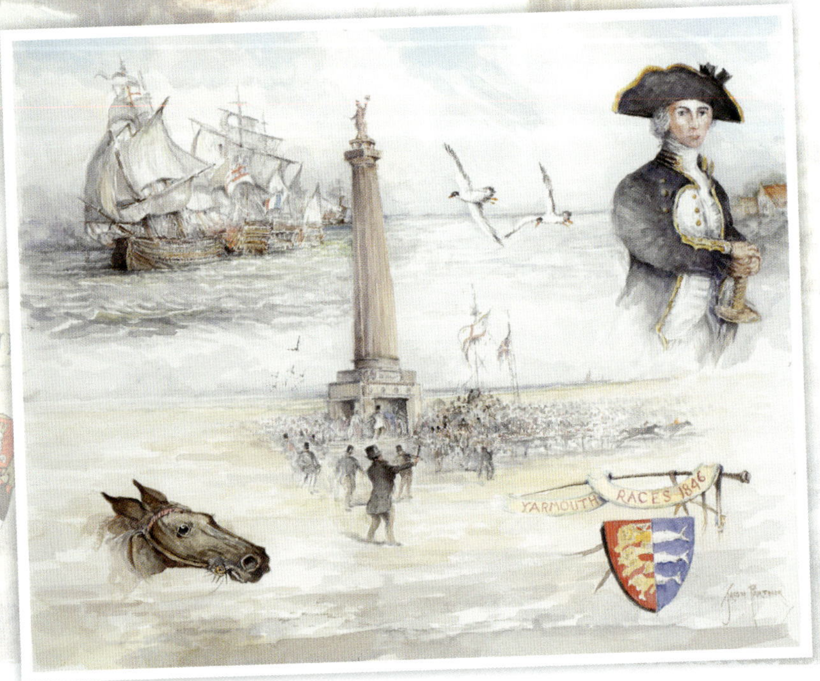

Nelson main scene

© From an original watercolour by Jason Partner.

Members of the Royal Navy,
Simon Clarke (Chairman),
of Gt Yarmouth Race Course,
and Colin Nelson presenting
the Nelson watercolour
by Jason in May 2005.

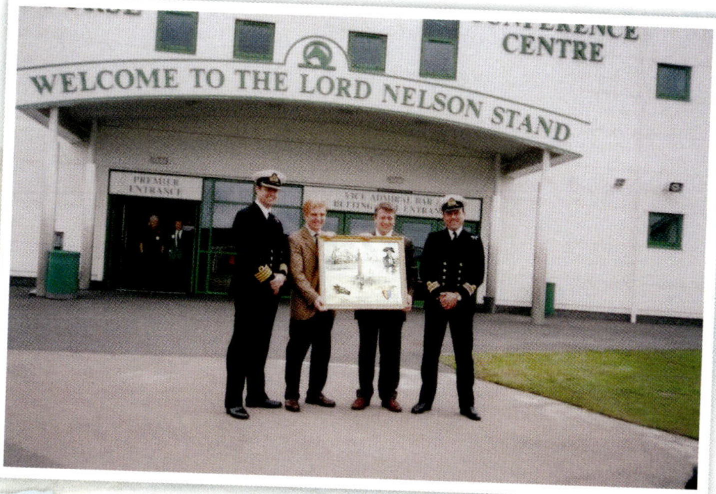

A Day at the Races

A 'Day at the Races' is an old film
starring the Marx Brothers, as I recall.
Great fun and laughter was had
by Groucho, Harpo, Chico and all.

Our day at the races was also a happy event
And like special days, so quickly it went.
Champagne to greet us, the Chairman to meet us,
as well as three Navy gents.

Our day was to honour Nelson, Norfolk's son.
So a watercolour by Jason Partner was done.
A tribute to both as it turned out to be,
Now it will be displayed for all to see.

The meal was delicious, and the wine flowed.
Then it was time to watch the horses go.
Bets were placed, up to the verandah we paced,
Hoping our horse wouldn't be too slow.

All too quickly the day came to a close,
And to present the final trophy,
Colin and Mary they chose.
Thank you everyone who gave us a day to remember.
It will remain in our memories forever.

Great Yarmouth
RACECOURSE

SEASIDE RACING AT ITS BEST

Jellicoe Road, Great Yarmouth, Norfolk, NR30 4AU
Tel: 01493 842 527 Fax: 01493 843 254 E-mail: info@greatyarmouth-racecourse.co.uk

Mr Colin Nelson
11 Siskin Green
Oulton Broad
Suffolk
NR33 8PP

20th May 2005

Dear Colin & Mary,

I'm writing to you on behalf of everyone here at Great Yarmouth Racecourse to thank you for making our first anniversary of the Lord Nelson Grandstand both a great success and a memorable day for the Racecourse and its visitors.

As you know the day went very well and even though the weather was not on our side in the morning, the sun did appear to make it a wonderful afternoon. I have enclosed some photographs for you as a memento of your day, both of the painting presentation, and of the presentation you both kindly made to the winning trainer of the final race, on behalf of the race sponsors.

Our Chairman, Mr Simon Clarke, also had a wonderful day and was as thrilled with the painting, as he was with your company. He sends his very best wishes to you both.

May I take this opportunity to thank you again for the permanent loan of the painting by Jason Partner, which will be on display in the Trafalgar Restaurant in time for our next race meeting on 1st June.

I hope to see you back at the racecourse in the very near future.

Yours sincerely,

Glenn Tubby
General Manager

Directors: Simon W Clarke, (Chairman), Rod G. Street, Anthony B Kelly FCMA, Christopher S. Hall, TD DL, James R. Shrimplin, Charles Reynolds
Registration: England 4266183

visit our web-site on: www.greatyarmouth-racecourse.co.uk

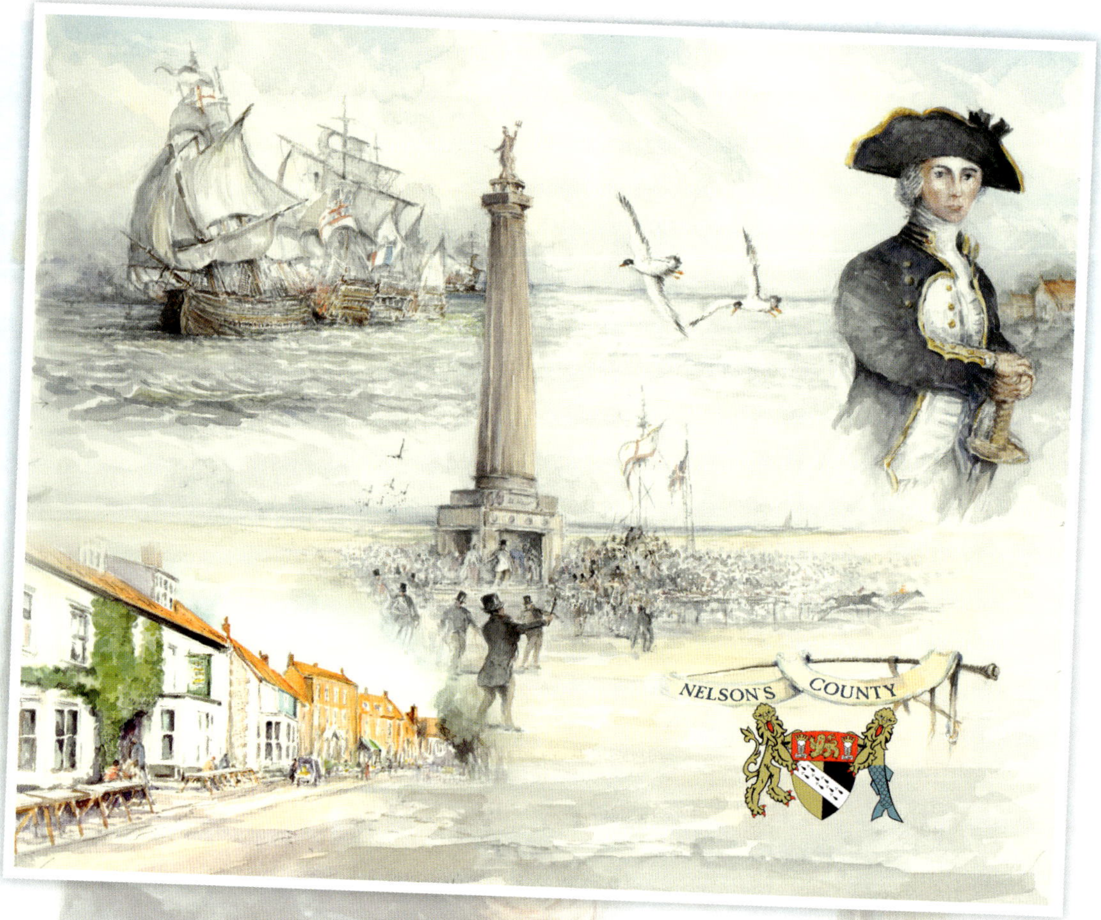

Nelson's County

© From original watercolours by Jason Partner.
With kind permission of Mr & Mrs Nelson
The Battle of Trafalgar, Young Nelson,
Nelson's Monument (Norfolk Pillar)
& The Hoste Arms in Burnham Market.

Nelson's famous signal to the Fleet at the Battle of Trafalgar in 1805.

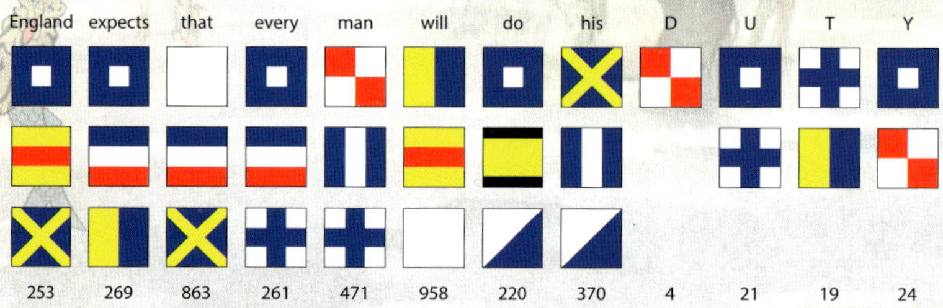

Admiral Horatio Lord Nelson

On 29th September 1758, Edmund and Catherine Nelson welcomed a son, Horatio, into the world. He was born in the parsonage house of Burnham Thorpe in West Norfolk.

Horatio and his siblings enjoyed an idyllic rural country life until Boxing Day, 1767, when his mother Catherine died suddenly.

Edmund was left with eight children to look after and very little money to do so. Catherine's family were well connected; she was a relation of Robert Walpole, the 'first' Prime Minister, and her brother Maurice was a famous Sea Captain. He suggested that, to help Edmund out, he should take one of the boys to sea. Everyone was surprised when the sickly Horatio seemed keen.

Nelson was educated at the Royal Grammar School, Norwich, and then the Paston School, North Walsham. Aged 12, with his education deemed complete, he left Burnham Thorpe to begin his naval career under his uncle Maurice's care.

In 1787, England was at peace. Nelson and his new wife Fanny returned to England and, later, to Burnham. They lived there for five years, during which time Nelson fished, sailed, farmed a few acres and read the papers, hoping for war and a recall to active service. In 1793, with France in the grip of revolution, Nelson was recalled, only to lose the sight in his right eye at Calvi and his arm at Cadiz.

He made his name at the Battle of the Nile in 1798 after which he returned to England via Yarmouth where he was given the Freedom of the Borough. In 1801 he visited the town twice, before and after the Battle of Copenhagen.

Nelson finally lost his life on 21st October 1805 at the Battle of Trafalgar after hoisting his famous signal:
'England expects that every man will do his duty.'

His dying words were:
'Thank God I have done my duty.'

Text by a former Curator of the Nelson Museum, Great Yarmouth, Norfolk.

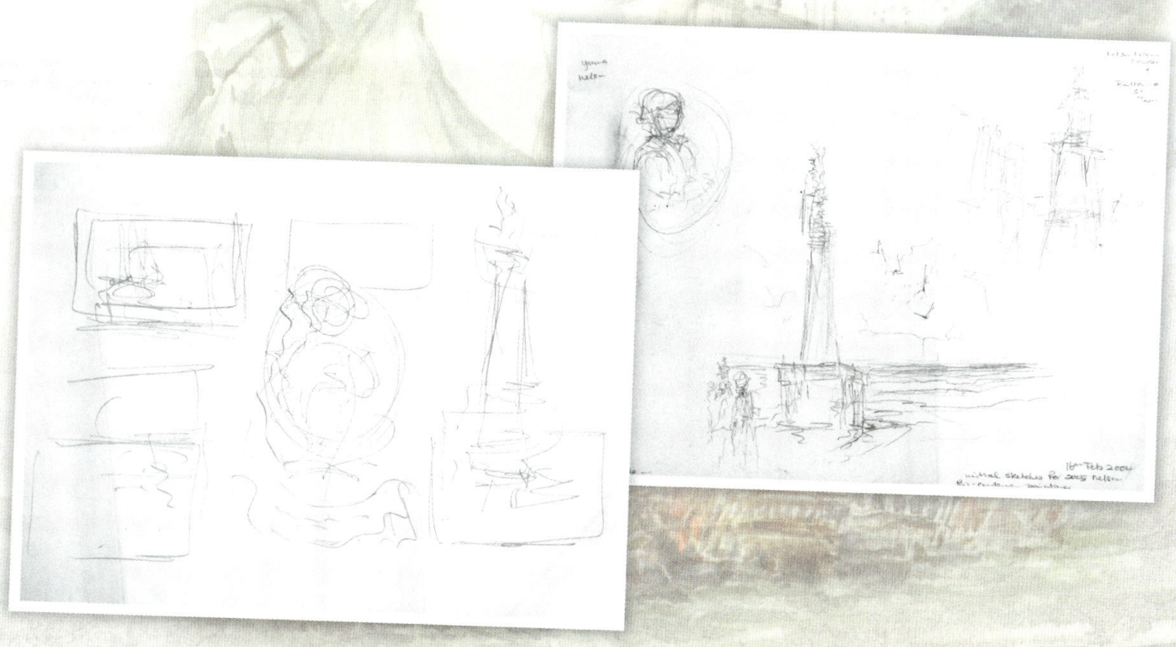

Jason's initial pencil rough drafts of Nelson's County 2004.

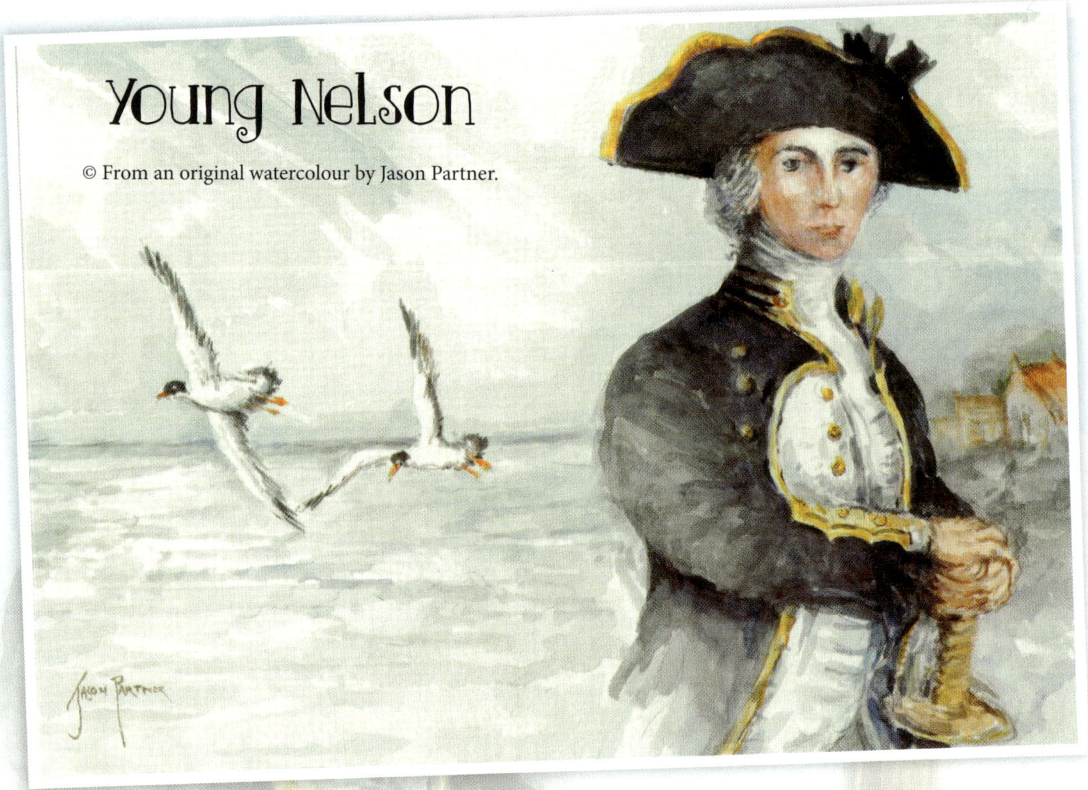

Young Nelson

© From an original watercolour by Jason Partner.

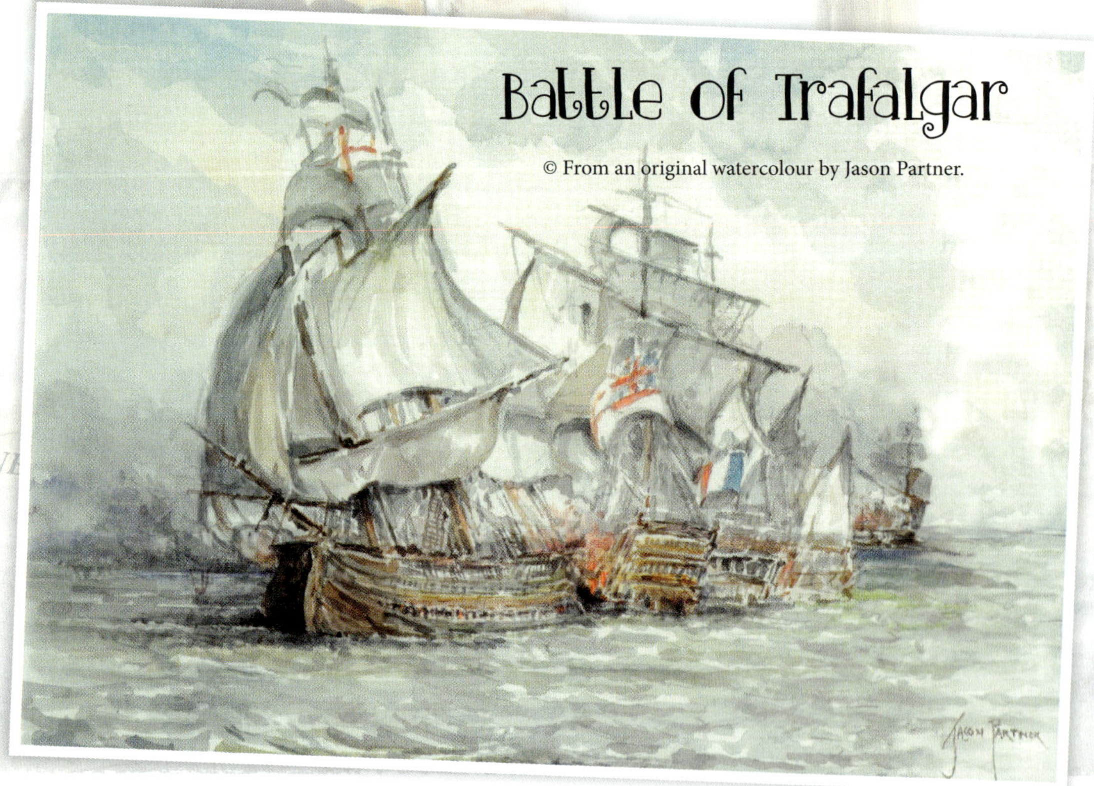

Battle of Trafalgar

© From an original watercolour by Jason Partner.

Nelson's Monument

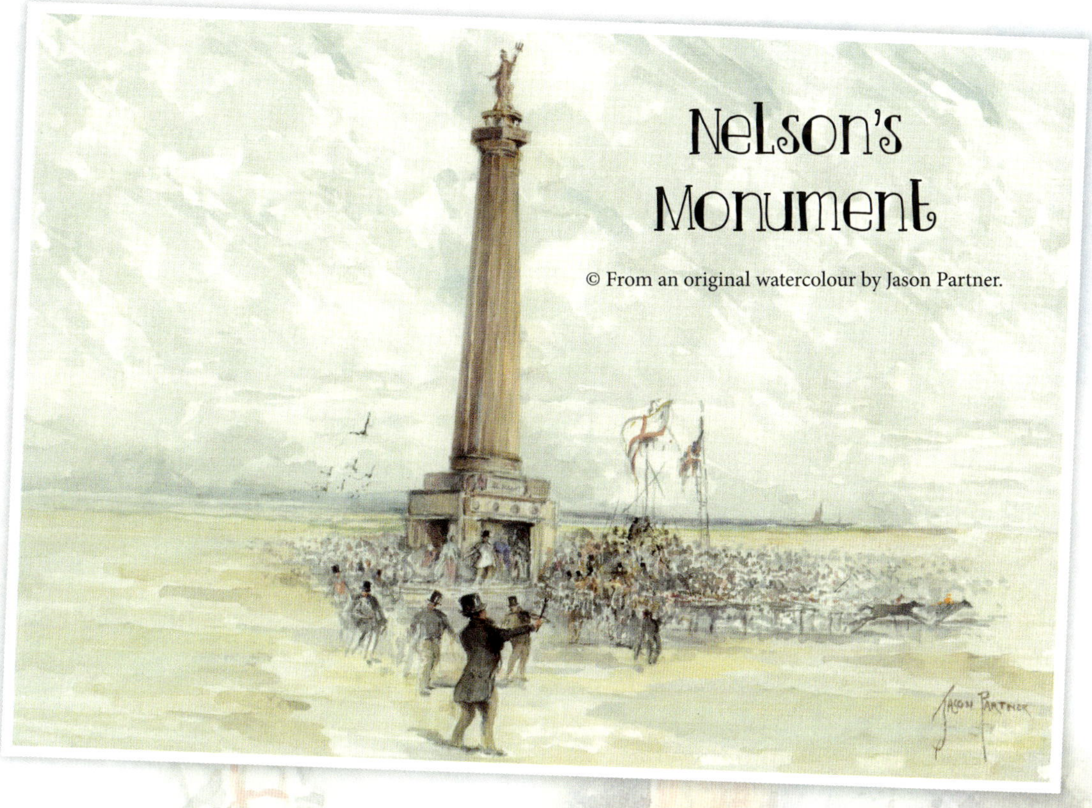

© From an original watercolour by Jason Partner.

Over the years the column has been referred to by various names: Britannia Monument, the Nelson Memorial or Monument and the Norfolk Naval Pillar.

It was built by William Wilkins between the years 1817 and 1819 in memory of the victor of the Battle of Trafalgar.

William Wilkins (1738-1839) was Norfolk-born himself, as was Admiral Lord Nelson, whom the Monument commemorates.

This magnificent structure stands 44 metres high (144 feet) and is located at the Denes, Great Yarmouth, Norfolk, England.

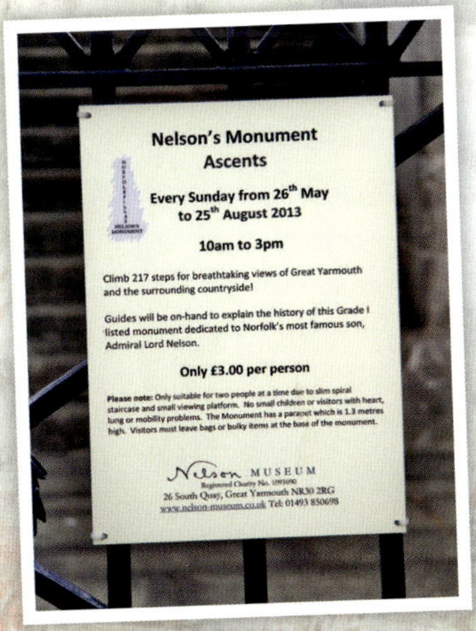

Photograph taken at the entrance gates to Nelson's Monument, the Norfolk Pillar, in August 2013.

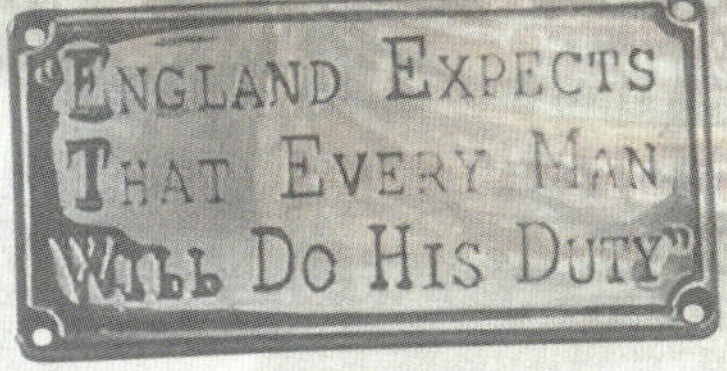

Archant archives...

Norfolk and its light

22 SEP. 1977

Lack of pollution was the reason why the light in Norfolk was so good, the Aylsham artist Jason Partner suggested to Norwich Rotary Club yesterday.

He spoke of the quality of light to be found in the county as he showed members a selection of his watercolours, many of them depicting the creeks and villages of North Norfolk.

His tip to anyone wanting to paint watercolour landscapes was — keep it simple. "The most simple subjects often make the best pictures," he said, adding: "A watercolour should never look overworked. It should look as if it has been dashed off. That is the joy of watercolour."

But he warned that a lot of hard work went into achieving that effect. He sometimes spent up to two or three days on a picture.

SOLD 57 PAINTINGS IN A DAY

ENN 27/3/75

OF THE 60 paintings on show at an exhibition which opened at the Assembly House, Norwich, on Monday, there were only three left by mid-afternoon; Norfolk artist Jason Partner could only say for the second successive year that the exhibition had been "fantastic."

It was the sixth year that Mr. Partner, whose home is at Aylsham, has had an exhibition of his water colours in Norwich and over those years the number of people interested in his work has increased.

"It has been lovely to see my clients become froends and buy my pictures over the years," he commented.

Apart from selling out of paintings, Mr. Partner gained a number of commissions, mostly keeping to his speciality of the Suffolk and North Norfolk coast.

He was born in Leicestershire but it was when he came to Norfolk that he found his real inspiration for painting. His home is at The Moorings, Clover Road, Aylsham, from where he has been seeking subjects throughout the countryside.

His technique now is to find a likely scene and, having sorted out the best composition, to sketch it roughly. When he returns to his studio the proper painting takes shape, mainly in the style of the old school of English water colour artists.

Aylsham artist's own show in U.S.

-3 OCT. 1975

Jason Partner, the Aylsham artist whose paintings have proved so popular in past exhibitions in Norwich, has now gained a trans-Atlantic reputation and is leaving for America today to hold a one-man show in Boston, Massachusetts.

Mr. Partner first began to sell his popular work in America about a year ago when Mr. Wililam Ash, owner of the English Gallery, Boston, saw an article about the painter's work in "The Arts Review."

"He took some pictures back with him and they went pretty well over there. Then he decided to arrange a one-man exhibition for me," said Mr. Partner. "They seem to really value our English water-colours in America. It will be exciting to meet people I don't know who have bought some of my paintings. I understand I'm going to meet the Governor of Kansas, who has some of my works."

Before going to Boston the artist will be spending some time in Nova Scotia. "I'm looking forward to painting in Nova Scotia and around Cape Cod, especially as the colours will be so good as it is the fall," he said.

Mr. Partner's watercolours are soft, delicate and fresh. There is a "wet" quality about many of them, particularly in the landscapes of the North Norfolk coastal villages. He has captured the sense of space of the open countryside and the stillness of the land which only birds and animals inhabit.

TELECOM'S CHOICE IS A FAMILIAR NUMBER

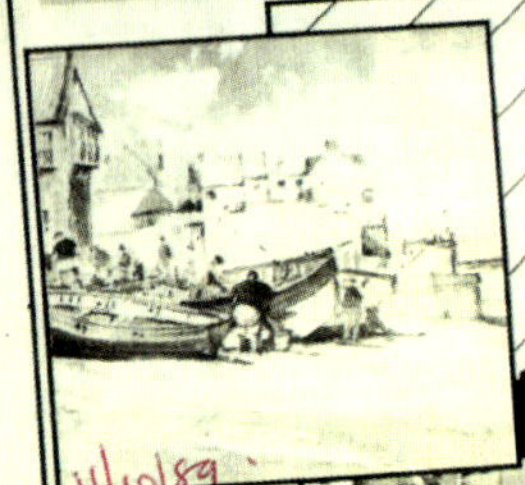

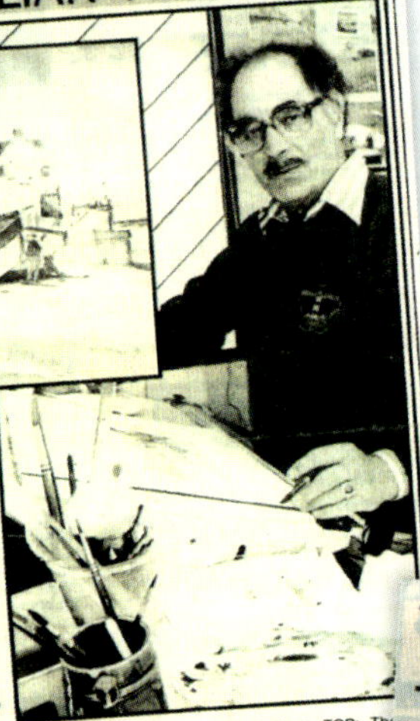

11/10/89

THIS picture is going to take on a familiar look over the next few months — it's the front cover of the new Norwich area phone book.

More than 250,000 homes are this week receiving the book, fronted by Aylsham artist Jason Partner's "Fishing Boats in Sheringham".

The original painting will now be raffled by British Telecom to raise cash for a £250,000 bone marrow transplant unit at Norfolk and Norwich Hospital.

BT staff have already raised £18,000 for the appeal.

Watercolour artist Jason Partner. TOP: Th phone book cover.

TICKLED

"Every time I paint it's as though I'm seeing the landscape for the first time," said Mr Partner, aged 65, who moved to the area 30 years ago.

"I'm just as tickled and enthusiastic to be in Norfolk. I came here after I fell in love with Blakeney salt marshes while I was holiday.

"I don't suppose I'll ever retire. I love painting and just hope I can go on and on."

BT spokesman Paula Garham said: "We saw the painting and thought it appropriate becau captures the spirit the area. We were pleased to use th work of a local ar

"We wanted something that's pleasing to the e especially when phone book is g to be in the hom the next 18 mo

Artist helps wherry fund

18. NOV. 1985

LOCAL artist Jason Partner has come to the rescue of the Norfolk wherry Albion.

The artist and the Artful Brush Gallery in Norwich are boosting the campaign to save the Albion by donating 10 per cent of the price of a special limited edition of 500 prints by Mr. Partner to the Norfolk Wherry Trust.

The prints portray a sailing wherry on a quiet reach on the Bure at Acle and it could raise more than £3500 to the project to restore the 87-year-old Albion.

The wherry is often regarded as the symbol of Norfolk but most have now succumbed to the ravages of time. The Albion, the only trading wherry still sailing, is in urgent need of restoration and attention.

The Trust hopes to build a special watershed to shelter the wherry from the winter elements. Experts say a shed could double or treble its life.

Mr. Partner watched as the Trust chairman, Major James Forsythe, unveiled the first of the new £75 prints at the Artful Brush Gallery on Saturday.

Major Forsythe said: "Keeping the Albion is like working on the Forth Bridge — as soon as you finish one end you have to make a start again on the other.

"We are always in need of money and this generous gesture will be a great help to us."

Major Forsythe said the new shed at Ludham could cost £10,000 if voluntary help was forthcoming — otherwise the price would be much higher.

Mr. Partner said his interest in the project was started through his enjoyment of sailing.

"It is a very good thing and I am pleased to be able to help a bit," he said.

Jason Partner of Aylsham is a not too distant neighbour of Ian Houston's in North Norfolk. He, too, is an accomplished watercolourist in the traditional mould, and, like Ian Houston, he finds no shortage of buyers for his work—the rash of red spots which appeared on his pictures on the first morning of his exhibition at the Assembly House this week reached epidemic proportions.

CONFIDENCE

Mr. Partner's smaller landscapes are particularly effective but his expertise is equally apparent in larger works such as "The Ringstead Downs under Snow," which has been chosen by the Norfolk Naturalists' Trust for their 1974 Christmas card. Here, the confidence which comes from a sound technique is clearly displayed in the isolated flicks and dashes which set the picture off.

If it is meticulousness one wants then the other exhibitor at the Assembly House this week—K. W. Hastings, who has a studio and gallery at Gorleston—is the man. He is quite happy to paint every blade of grass in a picture, although the brightness of his colours tends to undermine his realism. In the face of such painstaking care one inevitably thinks of certain naive painters despite Mr. Hastings' professional approach.

F.G.

7 APR 1974

Master of every landscape

Famous artist holds first exhibition at Holt

12 APR 1993

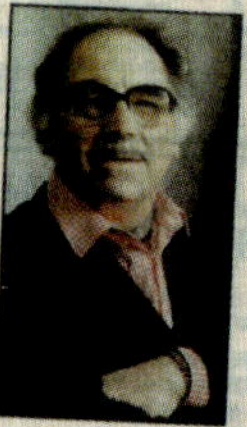

Jason Partner... technique involves generous use of water and limited range of colours.

Jason Partner can count Royalty and top politicians among his greatest fans — as well as many more admirers worldwide.

But the watercolour artist who has works in the collections of the Queen Mother and John Major and has exhibited worldwide will be staging his first at Holt Picturecraft Gallery from Saturday.

"I have had 27 exhibitions at the Assembly House, Norwich, and regularly stage them in Boston and Canada.

"I have also known Mike Hill at Picturecraft for a long time. He said to me: 'Come on, you have never had one in my place', so the decision was made.

Leicestershire-born Mr Partner was greatly influenced by the principal of Leicester College of Art, Daniel Watson. His technique involves the generous use of water and a limited range of colours.

But with great control he creates a lightness in his work which has now established him as a very popular lecturer and demonstrator both at home and abroad.

The mastery of the art is attained with apparent ease and he can faithfully portray the local landscape in all its moods, the power of the heavy horse, the majesty of a Thames barge in full sail, or wildfowl flying against a backcloth of mist on the Norfolk Broads.

Aylsham-based Mr Partner first visited

(9-5 daily including Sunday) and on that Wednesday he will stage a demonstration of the art of watercolour (7.30pm) in aid of the Cystic Fibrosis Trust.

Tickets are available at £5 each which includes a cheese and wine buffet.

■ Picturecraft Gallery is based in Lees Courtyard, off Bull Street, Holt. Admission is free, a large car park is provided and disabled access is easy and welcomed.

David Blyth

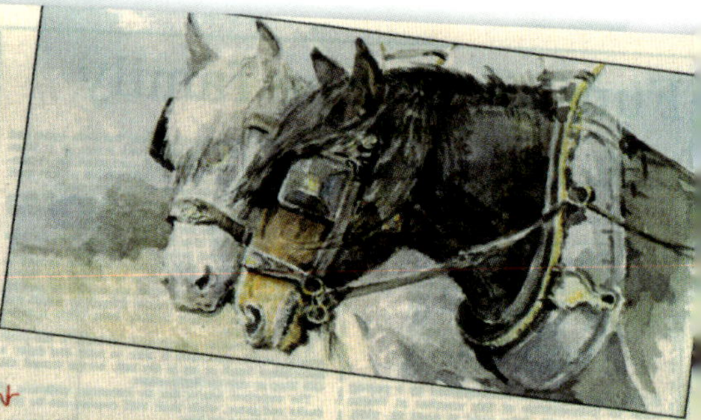

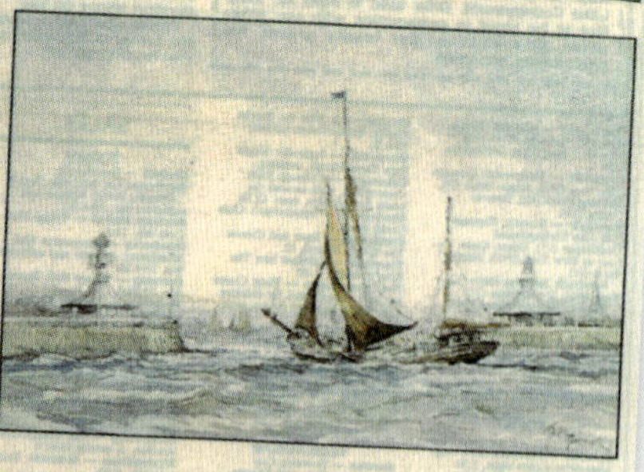

Ploughing horses' heads by Jason Partner and Fishing smack entering Lowestoft Harbour.

Artist turns author

30 APR. 1982

AYLSHAM artist Jason Partner, a regular and very popular exhibitor in Norfolk, has now turned author. The result is a short, illustrated paperback, **Jason Partner's Guide to Sketching and Water-colour Painting (Providence Press, £3.90)**. It is an orthodox introduction to the subject, very much aimed at enthusiastic beginners, but a special feature is the analysis the author makes of nine of his own landscapes which are reproduced here in colour. He urges the would-be artist to visit galleries, and he lists some of his own favourite painters, including Sir J. A. Arnesby Brown and Sir Alfred East. Mr. Partner celebrates his book's appearance — very appropriately — by having an exhibition of his own at the Assembly House, Norwich, this week.

F. G.

Jason's skill and popularity as an exceptional watercolour artist meant that he was frequently in the news!

Our thanks go to ...

The late Jason Partner - *for his legacy*

Mrs Jo Partner and family - *for their encouragement and support*

Keith Skipper - *for his lovely amusing Foreword*

Mr Tim Ridley - *for use of a photograph*

Joe Crowfoot - *for his contribution*

Pamela Dickerson - *for use of her collection of archive and her contribution*

Richard Clover - *for use of his photograph*

EACH - *for use of photographs*

Hazel Ashley - *for her contribution*

Mrs Gwen Wright and Staff - Barnwells Shop and Printers, Aylsham - *for their contribution*

Great Yarmouth Racecourse - *for use of photographs*

Archant - *for permission to use photographs and articles*

Bob Hutchinson - *for his enthusiasm and artistic graphic design of this book*

Barnwell Print - *for giving us advice and printing this book*

Without the help, support and contributions made by the above,
this book would not have been possible.
So many thanks to one and all.

What a wonderful legacy you have left us with, Jason, our ole partner!

Colin & Mary Nelson

Nostalgic Memories

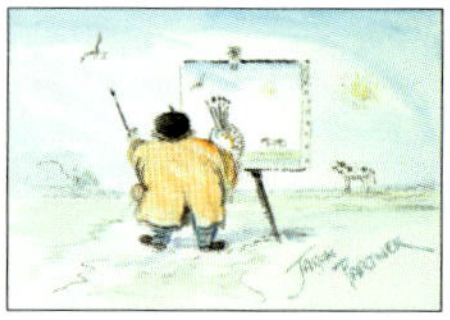